Register Now for Onlir to Your Book!

D1170240

SPRINGER PUBLISHING COMPANY
CONNECT™

Your print purchase of *Fieldwork and Supervision for Behavior Analysts* **includes online access to the contents of your book**—increasing accessibility, portability, and searchability!

Access today at:

**http://connect.springerpub.com/content/book/978-0-8261-3913-9
or scan the QR code at the right with your smartphone
and enter the access code below.**

0AKP8T0G

*Scan here for
quick access.*

If you are experiencing problems accessing the digital component of this product, please contact our customer service department at cs@springerpub.com

The online access with your print purchase is available at the publisher's discretion and may be removed at any time without notice.

Publisher's Note: New and used products purchased from third-party sellers are not guaranteed for quality, authenticity, or access to any included digital components.

LS

SPRINGER PUBLISHING COMPANY

View all our products at springerpub.com

Ellie Kazemi, PhD, BCBA-D, founded the MS in ABA program at California State University, Northridge (CSUN), and is a tenure-track professor in the Department of Psychology. She teaches undergraduate and graduate coursework on research methodology, behavior analysis, ethics, and organizational behavior management. She is very passionate about her role as a mentor and supervisor. Her efforts in developing a Structured, Competency-Based Supervision Model for emerging behavior analysts have gained tremendous attention from supervisors across the globe and at various universities. Dr. Kazemi is particularly qualified for her role as the leading author of this book based on her experiences developing practica coursework at CSUN, collaborating with community behavioral agencies to provide high-quality supervision to graduate students, and performing research and preparing peer-reviewed publications in the areas of staff training, performance feedback, and supervision. She is frequently invited to present workshops, tutorials, and keynotes on the topics of training, feedback, and supervision.

Brian Rice, MA, BCBA, received his master's degree in clinical psychology from California State University, Northridge (CSUN), and has been a Board Certified Behavior Analyst (BCBA) since 2011. Brian has served as a practica instructor in the CSUN Masters of Science, Applied Behavior Analysis program since 2014 and as a part-time faculty member in CSUN's Psychology Department since 2015. In his role as practica instructor, Brian conducts group supervision meetings based on the CSUN Competency-Based Supervision Model and monitors the individual field supervision experiences of his students at various community sites. In addition, Brian currently works full time as the Manager of Education and Professional Development at Easterseals Southern California. In this position, Brian is responsible for developing and implementing supervision processes to improve the quality of supervision of approximately 85 individuals receiving supervision from BCBAs in his organization. Brian also provides an 8-hour supervision workshop on best practices for competency-based supervision to BCBAs within his organization. In total, Brian has provided individual supervision for more than 35 emerging behavior analysts in the past 4 years as part of his continued work with children and adolescents with developmental disabilities.

Peter Adzhyan, PsyD, LEP, BCBA-D, has a master's degree in school psychology and a doctorate in educational psychology. He is a Board Certified Behavior Analyst (BCBA) and a Licensed Educational Psychologist. Dr. Adzhyan is currently working as a school psychologist for Los Angeles Unified School District (LAUSD), a post he has held for 17 years, and has 9 years of experience as a behavior analyst working with children and adolescents in various educational settings. As a behavior analyst, Dr. Adzhyan works with school psychologists, teachers, paraprofessionals, parents, and students by conducting functional assessments, carrying out trainings, and developing and implementing behavioral intervention plans for students with autism, attention deficit hyperactivity disorder (ADHD), emotional behavioral disorders (EBDs), and other behavioral disorders. Dr. Adzhyan was also part of the LAUSD team that developed a process of early referral, assessment, and support for students who engage in self-injurious behaviors. Dr. Adzhyan consults with LAUSD behavior support team members on cases that involve severe problem behaviors such as self-injury and aggression. He teaches courses and is a university-based practica supervisor at the CSUN MS-ABA program. He also teaches undergraduate courses at the Department of Psychology at CSUN. His research interests include use of Standard Celeration Charts (SCCs) within the Response to Intervention model to improve academic fluency; use of Precision Teaching with children with autism, EBD, and other behavior disorders; and developing and implementing behavior reduction treatment plans that are based on the principles of applied behavior analysis with children and adolescents with severe problem behaviors.

Fieldwork and Supervision for Behavior Analysts

A Handbook

Ellie Kazemi, PhD, BCBA-D, Brian Rice, MA, BCBA,
and Peter Adzhyan, PsyD, LEP, BCBA-D

SPRINGER PUBLISHING COMPANY

Springer Publishing Company, LLC
11 West 42nd Street
New York, NY 10036
www.springerpub.com

Acquisitions Editor: Rhonda Dearborn
Compositor: Newgen

ISBN: 9780826139122
ebook ISBN: 9780826139139

Editable worksheets to accompany the 10 BACB competencies are included in the online version available at http://connect.springerpub.com/content/book/978-0-8261-3913-9

Editable worksheets ISBN: 9780826138972

18 19 20 21 22 / 5 4 3 2 1

The author and the publisher of this Work have made every effort to use sources believed to be reliable to provide information that is accurate and compatible with the standards generally accepted at the time of publication. The author and publisher shall not be liable for any special, consequential, or exemplary damages resulting, in whole or in part, from the readers' use of, or reliance on, the information contained in this book. The publisher has no responsibility for the persistence or accuracy of URLs for external or third-party Internet websites referred to in this publication and does not guarantee that any content on such websites is, or will remain, accurate or appropriate.

Library of Congress Cataloging-in-Publication Data
Names: Kazemi, Ellie, author. | Rice, Brian (Professor of clinical psychology) author. | Adzhyan, Peter, author.
Title: Fieldwork and supervision for behavior analysts : a handbook / Ellie Kazemi, PhD, BCBA-D, Brian Rice, MA, BCBA, and Peter Adzhyan, PsyD, LEP, BCBA-D.
Description: New York, NY : Springer Publishing Company, LLC, [2019] | Includes bibliographical references.
Identifiers: LCCN 2018041171 | ISBN 9780826139122 (pbk.)
Subjects: LCSH: Behavioral assessment—Moral and ethical aspects—United States—Handbooks, manuals, etc. | Behavior analysts—Certification—United States—Handbooks, manuals, etc. | Behavior analysts—Professional ethics—United States—Handbooks, manuals, etc.
Classification: LCC RC437.B43 K39 2019 | DDC 155.2/8—dc23
LC record available at https://lccn.loc.gov/2018041171

Contact us to receive discount rates on bulk purchases.
We can also customize our books to meet your needs.
For more information please contact: sales@springerpub.com

Publisher's Note: New and used products purchased from third-party sellers are not guaranteed for quality, authenticity, or access to any included digital components.

Printed in the United States of America by Gasch Printing.

Contents

Preface

The simple truth is that we got the courage to write this book from the many colleagues and students who nudged, prompted, and encouraged us! A little more than 10 years ago, Dr. Adzhyan and I developed a structured supervision folder to guide our students and our own supervision practice. I posted the content of our folder on my laboratory website when we began to receive a high volume of requests from other students and supervisors who had come across one of our students. Brian Rice, one of my first supervisees, adopted our supervision folder upon graduation and has since made many contributions as a supervisor to the content, our CSUN practica students' experiences, and the field at large.

The three of us have had the distinct privilege, and occasionally the frustration, of supervising more than 150 students. Through our combined experiences, research, and, sometimes, trial and error, we have found that certain strategies and activities are more helpful than others for preparing emerging behavior analysts. This book is the culmination of what we have learned together supervising fieldwork experiences of individuals working with community partners, in public and nonpublic educational settings and schools, client's homes, clinics, community settings, and research laboratories.

We developed the 10 overarching competencies, and the task lists for each competency, with help from colleagues and students. As we developed the competencies, we quickly realized that we all had very different experiences in our graduate trainings and with our own supervisors, which naturally influence our supervision styles. However, all of us seem to agree about the core skills a competent, professional behavior analyst should have in his or her repertoire.

This handbook is written for you, the supervisee. Our objective is for you to work collaboratively with your supervisor(s) in preparation for your next step, whether that be a career as a practitioner or an academic. We focused on you, as our audience, to encourage you to prepare yourself for supervision by taking initiatives and asking for opportunities. We hope you find the self-reflection exercises and activities helpful. Supervision is a bidirectional learning process; we have shared our experiences with our supervisees through many of the activities and scenarios. In turn, we encourage you to discuss the scenarios with your supervisors and ask them if they have faced similar situations and how they would have dealt with the issues. We hope you use the scenarios as a basis to get to know your supervisors better.

We recommend that you read the introductory chapters, Section I, before or as you seek fieldwork placement for your supervision. In Section II, we have provided the information and the steps you need to take to become a competent supervisee and make the most out of your supervision experience. In Section III, we have outlined the 10 competencies we feel every behavior analyst should possess. We have left a lot of room for your supervisors and you to move through the competencies at your own pace and sequence depending on your baseline skills, the context of supervision, the population you serve, and your supervisor's clinical judgment and preferences. The competency task lists are not meant to be prescriptive; instead, they are guides to help you and your supervisor through your journey.

Editable worksheets to accompany the 10 BACB competencies are included in the online version available at http://connect.springerpub.com/content/book/978-0-8261-3913-9

Acknowledgments

Getting the opportunity to write this book has been a privilege we did not expect, and an accomplishment we would not have been able to achieve without the support of our supervisees, colleagues, mentors, friends, and family.

We are grateful to our students, some of whom are now colleagues, who have challenged us, provided us with excellent feedback, and taught us many things over the years. They are the catalysts for our contributions in this book.

Many thanks to our community partners who have collaborated with us in providing supervision to our students and who often remind us of the social significance of our roles as supervisors. We want to thank the clinical supervisors who have taken time to provide feedback on earlier iterations of the competencies. Also, we deeply appreciate the specific feedback we received from supervisors who used the supervision folder with their own supervisees.

We also want to thank Austin Chai and Jane Byon for their beautiful illustrations and Vahe Esmaeili, Ernesto Beltran Carrillo, and Victor Ramirez for reviewing earlier drafts of the chapters and providing prudent feedback from the perspective of a supervisee. We thank Dr. Linda LeBlanc, whose personal warmth, mentorship, and professional support helped bring this project to fruition.

Finally, we are especially grateful to Ashley Rice for organizing many of the documents for the supervision folder and for editing earlier versions of the competencies. She has been instrumental, personally and professionally, in our combined efforts to complete this book.

I

INTRODUCTION TO SUPERVISION

1

Preparing for Practica

Beginning your journey in practicum can be very exciting when you realize that supervision has a major influence on the development of your career and who you become as a professional. We are excited for you because entering your practicum marks the beginning of a new chapter of learning and represents a milestone in your training. Before you begin, there are certain things you need to know to take charge of your journey and start your experience on the right foot.

WHAT STEPS DO I NEED TO TAKE TO BECOME A CREDENTIALED BEHAVIOR ANALYST?

It is very important that you understand the credentialing process not only so that you can obtain a credential for yourself, but also because you will be responsible for teaching future generations of behavior analysts about the process when you become a supervisor. In addition, it is important that you learn the credentialing process as a professional representing the field of behavior analysis to clients, families, supervisees, and the community at large. You will find that something as simple as how you communicate about the training and experience you needed to become a behavior analyst can make a huge difference in how families feel about the treatment you offer. In fact, in a few minutes, you can make a lasting impression about your credibility, as well as the credibility of your profession. To gain the skills you need to become proficient at telling people about the professional requirements for behavior analysts, you first need to become informed, which you can do by reading this section.

The training and credentialing process in behavior analysis are similar to that of medical professionals or other licensed behavioral health providers such as clinical psychologists, clinical social workers, school psychologists, and marriage and family therapists (Kazemi & Shapiro, 2013). As you can see in Figure 1.1, to practice independently, your initial training begins with specific coursework requirements that are typically integrated into your graduate degree program. In addition, you are expected to gain practical experience under the tutelage and direct supervision of an experienced professional who has met certain board requirements and holds the credential you aim to obtain. Finally, you are required to apply to the credentialing board and provide evidence that you are ready to sit for the board examination because you meet the minimum requirements.

FIGURE 1.1 The degree, coursework, and supervision requirements to become eligible to sit for the board examination.

Degree   Coursework   Supervision

You may be wondering which credentialing board(s) gives you the credentials you will need to practice. Well, that depends on where you live. For this book, we decided to outline the minimum requirements for you as broadly as possible because we know that the readers of this book may live anywhere in the United States, or in the world, depending on the growth of the profession of behavior analysis. You should familiarize yourself with the specific credentials you will need to practice independently in your target region. The specific credentials you need differ depending on where you live and the specific credentialing requirements of your region. For example, some states, such as Hawaii, require you to be licensed to practice independently, and therefore you must apply to a licensing board and pass their examination(s). Some other states, such as California, have not regulated the profession of behavior analysis, so you can practice in these states independently with only your board certification as a behavior analyst (i.e., Board Certified Behavior Analyst [BCBA]).

Regardless of which credentialing board(s) serves as the regulatory system in your region, you will be required to complete your graduate degree, meet the educational and coursework requirements, complete a certain number of supervised experience hours, and pass the board examination *to meet the minimum criteria* to practice independently. As a point of reference, the Behavior Analyst Certification Board (BACB) is a nonprofit organization, established in 1998, that oversees the BCBA certification requirements for behavior analysts internationally. This organization provides guidelines to professional and consumers, monitors the provision of supervision for emerging certificants, and administers the certification examination (Behavior Analyst Certification Board, 2017). If you would like further information about this organization, go to www.bacb.com.

There are also some states that require you to have both a license and a certificate. You should discuss with your graduate program which credentials are required for behavior analytic practice in your region. It is in your best interest to spend some time learning how to evaluate the various credentials in behavior analysis that may be available to you in your region, which you can do by reading Green (2011). Finally, you would benefit from learning more about the differences between licensure and certification for behavior analysts (see Dorsey, Weinberg, Zane, & Guidi, 2009, and Green & Johnston, 2009, for great discussions).

In summary, to become a credentialed behavior analyst, at a minimum, you have to meet the following board requirements:

- Have a graduate degree in a related field
- Complete graduate-level coursework requirements (these may be coursework in your graduate degree program)
- Obtain fieldwork experience hours under the guidance of a supervisor
- Take and pass the board examination

Be aware that the requirements to sit for the board examination are likely to change every few years. The minimum requirements for every profession are increased every so often as more professionals enter the field and as the credentialing boards become more established. Also, you should recognize that credentialing boards require professionals to continue their education so they will stay on top of the most recent changes in the profession, including new research findings and practice guidelines. Therefore, after you obtain your credential, you will be required to complete a certain amount of continuing education units (CEUs) within a certain time frame to keep your credential. Tracking these changes and meeting the requirements for continuing education are the responsibility of each individual and, as such, you should be familiar with the standards and the sources to go to for keeping up your profession's standards.

Now that you have read about the requirements, understand the minimum criteria to practice behavior analysis, and know how to maintain your credential, we recommend that you set aside some time to engage in public rehearsal of this information (see Exercise 1.1). You need to rehearse publicly (or speak out loud) with yourself in the mirror, with imaginary listeners, or friends and family members who would provide you with honest feedback. The reason you should engage in public rehearsal is because different behaviors are used when reading, thinking, and telling someone about the credentialing process. When you speak publicly, you engage your vocal cords and can hear yourself speak. Unlike during thinking, when you speak publicly you are much less likely to stop mid-sentence or self-correct several times. Therefore, to become a better speaker and to achieve competence in "bedside manners," you need to practice publicly speaking about your work. To remind you to practice some things out loud, we have embedded practice exercises throughout the chapters.

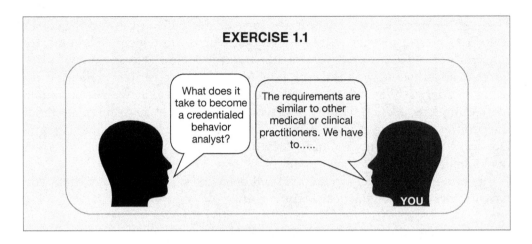

WHAT IS THE DIFFERENCE BETWEEN PRACTICUM, INTERNSHIP, AND FIELDWORK?

The terms *practicum* and *internship* are both used in most clinical programs to refer to supervised experiences that are integrated into university-based training. *Practicum* (plural *practicums* or *practica*) refers to the coursework associated with experiential learning, whereas *internship* or *fieldwork* refers to site placement that gives you access to "on the job" training. Your university may offer you practica coursework and require certain internship hours for you to fulfill your course requirements. Practicum usually provides you with additional monitoring and support through structured meetings with an experienced behavior analyst who has been hired by your university to teach the practica coursework. Your practicum meetings may include case consultations, peer review, role-plays, training, and other hands-on activities.

Your internship options depend on the arrangements your university has made with community partners, such as nearby hospitals, adult group homes, in-home behavioral agencies, and in-school public or nonpublic agencies. You may have the option to work at a university-based clinic or be able to access paid or unpaid internships. Universities differ in the types of internship experiences they can offer their students depending on the community surrounding the university as well as the types of experiential learning that have been historically available to the university students. The term *fieldwork* may be used to refer to experiential learning that is related to your practica or it may be independent of the university such that you are required to find and secure supervised fieldwork on your own. You should discuss with your graduate program whether you are required to take practica coursework, the structure of such coursework, and the available options for your fieldwork opportunities. Doing this will allow you to begin determining the best fit for you and your specific goals in the field of behavior analysis.

WHAT IS AND *IS NOT* SUPERVISION?

You may have some ideas about what clinical supervision looks like depending on your previous experiences and what you have seen or heard. Before anything else, it is good for you to jot down what you think of when you envision optimal supervision. Your preconceived notions of supervision are likely to influence how you approach your experience. Therefore, it is important that you take some time to self-evaluate your history with the concept of supervision before you begin (see Self-Reflection Exercise 1.1). Self-reflection, meaning taking the time to think about your own thoughts, history, values, motives, and actions, is important in your professional development. To help you take the time to become more self-aware and reflect on things that may affect your professional practice, we have developed self-reflection exercises throughout this book. Be sure to take the time to reflect and take written notes of what you learn about yourself (in this book or a supervision journal or binder) so that you may come back to your reflection(s) at different periods in your professional development.

SELF-REFLECTION EXERCISE 1.1

Before you move forward, take some time to self-reflect. My supervisor's primary role will be to _____. How would you fill in the blank?

1. _____

2. _____

3. _____

Self-reflect and think to yourself....

4. _____

5. _____

It is important, as you take the journey in supervision and thereafter, that you learn to take time to self-reflect and evaluate your own history and how it will affect your relationships with your supervisor, clients, peers, and future supervisees. If you do not take the time to complete this process of reflection, you may enter supervision with unrealistic expectations of how the process should work and, therefore, start your relationship with your supervisor on the wrong foot. In the following, we outline some examples of myths that supervisees have shared with us in their reflections.

Myth 1: Supervision is about me feeling empowered, confident, and prepared at all times. My supervisor will not ask me to take risks and will let me try new things only when I feel 100% ready.

The Truth: Supervision is about *learning from doing.* Your supervisor will encourage you to put your behavior out there so that you can be given feedback to improve. You will find that the more quickly you are willing to apply your new skills by putting your behavior out there, the more quickly your supervisor can assess how far you have gotten on your own and what things you can improve upon to grow.

> **Myth 2:** A good supervisor is my supporter and will always tell me how well I am doing, especially when I am nervous, down on myself, or feel dumb for having made some bad clinical judgments.

The Truth: A good supervisor will provide you with accurate feedback about your performance. This means that a good supervisor is willing to tell you when you have made an error and will help you learn how to correct such errors in the future. Telling you that you have made an error does not make your supervisor any less of a supporter of you. In fact, giving corrective feedback takes effort and is challenging for most supervisors. A good supervisor takes on the challenge knowing that accurate feedback will be most effective in helping you grow and the best way to support you.

> **Myth 3:** My supervisor's job is to be critical of my work.

The Truth: Your supervisor's job is to give you accurate feedback. That means that your supervisor will tell you when you have done something well as well as when you need to do something differently in the future.

> **Myth 4:** My supervisor will provide me with feedback on my clinical tasks only.

The Truth: Your supervisor will provide you with feedback on your clinical as well as ethical and professional skills. This will include, but is not limited to, your mannerisms, how you dress, and how you interact with others.

Remember...
The primary purpose of supervision is for you to gain the skills you need to become a competent professional!

After your self-reflection, it is important for you to learn what formal supervision involves and how it works. Supervision is a transition from learning theories, philosophy, concepts, assessments, procedures, and analyses in the classroom to applying what you have learned with clients. The *primary purpose of supervision* requirements, in addition to degree and educational requirements, for practice-based credentials is for you to gain the skills you need to become a competent practitioner. Ultimately, your supervisor is responsible for your activities with your clients as well as for your skills as a professional.

A *supervisor* is your coach, trainer, mentor, advisor, and sometimes even your counselor. What sets your supervisor apart from these other roles is that your supervisor improves your skills by evaluating your performance on an ongoing basis and by providing you with feedback to help you make improvements. That is why supervisors are generally considered the gatekeepers to becoming a professional. It is their job to evaluate their supervisees' performances and to determine when the supervisee is ready to sit for the board examination. Essentially, supervisors are tasked with the responsibility of decreasing premature entry of supervisees into a profession by screening their suitability.

NATURE AND FUNCTION OF SUPERVISION

In business, supervision is overseeing the work of staff, and its function is to increase work productivity and quality. In behavioral health professions, the *nature and function of supervision* is such that your supervisor is ethically, and in some cases by law, responsible for the following:

- The quality of services your clients receive
- Your therapeutic relationship with the clients and stakeholders
- Your actions with the clients and delivery of ethical practice
- Your professional growth, competence, and well-being
- Your work productivity, such as timely submission of your reports and progress notes

CHAPTER REVIEW

In this first chapter, we outlined the steps you need to take to become a credentialed behavior analyst. We also discussed the differences between practicum, internship, and fieldwork experiences. To set you on the path to success, we provided some guidelines to help you self-reflect before you begin your journey and offered information about what you should expect from supervision. You will find that supervised learning experiences are crucial for all practitioners (e.g., nurses, physicians, medical technicians, dentists, dental hygienists, counselors, therapists, social workers, and teachers) and a significant part of your training that will help you relate to other medical, mental, and behavioral health services providers.

REFERENCES

Behavior Analyst Certification Board. (2017). About the BACB. Retrieved from https://www.bacb.com/about

Dorsey, M. F, Weinberg, M., Zane, T., & Guidi, M. M. (2009). The case for licensure of applied behavior analysts. *Behavior Analysis in Practice*, 2(1), 53–58. doi:10.1007/BF03391738

Green, G. (2011). How to evaluate alternative credentials in behavior analysis. Retrieved from http://www.iabaonline.com/wp-content/uploads/2013/03/How-to-Evaluate-Alternative-Credentials-in-Behavior-Analysis-Green-G.pdf

Green, G., & Johnston, J. M. (2009). Licensing behavior analysts: Risks and alternatives. *Behavior Analysis in Practice, 2*(1), 59–64. doi:10.1007/BF03391739

Kazemi, E., & Shapiro, M. (2013). A review of board standards across behavioral health professions: Where does the BCBA credential stand? *Behavior Analysis in Practice, 6*(2), 18–29. doi:10.1007/BF03391799

Choosing the Type of Fieldwork You Want

There are significant differences between the types of experiences you will have depending on the fieldwork and the focus of your supervision site. Your university program may give you the opportunity to select between a university-based clinic and a community placement such as a clinical agency, school, hospital, community center, group home, or treatment facility. As with anything else in life, there is no perfect fieldwork experience. In addition, even though there are some general things we outline here about each type of fieldwork, know that there are always exceptions and recognize that you should do your homework before making a final decision. If you are given choices, you should select the fieldwork placement that is the best match for your needs and short-term goals (things you would like to achieve in the next 2–3 years) for supervision. We have outlined the pros and cons of each type of fieldwork experience to help you decide which experience may be the best option for you. Before you learn more about the differences between fieldwork experiences, spend some time self-reflecting and identifying your goals for supervision (see Self-Reflection Exercise 2.1).

Now that you have self-reflected about your strengths and determined some of your goals for supervision, you should try and select the fieldwork experience that is the best match for your goals (Figure 2.1).

Both university-based clinics and community placements will target your overall competence as a practitioner and emerging professional. However, these fieldwork experiences have different foci and funding mechanisms, which lend themselves to very different experiences for you. Just as with the word "supervisor," however, you may have some preconceived notions about some of the components of each type of experience (e.g., the word "research" may make you think of laboratory experiments

SELF-REFLECTION EXERCISE 2.1

The strengths I bring to my supervision experience are:

1. _____

2. _____

3. _____

4. _____

5. _____

Self-reflect and think to yourself....

Some things I'd like to achieve, or improve, during my supervision are:

1. _____

2. _____

3. _____

4. _____

5. _____

These become your short-term goals

FIGURE 2.1   Selecting fieldwork experience.

or cold scientists). We encourage you to keep an open mind and to get to know all of your options before selecting the site that is most suitable for your skills and goals.

UNIVERSITY-BASED SITES

The primary purpose of on-campus experience sites is to provide high-quality supervision to students and, in most cases, opportunities for collaborative and applied research projects (see Dubuque & Dubuque, 2018). As a result, university-based clinics usually provide focused services to specific populations (e.g., children younger than the age of four diagnosed with autism spectrum disorder) depending on the research projects and expertise of the faculty members involved with the clinic. Also, in most cases, families who look for university-based services are typically more educated and less wary of student interns and research. It is likely that they are faculty, staff, students, or alumni of the university or that they have heard about the university services through such individuals. In most cases, they have sought university services because they are looking for something other than what is available to them through their insurance provider. As a result, they are more likely to be involved in treatment planning, look favorably on treatment recommendations, and follow through with treatment protocols.

Supervisors at university-based practica are often faculty members or professional experts hired by the university to supervise interns. Therefore, they have a high level of control over your training and personal development. It is likely that your supervisor will spend a small amount of time on administrative tasks such as scheduling clients, discussing productivity with respect to financial cost–benefit, and paperwork. This is especially the case if the clinic is funded through grants and donations instead of a third-party payer (e.g., an insurance company). In such a setting, you are likely to obtain many more hours of supervision, typically with some involvement from a university faculty member who provides opportunities for research assistantships. You are also likely to have dedicated time with a supervisor to discuss ideas, review the research literature, and test out your ideas under the guidance of your supervisor with the clients. If you are considering a doctoral degree and a career as an academic and a researcher, this is definitely the right fieldwork for you because you will obtain applied research experience and mentorship from university faculty.

Some other advantages of university-based fieldwork are that you are likely to gain firsthand experience in applying the concepts and procedures you learned in your classes. Sometimes, your supervisor(s) may be also your faculty in your graduate program and may help you link your experience with coursework. It is also likely that you will feel more in charge of the treatment procedures you recommend and implement because you are in a setting that is more controllable by you than clients' homes or schools. Finally, you are likely to be the provider of the most recent evidence-based treatments available and cutting-edge research that has not yet been published. The disadvantage is that you may be less prepared for the world outside of the university, where the controlling agents often are the third-party payers and you have much less control over the context of services.

COMMUNITY-BASED SITES

Supervision in a community setting provides you with the opportunity to experience what a career as a behavior analyst working outside of a university setting will really look like. From the onset of your supervision, you will learn to work with human resources and administrative staff who have expertise in areas outside of behavior analysis and who enforce policies that affect your daily job. The primary focus of supervision in such a setting is client services, and your supervisor is likely to have administrative as well as clinical duties. In community settings, supervisors usually have little or no control over the number of clients they are assigned to, which staff are hired, and who they supervise. An increasing number of clinical supervisors also have administrative duties, which can be challenging to balance and sometimes decreases their capacity to focus on their clinical supervision. In addition, supervisors in community settings work with a wider range of both clients and staff.

Unlike in a university setting, some consumers may not be willing participants in the behavior change program, and the supervisor will have to adapt the program to facilitate their participation. Staff may also lack the motivation or skills to perform specific behavior procedures, and the supervisor is responsible for leading the team and ensuring procedures are implemented correctly. However, if your field placement is a supportive setting and you have a highly skilled supervisor, you will find that you can learn a lot about the realities of the job by experiencing the contextual challenges your supervisor faces. You could learn a lot about how your supervisor balances between responsibilities, juggles between stakeholders, manages time, problem-solves, and more.

Some other advantages of community-based fieldwork are that you are likely to learn, firsthand, how to work with diverse populations, ages, and families who may not access university services as readily. You are more likely to learn how to deal with challenging caregivers, unsatisfied customers, parents with concerns, and other difficult circumstances that affect your therapeutic relationship. In addition, you can learn how to tweak and use evidence-based interventions in contexts that are undoubtedly different from the ones in research studies (e.g., considering younger siblings in the household). If you are considering a career as a clinical director or clinical supervisor, this type of setting may be more suitable for you because you will learn about the ins and outs of community-based service delivery from the outset of your experience. The disadvantage of this type of fieldwork is that your supervisor is likely to have less time to give you and can focus less on your personal development during supervision. Also, the focus of community-based services is consumer care, so by design, your development and needs as a supervisee are not the priority.

In an ideal world, you would have the opportunity to receive supervision in a highly controlled setting, such as a university-based clinic, and then obtain supervision in a field experience after meeting competencies in the first setting. In addition to the gradual building of skills, such sequential supervised experience would give you access to multiple supervisors before practicing independently.

The advantage of having multiple supervisors is that you learn from the different perspectives they offer as well as learn whether the feedback they are giving you is reliable across supervisors. Some behavioral health professions, such as clinical psychology, require such multistep supervision experience such that students are required to obtain a certain amount of supervised experience in their pre- and post-doctoral degree programs. However, in behavior analysis, it is rare that you will have such an opportunity today because of the ever-increasing demand for credentialed behavior analysts.

Depending on your geographic region and the university you are attending, you may or may not be given choices for your supervision placement. If you are given choices between the different types of supervision, you should select your site based on your own strengths, goals, and hopes for supervision. We have provided the Quick Reference 2.1 checklist for you to consider the advantages of each type of fieldwork.

QUICK REFERENCE 2.1 ADVANTAGES OF EACH FIELDWORK PLACEMENT

University Based	Community Based
1. Work directly with faculty member(s) at the university in their area of expertise	1. Become exposed to different client populations and intervention approaches
2. Develop expertise in specific clinical area(s) and, in some cases, research area(s)	2. Practice balancing clinical and administrative tasks required of a community-based supervisor
3. Have more supervisory contact and access to indirect experience activities	3. Access clearly defined roles and growth opportunities within the organization
4. Access a connection between coursework and supervision experience	4. Observe utilization of procedures based on client, setting, and funding entity
5. Focus on developing competencies in a systematic manner	5. Address competencies as opportunities arise

NOW WHAT?

Now that you are more familiar with each type of fieldwork and the advantages and disadvantages of supervised experience at each of these settings, it is time for you to consider your own strengths and goals from Self-Reflection Exercise 2.1 and see if one of the fieldwork experiences is more suitable for you. We recommend that you take some time to self-reflect and identify the advantages of each type of fieldwork that really matter to you in Self-Reflection Exercise 2.2.

SELF-REFLECTION EXERCISE 2.2

Considering your strengths and goals from Self-Reflection Exercise 2.1 and the advantages of each fieldwork experience from the Quick Reference 2.1, jot down the top five advantages that best match your short-term goals:

1. _____

2. _____

3. _____   *Self-reflect and think to yourself....*

4. _____

5. _____

After completing the exercise, note which fieldwork experience option provided by your graduate program has the largest number of advantages listed. Don't get sidetracked by the bells and whistles and how fancy a fieldwork experience sounds. What matters is that you select the fieldwork that is the best match for your short-term goals. There is no way that you can have it all in a short period of time. Your best bet is to narrow down your options and gain the experience you need most immediately. Over time, you may change your mind and broaden your experiences as you grow as a professional. Right now, you are likely to obtain a stronger foundation in experiential learning if you begin your journey at a place that meets your immediate and short-term needs.

CHAPTER REVIEW

In this chapter, we described the types of experiences you are likely to have at a university-based site versus in community-based fieldwork. We also outlined some potential pros and cons associated with each type of setting. Finally, we provided self-reflection activities to help you select the type of fieldwork that would be best suited to your needs. We recognize that not all readers of this book will have the opportunity to select between these fieldwork experiences. However, knowing about the different types of fieldwork available for experiential learning can be very helpful to you as you grow as a behavior analyst and are put in a position to hire or supervise future emerging behavior analysts.

REFERENCE

Dubuque, E. M., & Dubuque, M. L. (2018). Guidelines for the establishment of a university-based practical training system. *Behavior Analysis in Practice*, 11, 51–61. doi:10.1007/s40617-016-0154-8

3

Selecting a Supervisor

In addition to selecting the type of fieldwork, you may be in a position to select a supervisor who will guide your experience and determine when you are ready to sit for the board examination. The following scenario is the one we have faced quite often.

VIGNETTE 3.1

Jossalyn is a second-year graduate student in applied behavior analysis. She is hard working and diligent about doing a good job at her internship site. Over the past year, she has noticed that despite her requests, her supervisor has not provided her with opportunities outside of the direct 1:1 work with her clients. Jossalyn has asked her practica instructor about the methods to approach her supervisor and followed the advice she was given. However, her supervisor keeps putting the issue to the side and giving her the same response—that is, the company limits the amount of nonbillable time.

Although Jossalyn's situation may seem unfair because she will need experience with the things outside of the 1:1 implementation to become a competent behavior analyst, the scenario illustrates the importance of identifying the correct supervisor for your experience. In addition, it is important that you evaluate the pros and cons of each supervisor in the context of the internship site that employs them. In some cases, if you are already in a setting where you provide behavioral services, you may have a supervisor overseeing your current work and may be wondering if you should approach that person for a formal supervised experience. Alternatively, you may be relieved of making a choice because your university has selected supervisors for you. Throughout your career as a behavior analyst, you are likely to seek supervision for any, or a few, of the following reasons:

- To obtain a graduate degree
- To become eligible to sit for certification
- To become eligible to sit for licensure
- To maintain employment
- To grow or gain promotion
- To become proficient with a new clinical population or procedure(s)

No matter which of the aforementioned circumstances best describe you, it is important for you to become informed about the various aspects of selecting a good supervisor for several reasons. First, as with any relationship, you may wonder if your supervisor is a good one and having appropriate criteria on which to base your judgment will help you determine if you have made the right decision. Also, knowing what to look for helps you set appropriate expectations of your supervisor. Actually, we hope the information in this chapter also helps you recognize the complexities of supervision so that you are much more appreciative of the time and effort it takes an individual to supervise well. Second, you can set future goals for yourself if you wish to supervise others upon becoming credentialed. A part of the evaluation process for choosing a supervisor is not just the development of your skill set, but also selecting the best model for effective supervision practices. Third, you may be in a position to seek supervision later in your career, if you decide to work with a new population or in a new context. Completing the evaluation for your initial supervision will benefit you in this situation, as you will undergo the whole experience all over again. Finally, you may find yourself in a position to speak with peers or other professionals about their relationships with their supervisors and the content of this chapter will help you provide them with some insight.

ETHICS OF SUPERVISION

What makes the supervision experience unique is the fact that you are required to obtain it formally, so as to become eligible for practice-based credentials such as the Board Certified Behavior Analyst (BCBA). In addition, a supervisor evaluates your performance and makes decisions about your activities throughout the supervision process. In fact, a supervisor is obligated to design and document feedback and reinforcement systems that improve your performance (Behavior Analyst Certification Board, 2017a). As a result of the nature of supervision, issues of power, trust, safety, and control play a central role in the experience. The supervisor has a lot of power when it comes to when and how you can obtain your credential as well as your reputation as an emerging behavior analyst. Furthermore, a supervisor's suggestions for change are requirements, not just recommendations. Therefore, selecting an ethical, competent, and professional supervisor is key to making your supervision experience a good one.

As a whole, the lack of supervision research and the minimal monitoring of supervision practices of supervisors have put ethical practice in supervision at risk. Unfortunately, a supervisor is especially at risk of being compromised because of the multiplicity of his or her roles and the contingencies that affect supervisory practice, such as the types of work activities that are billable, the activities that appear to be valued by the employer(s), and the outcomes that result in promotions. Perhaps for these reasons, supervisors are obligated to take full responsibility for providing effective supervision to their supervisees. For example, they must accept only the volume of work that is commensurate with their ability to supervise effectively (Code 5.02 of the Compliance Code, Behavior Analyst Certification Board, 2017a).

Supervisors have a lot of responsibilities and power in the supervisor–supervisee relationship. The power differentials between a supervisor and a supervisee can potentially even be enhanced if the supervisor is a member of the majority culture, race, ethnicity, gender, or sexual orientation but the supervisee is not (Toldson & Utsey, 2008). An ethical supervisor is self-aware of the differential power in the relationship and takes steps to limit potential harm to both supervisees and consumers of their services (Thomas, 2010). An example step would be for the supervisor to create and schedule opportunities for an honest evaluation of supervision by the supervisee (see Compliance Code 5.07, Behavior Analyst Certification Board, 2017a). By taking this step, the supervisor and the supervisee can proactively identify and address any issues that may arise. Another example step would be for the supervisor to obtain consultation or additional training in culturally competent supervision. When supervisors take any of these steps, it would be best for them to discuss their decision making because ultimately supervisors are responsible for modeling ethical behavior (Bailey & Burch, 2016; Cobia & Pipes, 2002).

The most challenging role the supervisor has is the role of a gatekeeper for certification, and an ethical supervisor takes this role very seriously. Your supervisor, therefore, will be responsible for noticing any impediments to you becoming a competent, independent practitioner. Some of the things that your supervisor may watch for include academic difficulties, mental health problems, ethical or legal misconduct, and familial and life circumstances that compromise your performance. In all of these cases, it is the ethical and professional responsibility of your supervisor to recognize, assess, and intervene (Kaslow et al., 2007; Thomas, 2010). It is also your responsibility, as the supervisee, to keep your supervisor informed of your status. An ethical supervisor will teach you to seek supervision the moment you self-detect that you may be having difficulties that compromise your performance. The supervisor will work with you to determine the appropriate steps you need to take to become a healthy, competent, and contributing member of the profession. An ethical supervisor teaches you to prioritize consumers of your services and how to determine when your performance may compromise them. On the one hand, you want your supervisor(s) to have this gatekeeping power because it is very valuable to the profession's vitality as a whole. On the other hand, as a gatekeeper, the supervisor is very powerful in determining your future, and this power may potentially be abused if the supervisor has not taken steps to limit problems that may arise from conflicts of interest, dual relationships, and breach of confidentiality (see codes 1.06 Multiple Relationships and Conflict of Interest, 1.07 Exploitative Relationships, and 2.06 Maintaining Confidentiality of the BACB Professional and Ethical Compliance Code for Behavior Analysts, 2017a).

SUPERVISOR COMPETENCE

Although supervision is extremely important for shaping emerging clinicians, specialized training for it lags behind (Scott, Ingram, Vitanza, & Smith, 2000). In a recent survey, DiGennaro Reed and Henley (2015) found that the majority of supervisors reported that their current place of employment did not provide training about effective supervision practices. In addition, of the respondents who reported that they received training to supervise staff, very few (less than 5%) indicated that they felt their training prepared them to supervise others successfully! The truth is that many individuals are promoted to supervisory positions because they had excellent clinical skills in working with clients, not because they had formal training in or demonstrated competence in supervision (Page, Pietzak, & Sutton, 2001). That is why most supervisors rely on their own background and experience and either use the methods their supervisors used with them (Campbell, 2011) or do their best to do something different from what they themselves experienced to spare their supervisees.

For these reasons, the BACB developed the Supervisor Training Curriculum Outline in 2012 (Behavior Analyst Certification Board, 2017c) and has begun to enforce additional requirements for post-credential candidates who wish to supervise. Figure 3.1 presents the current requirements for supervisors of experience for individuals pursuing certification.

FIGURE 3.1   Requirements for supervisors of experience for those pursuing certification.

1. At the time of supervision, supervisors must hold the BCBA or BCBA-D credential, or be a licensed or registered psychologist certified by the American Board of Professional Psychology in Behavioral and Cognitive Psychology who was tested in Applied Behavior Analysis, or be authorized by the BACB to provide supervision for a Verified Experience; AND

2. Pass an 8-hour, competency-based training covering the BACB's Supervisor Training Curriculum Outline; AND

3. Obtain 3 hours of continuing education related to supervision during each certification cycle.

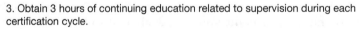

If your supervisor has met requirements 1 to 3 as outlined in Figure 3.1, his or her certificant registry will include the following statement: "Meets 2015 Standards for Supervision Requirements to supervise Exam Candidates as of Date," which will be the date the certificant became eligible to begin providing this type of supervision (Behavior Analyst Certification Board, 2017b). In addition to meeting these requirements, the supervisor may not be your employee, someone subordinate to you, or someone related to you—these restrictions are intended to avoid dual relationships and conflicts of interest that may arise as a result of such relationships. In its March 2018 newsletter, the BACB provided a number of documents to assist with the process of supervision. One such document, the Pre-Experience Checklist, has a list of steps you should take prior to starting your supervision experience. These steps include creating a BACB Gateway account, finding a supervisor who has met the BACB requirements to provide supervision for the BCBA certification, as well as seeking a resource to help you determine when you might be eligible to take the examination. By completing the steps in this document, you will be prepared better to start the supervision process.

According to the newsletter issued in October 2017, there were two primary changes to the supervision requirements: (a) a new policy section that outlines a supervisor's responsibilities, which is to reflect his or her accountability for supervised fieldwork, and (b) a restriction on BCBAs supervising within their first year after obtaining the BCBA certification. Given that these standards will be implemented in the near future, we recommend that you begin to take them into account, to the extent that you can, prior to their implementation date as you select a supervisor.

More often than not, the board requirements for supervision do not result in a performance evaluation of supervisory skills. It is left up to the supervisors to determine whether they *feel knowledgeable* and skilled enough to supervise. Therefore, in Quick Reference 3.1, we have provided a list of supervision skills we feel are important.

QUICK REFERENCE 3.1   SUPERVISION SKILLS

- Knowledge of the requirements for becoming credentialed and the most recent board standards
- Knowledge of the role and functions of supervisors in behavior analysis
- Knowledge of legal, ethical, and regulatory guidelines (e.g., school policies) that apply to their role as supervisors as well as to their consumer services
- Knowledge of the principles, philosophy, and methodology of behavior analysis as they relate to practice
- Competence in all areas of consumer care
- Competence in relationship skills (e.g., building rapport and trust)
- Competence in application of behavior analysis (e.g., conducting behavior assessments and prescribing appropriate function- and evidence-based behavior interventions)
- Skills in minimizing, mitigating, and resolving conflicts that may arise between the supervisor and the supervisee, the consumer and the supervisee, coworkers, and others

(continued)

QUICK REFERENCE 3.1   SUPERVISION SKILLS (*continued*)

- Competence in case of conceptualization, problem solving, and family systems
- Competence in crisis management
- Competence in integrating multicultural and diversity factors, such as ethnic, cultural, and religious values, in consumer services as well as the supervisory relationship
- Competence in minimizing harm to consumers and supervisees by limiting or resolving an ethical dilemma
- Competence in behavior skills training (BST) and giving feedback
- Professional skills (time management, oral and written verbal communications, recording documentations)

In surveys, supervisees have reported satisfaction with supervisors who demonstrate several of the skills outlined in Quick Reference 3.1 (Kazemi, Shapiro, & Kavner, 2015). Not surprisingly, items such as a supervisor's ethical and professional conduct are most important when considering supervisees' satisfaction with supervision. Supervisees report satisfaction with supervisors who treat their supervisees, peers, clients, and all parties involved at the workplace respectfully with regard to limiting gossip, being transparent, and maintaining confidentiality. Also, supervisees note how the supervisor treats his or her peers and develops relationships in the workplace that limit harm to supervisees and consumers.

Other qualities of a supervisor include being competent. At a minimum, a supervisor should be knowledgeable about the requirements for becoming credentialed by the regional and national boards and be well aware of the roles and functions of supervisors in behavior analysis. Also, a competent supervisor should have a strong foundation in behavior analysis because he or she is responsible for taking the material you learn in the classroom and showing you how it applies in your practice. There is ample evidence that BST, specifically components such as modeling and feedback, is the best way to teach performance skills, and it is important that a competent supervisor is skilled in this area (Sarokoff & Sturmey, 2004; Ward-Horner & Sturmey, 2012). A competent supervisor stays on top of the latest research in behavior analysis and gives consideration to important factors such as culture, ethnicity, and religion in his or her supervision practice. Lastly, a competent supervisor manages his or her time well so as to be able to meet the needs of consumers, supervisees, and other stakeholders (e.g., insurance companies), and can communicate, orally and written, with stakeholders regarding the clients' care and day-to-day activities.

It is an unfortunate reality that not all supervisors are quality supervisors or necessarily meet the minimum standards. A number of studies indicate that 50% of individuals report having experienced bad supervision (Nelson & Freidlander, 2001). Poor supervision has detrimental effects such that it negatively impacts consumers' progress and intervention outcomes. Poor supervision also impacts the skills of supervisees as a result of insufficient practice and guidance. In addition, supervisees who experience poor supervision do not have good role models to become effective supervisors in their own practices. In Quick Reference 3.2, we have provided a list of red flags or characteristics of a bad supervisor. In Chapter 6, we outline some strategies for you to approach your supervisor to provide feedback if you see some of the following red flags.

QUICK REFERENCE 3.2   CHARACTERISTICS OF A BAD SUPERVISOR

- Untrustworthy such that the supervisor is not professional or ethical
- Excessively critical and fails to notice improvements
- Disorganized, so that supervision, client, and work goals are unclear or missed
- Poor at resolving conflict
- Unavailable for meetings, feedback, or changes to consumer interventions
- Inconsistent

HOW WOULD I KNOW IF I AM GETTING GOOD SUPERVISION?

It is important that you have realistic expectations of your supervisor and recognize the factors that may affect his or her supervisory practice in your relationship. It is as much your responsibility as it is your supervisor's to read and make sure you understand the Experience Standards outlined in all of the forms provided to you by the BACB to support your supervision experience. There is no perfect supervisor, just as there is no perfect partner, friend, parent, or supervisee. Good supervision experience requires that both the supervisor and the supervisee work on the relationship, give each other clear expectations, keep channels of communication open, follow through with promises, and give each other the benefit of the doubt. The key is to have a discussion with your potential supervisor about how he or she will provide you with opportunities for meeting the Experience Standards outlined by the BACB. A good supervisor is someone you trust to approach and discuss your difficulties. Sometimes supervisors are highly knowledgeable and competent, which can make their supervisees feel intimidated. A good supervisor self-detects such limitations and takes steps to make the supervisee feel comfortable enough to approach any issues. The single most important quality of a good supervisor is that he or she builds a relationship with you such that you trust that the supervisor has your best interest at heart.

The second most important attribute is your supervisor's ability to face and resolve conflicts. Sometimes, the amount and type of support your supervisor is given by his or her employer to provide supervision may help or hinder the supervisory process. For example, Jossalyn, from Vignette 3.1, may learn that her supervisor has tried advocating on her behalf. However, the supervisor was ineffective in relaying to her employer the importance of giving Jossalyn experience in activities other than the 1:1 implementation. More importantly, the supervisor had not directly addressed the problem with Jossalyn or helped problem-solve. A good supervisor acknowledges such hindrances and takes steps to resolve and remove barriers. For example, Jossalyn's supervisor may have learned that if Jossalyn agreed to provide 1:1 work for 12 hours or more per week, the employer would allow her to engage in 2 to 3 total weekly hours of nonbillable work (e.g., developing measurement tools, revising curriculum based on the client's progress, and helping with portions of the progress report). In addition, if your supervisor identifies an issue in your participation in supervision, he or she should be capable of approaching the issue and working with you to address it. A good supervisor will encourage your development in this area, specifically by teaching you how to bring up and address any work-related dilemmas as part of supervision. Lastly, as you develop your skills, a good supervisor will expect you to collaborate with him or her and make you an active participant in guiding the course of your supervision.

Finally, we recommend that you have a discussion with your supervisor regarding the requirements of supervision as provided in the BCBA/BCaBA Experience Standards document. It is imperative that you and your supervisor familiarize yourselves with this document at the start of your supervisory relationship and discuss how specific standards will be met. For example, given that restricted hours (i.e., 1:1 work with clients) is capped at 40% of your total experience time, a good discussion would be how you can meet that requirement during your supervised experience. As previously mentioned, the standards for supervision can, and do, change periodically. It is your responsibility to work with your supervisor and to remain abreast of these changes to ensure that your supervision experience meets the standards set by the BACB.

NOW WHAT?

In this chapter, we reviewed specific areas for you to take into account when you choose your supervisor(s). An important final step is the actual decision making of who will be supervising your experience. Whether you get the opportunity to select your supervisor or one is assigned to you, we recommend that you speak to your supervisor about how he or she approaches the supervision process. In Quick Reference 3.3, we have listed some specific questions you may want to ask your supervisor.

QUICK REFERENCE 3.3   QUESTIONS TO ASK A POTENTIAL SUPERVISOR

1. What is your primary role in your organization?

2. How do you typically assess the competencies of your supervisees?

3. Are there any limitations you foresee occurring in our supervisor–supervisee relationship? Specifically, do you feel you face any barriers with regard to doing field observations, overseeing my indirect work hours, or giving me opportunities for

---

(continued)

**QUICK REFERENCE 3.3   QUESTIONS TO ASK A
POTENTIAL SUPERVISOR (*continued*)**

specific competences (e.g., designing, conducting, and interpreting functional analyses)?

4. What would you say is your area of expertise?

5. Have you met the BACB minimum standards to provide supervision?

6. My goals for supervision are _____. How would you envision us working toward those goals?

7. What would be your expectations of me if I were your supervisee?

CHAPTER REVIEW

In this chapter, we discussed everything you need to know to select a supervisor who is a good match for you. We discussed the importance of ethics in supervision and how the ethical conduct of a supervisor can affect you. We outlined the minimum requirements the BACB has for certificants to become eligible to supervise as well as the skills of a competent, good supervisor. Finally, we provided a list of potential questions to ask supervisors whom you decide to interview before selecting a supervisor. Given the importance of the role of a supervisor and his or her power in your relationship, we hope you to take some time to digest the information in this chapter and set yourself on a course for success. The information provided in this chapter is prescriptive both for finding the right supervisor and for becoming one! We hope that by illustrating the many complexities of the role of a supervisor, we have been able to increase your appreciation for your supervisors as well.

REFERENCES

Bailey, J., & Burch, M. (2016). *Ethics for behavior analysts* (3rd expanded ed.). New York, NY: Routledge.

Behavior Analyst Certification Board. (2017a). Professional and ethical compliance code. Retrieved from https://www.bacb.com/wp-content/uploads/2017/09/170706-compliance-code-english.pdf

Behavior Analyst Certification Board. (2017b). Requirements for supervisors. Retrieved from /https://www.bacb.com/supervision-requirements

Behavior Analyst Certification Board. (2017c). Supervisor training curriculum outline. Retrieved from https://www.bacb.com/wp-content/uploads/2017/09/supervisor_curriculum.pdf

Campbell, J. M. (2011). *Essentials of clinical supervision* (Vol. 28). Hoboken, NJ: John Wiley & Sons.

Cobia, D. C., & Pipes, R.B. (2002). Mandated supervision: An intervention for disciplined professionals. *Journal of Counseling and Development, 80*, 140–144. doi:10.1002/j.1556-6678.2002.tb00176.x

DiGennaro Reed, F., & Henley, A. J. (2015). A survey of staff training and performance management practices: The good, the bad, and the ugly. *Behavior Analysis in Practice, 8*(1), 16–26. doi:10.1007/s40617-015-0044-5

Kaslow, N. J., Rubin, N. J., Bebeau, M. J., Leigh, I. W., Lichtenberg, J. W., Nelson, P. D., . . . Smith, I. L. (2007). Guiding principles and recommendations for the assessment of competence. *Professional Psychology: Research and Practice, 38*, 441–451. doi:10.1037/0735-7018.38.5.441

Kazemi, E., Shapiro, M., & Kavner, A. (2015). Predictors of intention to turnover in behavior technicians working with individuals with autism spectrum disorder. *Research in Autism Spectrum Disorders, 17*, 106–115. doi:10.1016/j.rasd.2015.06.012

Nelson, M. L., & Friedlander, M. L. (2001). A close look at conflictual supervisory relationships: The trainee's perspective. *Journal of Counseling Psychology, 48*(4), 384–395. doi:10.1037/0022-0167.48.4.384

Page, B. J., Pietzak, D. R., & Sutton, J. M. (2001). National survey of school counselor supervision. *Counselor Education and Supervision, 41*(2), 142–150. doi:10.1002/j.1556-6978.2001.tb01278.x

Sarokoff, R. A., & Sturmey, P. (2004). The effects of behavioral skills training on staff implementation of discrete-trial teaching. *Journal of Applied Behavior Analysis, 37*, 535–538. doi:10.1901/jaba.2004.37-535

Scott, K. J., Ingram, K. M., Vitanza, S. A., & Smith, N. G. (2000). Training in supervision: A survey of current practices. *The Counseling Psychologist, 28*(3), 403–422. doi:10.1177/0011000000283007

Thomas, J. T. (2010). *The ethics of supervision and consultation: Practical guidance for mental health professionals.* Washington, DC: American Psychological Association. doi:10.1037/12078-000

Toldson, I. A., & Utsey, S. (2008). Race, sex, and gender considerations. In A. K. Hess, K. D. Hess, & T. H. Hess (Eds.), *Psychotherapy supervision: Theory, research, and practice* (2nd ed., pp. 537–559). Hoboken, NJ: Wiley.

Ward-Horner, J., & Sturmey, P. (2012). Component analysis of behavior skills training in functional analysis. *Behavioral Interventions, 27*(2), 75–92. doi:10.1002/bin.1339

4

Applying, Interviewing, and Securing Fieldwork

Depending on the type of program and the particular institution you attend, you will spend anywhere between 10 and 30 hours per week in your supervised experience. Thus, choosing the appropriate supervisor and fieldwork experience are vital. In this chapter, we discuss all aspects of securing fieldwork experience.

EVALUATING DIFFERENT INTERNSHIP SITES

The process of applying to specific internship sites will vary depending on your university and, in some cases, the specific sites. Some universities and agencies will have a formal application process, whereas others have an informal process and ask that you show up on a certain date and time for an interview. Typically, more established organizations or sites are likely to have more formalities because they have learned to streamline the process over time. A formal application process typically requires that you submit a cover letter, a complete application, your curriculum vitae (CV), and some references or letters of recommendation prior to being granted the opportunity to interview. It is also likely that you will be required to submit all of these items, or some of them, during a less formalized process. In this chapter, we provide some guidelines regarding each of these documents. But, before you begin the application process, you should conduct a thorough review of the following information, which will help you during the application process as well as your fieldwork experience.

Know the BACB Requirements

It is extremely important that you become familiar with the board(s) that will govern your activities as a credentialed behavior analyst. Although the requirements for credentialing differ from state to state, we will focus on the Behavior Analyst Certification Board (BACB; www.bacb.com) because it has been the primary certification board for behavior analysts, is an international organization, and is accredited by the National Commission for Certifying Agencies (NCCAs; www.credentialingexcellence.org). As we mentioned previously, board standards change every few years, and it is your responsibility to stay on top of the changes. The primary way you can do this is by subscribing to alerts for and reading the BACB Newsletters (www.bacb.com/newsletter/). For example, in October 2017, the BACB announced revised standards that will apply to anyone applying for certification on or after January 1, 2022. In this book, we outline standards that apply currently as well as those that will go into effect in January 2022, based on the October 2017 newsletter. When you are selecting a site for your fieldwork, you want to be sure that the majority of the activities you engage in meet the BACB requirements and that you have access to eligible supervisors (individuals who meet the minimum requirements, as discussed in Chapter 3) at the site.

Research the Organization as Your Potential Internship Site

Depending on the program or university you attend, you will have different options for fieldwork. Some universities screen community partners and develop relationships with the organizations that they approve for supervision of their students. In such cases, the university may provide you with a list of potential sites, and you are encouraged to select the sites based on your geographic location, the population you'd like to serve (e.g., early childhood, geriatrics), the expertise you'd like to gain (e.g., autism spectrum disorder therapy, addiction, literacy intervention), and the setting in which you hope to gain the experience (e.g., university campus, clients' homes or schools). If your university has not vetted the fieldwork sites (and even if the sites have been screened by your university), you need to conduct some preliminary research on the site to determine how well it fits what you need for your experience. We have provided a list of steps to take that we use to screen community agencies that partner with California State University, Northridge (CSUN), to provide supervision to our graduate students (see Quick Reference 4.1). In addition to the following resource, Brodhead, Quigley, and Cox (2018) offer some great tips for identifying organizations that will foster ethical practice.

PREPARING TO APPLY

After completing your evaluation of specific internship sites, you should prepare for the application process. As previously mentioned, there are specific documents

---

QUICK REFERENCE 4.1   REVIEW THE ORGANIZATION'S WEBSITE AND OTHER ADVERTISEMENT MATERIAL FOR THE FOLLOWING:

- See if there is an organizational chart or a list of employees and their positions to determine whether the credentials those employees hold match or are close to the minimum criteria outlined in the Practice Guidelines provided by the BACB (page 26, www.bacb.com/wp-content/uploads/2017/09/ABA_Guidelines_for_ASD.pdf).

- Does the organization provide ongoing training and professional development opportunities in behavior analysis to employees?

- Does the organization refrain from advertising or offering treatments that are popular but not evidence based (see the National Standards Project Report, 2015, for a list of evidence-based treatments for autism spectrum disorder [ASD]; www.bacb.com/newsletter)?

- Does the organization include testimonials only from clients who are no longer receiving services?

- Does the organization have job descriptions for behavior analysts that are accurate and describe ABA and their services in a manner that is conceptually systematic with the science of behavior analysis?

---

that you should have ready before applying to an internship site. In the following sections, we detail some specifics regarding the documents you are recommended to have ready: a cover letter, a CV, and letters of recommendation. Although the field placements may request other documents, such as work samples, the following documents are relatively standard for hiring.

BUILDING YOUR COVER LETTER

When you are applying for any position, you should put together a brief (typically one-page) cover letter. The purpose of the cover letter is to introduce yourself and to draw attention to the most important parts of your supplemental material (e.g., your CV). Just as with any business letter, your cover letter should include the date; a salutation or a greeting at the beginning of the letter; one or more paragraphs describing your qualifications, why you are applying for the position, and what you can bring to the company; and a professional closing statement. Be sure to disclose in the letter which other documents the agency will be receiving from you in addition to your cover letter. You should include your contact information (email address and phone number) and end with a signature or a closing salutation. The cover letter is the first document the organization receives from you, so keep it brief and be sure to edit your letter to avoid spelling and grammatical errors. See Figure 4.1 for a sample cover letter.

FIGURE 4.1   An example cover letter.

Your Full Name
Address
Email
Phone number

Date of letter (Month DD, YYYY)

Dear Sir or Madam:
      Discuss who you are. Do not include that you are writing this to apply for the job, they already know that. Mention your qualifications, which include your most recent academic achievements, such as getting your master's degree or obtaining a BCBA credential.
      Discuss the reasons you are choosing to apply to this company. Mention its goals, what you have found when researching the organization, and how those goals match with your own at this position. Discuss what you can contribute to the company that may be something new or strengthen the company's work. Lastly, mention the other documents that the organization will be receiving from you in addition to this letter.

Thank them for their time and consideration,

Sincerely,
Your Full Name

BUILDING YOUR CV

The purpose of a CV is to show a prospective internship site or employer that you have the necessary qualifications and experiences to meet the requirements for the position for which you are applying. Compared to a resume, which is short and bulleted, a CV is typically more detailed and leaves room for you to market your strengths. A good CV has the following characteristics:

- Attracts the reader's attention
- Creates a good impression of your experiences
- Presents your skills and qualities clearly and concisely

CV Tips

1. Use a professional email address (e.g., Jan.garcia@gmail.com, **NOT** partygal12@ aol.com).

2. Include only experience relevant to the position.

3. Keep style and formatting consistent. **DO NOT** include items such as birthday, ethnicity, or home address if you are placing your CV on the web.

Although there is no standard for a CV, how you format yours and the content you select to include matter. Keep in mind that the decisions you make regarding format and content should be determined based on how you think you can sell yourself for the position you seek. The following subheadings are included in most CVs.

Personal Contact Information

Include your full name, contact details such as the best number to reach you, your email address, and mailing address.

Education

In this section, you include your education, listed in reverse chronological order, with your most recent experiences and qualifications first. Listing your education in reverse chronological order allows for your prospective site to quickly evaluate your highest level of education, a key component when the company is determining whether you meet minimum criteria for the position. In addition, you must include the name of the institution, the dates you attended, the degree obtained, and the city and state where the institution is located. When developing this section, think about the relevance of each of your qualifications and include college only.

Employment or Work Experience

Similar to the "Education" section, you should list your work experience in reverse chronological order and highlight the experiences relevant to the position you are seeking. You typically list a maximum of 5 years of experience unless an experience you had more than 5 years ago is extremely relevant, highly prestigious, or more relevant than the experiences you had in the last 5 years. If you have had several different jobs, list the roles that are relevant to the position you are applying to obtain. If you have only a few work experiences, include volunteer work and change the subheading to "Employment and Volunteer Experiences." If you have research experience, you would include it in this section as well, either within the "Work Experience" section or in a separate section dedicated to your research experience if you are applying to research positions. You need to include the dates you worked, the title of your job, and the specific roles and responsibilities you had. Select your roles and responsibilities to highlight your skills. For example, everyone in a sales position may have greeted customers, worked on sales of merchandise, and helped clean up the store at the end of the day. But if you were trusted with opening and closing the store, training staff, and assisting the manager, or if you played other additional roles, outline those specific roles to demonstrate that you stood out or were a dependable employee. We have provided a list of powerful words with which to describe your skills and experiences in Quick Reference 4.2.

QUICK REFERENCE 4.2   ACTION WORDS TO USE IN YOUR CV

Roles and Responsibilities		Skills and Abilities
ınaged	➢ Supervised	➢ Trained in
oordinated	➢ Delegated	➢ Proficient at
Assigned to	➢ Analyzed	➢ Initially, employed to
Designed	➢ Developed	➢ Organized
➢ Created	➢ Conducted	➢ Negotiated
➢ Researched	➢ Led	➢ Initiated
➢ Improved	➢ Implemented	➢ Presented
➢ Identified	➢ Ensured	➢ Resulted
➢ Monitored	➢ Supported	➢ Instrumental in
➢ Strengthened	➢ Resolved	
➢ Planned	➢ Prepared	

References

Select your references carefully because the title, position, and the reputation of the individual influence how you are perceived. When selecting your references, it is imperative that you avoid ethical problems such as asking individuals who have personal relationships with you or are your clients. As an example, refrain from using a relative as your reference because your dual relationship with that person, meaning the fact that you are related and worked for the person, biases the recommendation and it will not be deemed as valid. Also, avoid asking clients, or caregivers of clients, to be references, because they would want to be seen as favorably by you and would not want to jeopardize their relationship with you. Furthermore, by asking a client or a parent to serve as your reference, you are asking them to break their confidentiality. Typically, the best references are individuals who can comment on your specific skills and attributes that are relevant to the position you seek. Some individuals to consider would be your former professors, employers, or supervisors.

Other Subheadings

Include the subheading of "Professional Certification" if you have relevant professional certification(s), such as Crisis Management Intervention (CPI), Cardiopulmonary Resuscitation (CPR), Registered Behavior Technician (RBT), or Board Certification at the Assistant Level (BCaBA). In addition, include the certification date for each item. Include the subheading of "Awards and Honors" if you have received high honors or achievements that are relevant to the position you seek or demonstrate strengths about you that relate to the position. Include a section for your "Publications" if you have served as an author on a poster, symposia, peer-reviewed article, or a chapter. Use the *Publication Manual of the American Psychological Association* for appropriate referencing of your publications.

Grammar and Formatting

When writing your CV, try to use the active versus passive tone of voice and keep things consistent (e.g., how you begin each sentence with a sub-bullet). Use the past tense when you are referring to work experiences that occurred in the past and the present tense only for the positions you have at the time you are writing your CV. Try to keep your CV easy to read and digest. Use a simple font (also referred to as a sans serif in typography), such as Calibri, Arial, or Cambria. Keep the font size at 12 or 12.5 points, and use bold, italic, and underlining sparingly and systematically. For example, make all of the headings bold. Also, keep your margins between 0.5 and 1 inch. Edit your work, giving yourself enough time to review your CV and revise it. Nothing works against you more than typos, gross grammatical errors, or formatting issues, because these errors demonstrate a lack of time management skills and attention to detail.

If your university provides you with practica coursework, you may have the opportunity to develop your CV, obtain feedback from your peers and instructor, and revise your CV before sending it out. If you are not able to use practica, we recommend that you identify two or three peers who are willing to serve as your peer reviewer, as long as you return the favor. Note that your CV is a work in progress: It should be developed and revised as you develop as a professional. We recommend that you set a schedule to revise your CV annually, because otherwise it becomes daunting to search, find, and include your activities accurately (Figure 4.2).

ASKING FOR LETTERS OF RECOMMENDATION

If your internship sites require letters of support from faculty members or others, give the recommenders ample notice before the deadline for your submission. Ample notice is 10 to 14 days, although some individuals ask for up to 30 days' notice in advance. Provide your recommenders with a copy of your CV and a description of the organization. Also, provide your recommenders with key information you hope they will include about you, such as the length of time they have known you as well as a brief list of the roles and responsibilities you have had that they can speak to. Most recommenders prefer to send their letters directly to the organization requesting the recommendation. Therefore, either provide electronic addresses and the person to whom the emails should be addressed or provide your recommenders with what they need for snail mail, such as addressed and stamped envelopes. The more diligent you are about how you ask your recommenders for their letters, the more likely they are to write strong letters of support, because there is likely to be a recency effect with regard to what they recall regarding your professional conduct.

FIGURE 4.2 An example curriculum vitae.

Full Name
Address: 123 My House St., City, State, Zip Code
Email: Myname@email.com
Phone: (555) 867-309

Education

Master of Science in Applied Behavior Analysis **Full Name of Institution** (City, State of institution)	Dates of Attendance: Mo/Yr-Mo/Yr
Bachelor of Arts in Psychology **Full Name of Institution** (City, State of institution)	Year Graduated

Experience

Most recent relevant experience company name	Dates Employed: Mon/Yr-Mon/Yr

Title of position
* Implemented...
* Supervised...
* Managed...
* Led...

Next most recent relevant experience company name	Dates Employed: Mon/Yr-Mon/Yr

Title of position
* Implemented...
* Assigned to...
* Planned...

Certifications

* **Registered Behavior Technician (RBT)**	Date received: Mon/Yr
* **Crisis Management Intervention (CPI)**	Date received: Mon/Yr
* **Cardiopulmonary Resuscitation (CPR)**	Date received: Mon/Yr

Publications
* Author, A. A., Author, B. B., & Author, C. C. (Year). Title of article. *Title of Periodical, volume number* (issue number), pages. http://doi.org/xx.xxx/yyyyy

References
Name, Credentials
Company/Institution
Relationship to You
Contact Information

PREPARING FOR THE INTERVIEW

Before the Interview

Prepare yourself for the interview by reviewing your notes from when you researched the site. We advise that you imagine being asked a question and answer it out loud, edit your answers, and restate your revised answers out loud. After practicing alone, it is a good idea to ask a peer to perform a mock interview with you and to provide you with honest feedback. In Quick Reference 4.3, we list some common questions you may be asked at any interview. Also, be sure to read Brodhead et al. (2018) for tips on how to identify ethical practices in organizations prior to employment or obtaining an internship. Prepare to answer common questions, like the ones listed in Quick Reference 4.3, but do not memorize your answers. That way, you can be flexible and adapt your answers to the interview questions. Also, be mindful of the function of the interview, which is to determine if you have the prerequisite skills and the determination to be worth the investment the organization has to put forth to supervise you.

QUICK REFERENCE 4.3   COMMON INTERVIEW QUESTIONS

- What experiences have you had that prepare you for this position?
- Can you tell us about yourself and why you selected this particular site?
- What are your immediate and long-term goals?
- What strengths will you bring to our organization?
- What would you say are some of your weaknesses?
- Scenario-based questions intended to see how you speak about the situation and solve a problem (e.g., tell us about a conflict you faced and how you handled it. Describe a difficult case and how you handled it.)
- What questions do you have for us?

The Interview Date

Excellent interviewers look for behaviors you demonstrate during the interview that are indicative of how you will behave if you are offered the position. Promptness and timely arrival to scheduled meetings is very important. So, arrive early to the site to be sure you have enough time to find the location, find the office of the interviewer, and check out the organization as a whole. Your professional conduct, including how you dress and present yourself, is important to every organization, because you will represent the organization as its employee. Dress professionally for your interview to demonstrate to the interviewer that you have put time and effort into preparing for the position as well as to show that you have professional conduct skills. Greet everyone and introduce yourself, because your professional conduct with administrative staff and other employees is exemplary of how you will conduct yourself when you are sent to a school, a client's home, or to other settings.

During the interview, be mindful of your active listening and oral communication skills; they are prerequisites for any professional behavioral service provider! Oftentimes, an interviewer's wording of a question or follow-up to a response gives you a clue as to the function of a question. So, pay careful attention to the interviewer's needs as a listener by attending to his or her tone of voice and body language. There is usually an opportunity for you to ask questions during the interview. Have a list of questions ready (these should be based on the research you conducted on the organization). Refrain from asking questions to which you can find answers by conducting a quick web search. Again, as a professional, there will be many times you will be working with clients or stakeholders, and you will need to review materials or conduct searches to become more informed as a member of the service-providing team. The questions you ask during the interview demonstrate the level to which you put time and effort into conducting searches independently and how well you use other individuals' time. In addition, asking questions provides more information to be used in determining the goodness of fit between you and the organization. Some good questions for you to consider asking are outlined in Quick Reference 4.4.

QUICK REFERENCE 4.4   GOOD QUESTIONS TO ASK DURING AN INTERVIEW

- What are the growth opportunities available in your organization for someone like me?
- How much time is usually devoted to assessment, and to direct and indirect services?
- Are there opportunities or support for participating in professional development activities?
- Does the organization hire strong interns after they graduate?
- What are some of the challenges the site faces with supervision of interns?
- Add questions from Brodhead et al. (2018).

Finally, be sure to inform the site of your enrollment in a graduate program and be prepared to discuss the requirements of your program. For example, as part of your graduate degree program, you may be required to attend classes, potential culminating examinations, symposia or university-hosted conferences, and other events to gain the most from your graduate education. It is important for you to divulge the requirements of your program and discuss with the site how the organization can help you by accommodating those needs. No site will be able to provide you with internship hours at exactly the time you need or to allow you to reschedule clients to study for your examinations. Be mindful that you are providing services to clients and that their needs must be prioritized. Be flexible, but transparent about your own boundaries. The scheduling negotiation should begin with open communication between you and the site and a willingness, on your part, to be flexible, but realistic so as not to sabotage your academic achievement.

WHAT IF YOU WERE NOT OFFERED A POSITION?

Most university programs that oversee your fieldwork experiences offer multiple opportunities for interviews and have different tiers of competition. At some universities, the university-based fieldwork opportunities are the most competitive. In other universities, the sites that offer the highest stipends for student pay or those that are geographically closer to the campus are more competitive. Your best bet is to have backup plans and to interview at multiple levels to secure a position. If you find that you did not secure the position(s) you wanted, you should try to meet with your practica instructor, program advisor, or internship coordinator and ask for some tips and feedback on your application for the future. In some situations, especially if the site has a formal internship agreement with your university, these individuals may be able to reach out to their contacts at the sites to access additional feedback regarding your interview. Your best bet is to make time to stay connected with individuals close to you and to seek the support of faculty, advisors, and peers. Asking for help demonstrates maturity and professionalism on your part; it is not a sign of weakness. Lean on your support system and implement the feedback and suggestions you receive.

In some cases, despite your best efforts, you may not secure a position you desired. Avoid stressing yourself out by asking questions that have circular answers, such as "What if I did XXXX?" or "What if I was feeling better during XXXX?" Although it is difficult to take a different perspective when you feel rejection, it is important to recognize that the selection process is bidirectional, and that while you may be an excellent candidate, sometimes you may not be the right match. Also, your fieldwork decision, albeit important, will not completely shape your career. Each site and experience will offer unique learning opportunities, and you can grow in any supportive environment if you focus on finding those opportunities and devote your internship to self-growth.

CHAPTER REVIEW

In this chapter, we walked through the process of preparing, applying, and interviewing for a position at a fieldwork placement site. Although it may seem possible to "wing it" as you evaluate different sites and apply for positions, appropriate preparation and practice can make a huge difference in the trajectory of your experience and the likelihood that you secure your first choice fieldwork placement. To paraphrase a quote from Benjamin Franklin, if you fail to prepare for this process, you are preparing to fail during your fieldwork placement.

REFERENCE

Brodhead, M. T., Quigley, S. P., & Cox, D. J. (2018). How to identify ethical practices in organizations prior to employment. *Behavior Analysis in Practice, 11*(2), 1–9. doi:10.1007/s40617-018-0235-y

5

Formalizing Supervision and Record Keeping

A crucial part of supervised experience is accurate record keeping of your activities and the supervision you receive. The scenario in Vignette 5.1 is an illustration of what may happen should you neglect to follow the steps outlined in this chapter.

VIGNETTE 5.1

Jan was ready to sit for the BCBA examination and set up a meeting with her supervisor to have him sign her Experience Verification form. During the meeting, Jan's supervisor informed her that her performance had been subpar and that he would not sign her verification form because he did not feel she was ready. Jan contacted the BACB, which asked her to send copies of the supervision contract and all of the signed Experience Supervision forms. Jan informed the BACB that she had never signed a contract and her supervisor had stated that the forms would all be signed after the accrual of all hours. Jan was very frustrated when she realized that she had not followed the appropriate procedures for accruing supervision hours and that she would have to restart.

To avoid falling way behind and feeling the frustrations Jan felt, you should read the procedures outlined on the Behavior Analyst Certification Board (BACB) website carefully and ask your graduate program and supervisor questions about your hours intermittently throughout your supervision experience. It is very likely that your graduate program, your supervisor, and your site will require you to be responsible for keeping track of your hours. Some of your supervision hours may be billable by the site, which means you would have to complete additional forms to be paid and for the site to be compensated for the services. Also, some of your hours may not count toward your supervision hours because they are not behavior-analytic in nature or are exclusively administrative. Therefore, accurate record keeping of the supervised hours you accrue will take time and organization skills. However, you will find that maintaining accurate records of the range of services you provide is not vital just during your fieldwork and internship experiences; these skills will also be essential as you move into your future career. By mastering this skill at the start of your supervised experience, you may save yourself hours of meticulous and tedious document review when applying for certification. In this chapter, we discuss how you can meet the requirements to begin to obtain supervision, formalize your supervision experience, complete the forms required by the BACB, and keep track of all of your activities.

BEFORE YOU CAN BEGIN ACCRUING HOURS

To begin accruing supervised experience hours formally, you will need to have started the qualifying coursework (i.e., attended the first graduate-level class in behavior analysis), secured a qualified supervisor, and completed a supervision contract. Some fieldwork placements have additional policies that stipulate when you can begin to accrue hours, such as requiring the completion of certain coursework or paperwork. Be sure to ask your graduate program advisor, internship coordinator, and/or fieldwork contact about their policies regarding the onset of your supervised experience hours. In addition to your placement, your supervisor may have other requirements, such as particular prerequisites you must meet, before you can begin to officially accrue hours. Whatever the terms may be, we encourage you to include them in your initial contract so that it is clear to you, and your supervisor, when you can begin to accrue hours formally. As mentioned in Chapter 3, we highly recommend utilizing the BACB Pre-Experience Checklist to determine your eligibility to begin supervision with a Board Certified Behavior Analyst (BCBA).

FORMALIZING THE SUPERVISED EXPERIENCE

Supervision Contract

According to the BACB, the supervisee and the supervisor must develop and sign a written contract prior to the onset of experience. The function of the contract is to protect you and your supervisor by creating an occasion for you to discuss your roles, responsibilities, and expectations clearly. You may be given a contract by your internship site or asked to develop a new one by editing a preexisting template. You want to be sure the following components suggested by the BACB are present in your contract (Behavior Analyst Certification Board, 2018c):

1. State the responsibilities of the supervisor and supervisee, including completion of the online experience training module by both the supervisor and

the supervisee as well as completion of the 8-hour supervision training by the supervisor.

2. Include a description of the appropriate activities and instructional objectives.

3. Include a statement of the BACB requirements on restricted and unrestricted activities.

4. Include the objective and measurable circumstances under which the supervisor will sign the supervisee's Experience Verification form when the experience has ended.

5. Delineate the consequences should the parties not adhere to their responsibilities (including proper termination of the relationship).

6. Include a statement requiring the supervisee to obtain written permission from the supervisee's on-site employer or manager when applicable.

7. Include an attestation that both parties will adhere to the Compliance Code.

In addition to the aforementioned components, we usually encourage supervisees to include the following items in their contracts:

1. If there are multiple supervisors, what their roles and responsibilities will be and what is expected of the supervisee with regard to communication.

2. Procedures for cancellations or rescheduling of supervision meetings.

3. When and how experience forms should be presented to be signed during each supervisory period.

4. The details of the supervision experience, including the type of experience (e.g., university-based concentrated supervised fieldwork versus supervised fieldwork), the total number of hours required, the weekly hours required, the supervisory period, the percentage of fieldwork hours required to be spent in supervision, and the competencies that must be met.

5. When and how the performance of the supervisee will be evaluated in addition to the Experience Supervision form.

The BACB provides some sample contracts on its Supervision Resources page (www.bacb.com/supervision-resources). Most fieldwork settings have developed contracts of their own, which they may have reviewed with lawyers or human resources professionals. In such cases, you may be given a copy of the contract and asked to review and sign it. Although the fieldwork setting may have a preexisting contract, that does not mean the contract cannot be discussed and modified. Ideally, you will conduct this review with your practica instructor or someone familiar with supervision contracts. Be sure to compare your contract to the BACB requirements to ensure that you do not agree with anything that is not in line with the board's minimum requirements. If you run into a situation where you are unsure or uncomfortable with the contract language, discuss it with the organization and supervisor. Do not hope that the questionable issue will not come up if it is rare, but rather focus on addressing any possible issues proactively. The supervision contract sets the tone for your entire experience. As such, you should take the time to ensure the document sets you up for success. In situations where the organization is unable or unwilling to change the contract and the terms do not meet BACB's minimum standards, we recommend pursuing alternative placement options. As stated previously, you should avoid signing any documentation without reading it for yourself or if you feel uncomfortable with any portions.

Paperwork and Proper Documentation

You and your supervisor are responsible for completing documentation, for completing the Monthly Experience Verification forms during each supervisory period, and for keeping copies for at least 7 years from the date of the last supervision period. When you apply to the BACB to sit for the examination, you complete the Final Experience Verification form, which is a summary of all of your supervision hours. You should keep a copy of your supervision contract, signed Monthly Experience forms, and final Experience Verification form in one place. In addition to these forms, the BACB announced in its March 2018 newsletter that supervisees would be required to maintain documentation of all independent and supervised fieldwork hours using both the BACB Experience Tracker (found on the BACB website) and a unique tracking system utilized by both the supervisor and the supervisee. The BACB reserves the right to audit and ask to see all of these documents within the 7-year period. We recommend that you select a secure storage location for all of the documents you are required to keep. In particular, we suggest that you select an encrypted cloud-based storage system to save your files, so that you will not lose them in the event of a computer or hard-drive failure.

In the October 2017 and March 2018 BACB Newsletters, the BACB outlined the changes in supervision procedures that will go into effect for all testing periods starting January 2022. Given the movement toward these new standards, we will focus on how you can meet the new requirements that will go into effect. If, at this time, you are accruing experience under the previous standards, we highly encourage you to review the BACB March 2018 newsletter and Experience Standards Form thoroughly. In Table 5.1, we have provided a snapshot of the minimum requirements to be met under the pre-January 2022 standards.

If you are planning to begin your supervision experience after January 1, 2020, we recommend that your supervision experience meets the standards set in the October 2017 BACB newsletter. We make this recommendation to ensure that you are meeting the minimum standards regardless of when you take the examination. The BACB allows a 5-year period to accrue your experience hours and pass the certification examination. In the event that you have to suspend your experience accrual for a period of time, meeting the standards set forth in the October 2017 newsletter ensures your eligibility in the event that you take the examination after the January 2022 testing periods. If you take the examination prior to that time frame, meeting the October 2017 standards will result in you meeting the standards listed in the March 2018 newsletter. These standards differ from the previous standards in a few key ways. First, the university-based and intensive practicum options will

TABLE 5.1 BACB March 2018 Version

	Supervised Independent Fieldwork	Practicum	Intensive Practicum
Experience hours required to qualify	1,500	1,000	750
Experience hours per supervisory period	Minimum of 20 hours to a maximum of 130 hours		
Supervisory period	1 calendar month		
Minimum number of supervisor–trainee contacts per supervisory period	Two contacts	Four contacts	Eight contacts
Observations of trainee with client per supervisory period	Two observations	Four observations	Four observations
Supervision hours per supervisory period	5% of hours	7.5% of hours	10% of hours
Course grade	N/A	Official documentation reflecting a passing grade (C or better) in all Verified Experience courses	

N/A, not applicable.

be combined into a single experience category labeled as Concentrated Supervised Fieldwork. The Supervised Independent Fieldwork has been renamed as Supervised Fieldwork. Second, the required fieldwork hours to qualify for the examination have been increased to 2,000 total hours for Supervised Fieldwork and 1,500 hours for Concentrated Supervised Fieldwork. Third, the required number of supervisory contacts has increased for both experience types. Fourth, the maximum percentage of restricted activities (i.e., 1:1 work with clients on behavior programming) was increased from 50% to 60%. Finally, all supervision hours are to be calculated on a monthly basis, as opposed to weekly or biweekly. Table 5.2 provides a snapshot of the summary of the changes being made to the supervision requirements.

The BACB offers a variety of resources to assist with tracking your supervision experience, some of which are required documents for either eligibility to take the examination or documents that can demonstrate you met the required experience hours should you be audited. The first document is the Monthly Experience Verification form. This form is required to be completed every month to document your total experience hours and total supervision during a monthly period. The form comes in two versions. Version 1 (Individual Supervisor) is to be used for a single supervisor signing off on hours, and Version 2 (Organization with Multiple Supervisors) is to be used if you have more than one BCBA at your organization (e.g., school, work site) who will be signing off on your time. If you use the Organization with Multiple Supervisors form, you will need to indicate one individual as the responsible certificant for your supervision. The second document that is required is

TABLE 5.2   BACB October 17, 2018 Version

	Supervised Fieldwork	Concentrated Supervised Fieldwork
Fieldwork hours required to qualify	2,000	1,500
Fieldwork hours per week	10–30 hours	15–30 hours
Supervisory period	1 calendar month	1 calendar month
Percentage of fieldwork hours spent in supervision (calculated per monthly supervisory period)	5%	10%
Number of supervisory contacts per period (contacts must be at least 15 min)	4	6
Unrestricted activities	At least 60% of supervised fieldwork hours must be spent engaged in unrestricted activities	
Individual/small-group supervision	Supervision may be conducted in small groups for no more than 50% of the total supervised hours in each supervisory period	

your Final Experience Verification form. This form comes in the same two versions as the monthly form, but, unlike the monthly form, it is to be submitted only after your experience concludes. Your total experience and supervision hours from all of your monthly forms are to be recorded on this form and signed by your supervisor.

In addition to the forms for tracking hours, the BACB introduced an Excel Tracking document with the March 2018 newsletter (see Figures 5.1 and 5.2). This document is required by the BACB as an indication of the various types of experiences accumulated during your supervision time frame. Each worksheet and section has instructions that detail the use of the form. The Excel Tracking document is where you will record all of the behavior-analytic work you complete throughout your supervision experience and report the type of work you have done (restricted versus unrestricted) as well as the supervision format (individual versus group). Finally, this document will help you determine if you have met all the requirements needed to count your hours during the monthly time period. This is indicated in the data analysis worksheet, column BG (labeled audit categories). If your experience in a month does not meet the specified requirements, this section will alert you to the specific issue as well as identify what is required to fix that issue.

The last document you are required to keep is one that the BACB has not provided, but reserves the right to request in the event of an audit. This document is a unique tracking system created by the supervisor and supervisee, with both individuals completing specific sections. The requirements for this document can be found in Quick Reference 5.1. Given the requirement for this document, we have some recommendations for what to include beyond the BACB requirements:

1. In addition to documenting restricted versus unrestricted activities, keep notes on the specific tasks you are completing during each session.

FIGURE 5.1 Experience Tracker: Experience log worksheet (BACB March 2018 version).

Experience Tracker: Experience Log

Version 1.0

Log your experience into the table below in the order it was obtained. Note that some values will calculate automatically based on the data entered and will default to categories with limitations (i.e., restricted hours and group supervision hours). Be sure to select an experience type, setting, and supervisor for *every experience entry* even if a supervision session did not occur.

Experience Type	Setting	Supervisor	Date of Experience	Experience Start Time	Experience End Time	Experience Hours	Unrestricted Hours	Restricted Hours	Method of Supervision	Supervision Start Time	Supervision End Time	Supervised Hours	Individual Supervision Hours	Group Supervision Hours	Independent Hours	Client Observation?	Experience Notes

FIGURE 5.2 Experience Tracker: Data analysis worksheet (BACB March 2018 version).

Experience Tracker: Data Analysis
Version 1.0

The table below shows the experience logged and the adjusted experience based on the BACB's Experience Standards. Details regarding why some or all of the hours in a given month were not countable can be found by referencing the letters in the "Audit Categories" column against the table in "Audit Categories" tab in the Experience Tracker. Note that just because an audit category is cited does not necessarily mean there was noncompliance with the standards. It may mean that only some of the hours accumulated during the supervisory period were countable (e.g., hours accumulated when a supervision contract was in place) or that a given standard has not been met yet (e.g., the percent of experience hours accrued has not reached 100%). Note that hours initially logged during a supervisory period will not display under the adjusted experience section of the table until minimum standards have been met (e.g., at least 20 hours have been accrued during the supervisory period).

LOGGED EXPERIENCE
(Aggregated data from the "Experience Log" tab)

Year	Month	Experience Type	# of Independent Hours	# of Supervised Hours	Experience Hours	# of Unrestricted Hours	# of Supervision Contacts	# of Client Observations	% of Experience Supervised	% of Group Supervision

ADJUSTED EXPERIENCE
(Logged data based on compliance with the Experience Standards)

# of Independent Hours	# of Supervised Hours	Experience Hours	% of Unrestricted Experience Hours	% of Experience Hours Accumulated	Audit Categories

2. For supervised hours:

   a. Indicate the BACB 5th Edition Task List items targeted by your supervisor.

   b. Have your supervisor keep a record of any feedback delivered to you during the supervisory contact.

3. Include a rating scale of your performance in key areas of supervision:

   a. Receptiveness to feedback

   b. Professionalism with consumers

   c. Use of behavior-analytic principles with consumers

   d. Others agreed upon by you and your supervisor

4. Store the document in a shared cloud-based storage system (e.g., Dropbox, Google Drive, Box). By doing this, you and your supervisor can make edits on the same document without e-mailing the different versions back and forth.

QUICK REFERENCE 5.1 TRACKING SYSTEM REQUIREMENTS

- Independent hours:
  - Session date
  - Session start time
  - Session end time
  - Experience type (Supervised Fieldwork or Concentrated Fieldwork)
  - Setting name
  - Supervisor name
  - Activity category: restricted or unrestricted
- Supervised hours:
  - Supervisory contact date
  - Supervision start time
  - Supervision end time
  - Format (e.g., in person, online, phone call)
  - Experience type (Supervised Fieldwork or Concentrated Fieldwork)
  - Supervision type: individual or group
  - Activity category: restricted or unrestricted (when supervision involves observing the trainee in an activity)
  - Summary of supervision activity
- Supervisory period as a whole:
  - Total hours of group and individual supervision
  - Total number of contacts
  - Total number of observations of trainee with the clients

5. Collaborate with your supervisor on creating the document. The more personalized it is to you and your needs, the easier it will be to utilize.

CHAPTER REVIEW

In this chapter, we focused on how you should go about setting up and documenting your supervision experience to help you avoid the mistakes Jan made in Vignette 5.1. Taking the time to formalize your experience by developing a supervision contract at the outset ensures that you and your supervisor will start off on the same page with regard to your expectations. Creating, tracking, and storing your supervision experience per BACB standards protects you against uncertainty regarding your total hour accrual and helps you idetermine whether you have met the standards adequately. Although the content presented in this chapter may seem like general guidelines, we advise you to treat it as prescriptive to save you time and hours of frustration when you near the end of the supervision experience. When evaluating the content of this chapter, think to yourself: Is it better to spend 10 hours now to be proactive and protect myself or 30 hours later to try and fix an issue?

REFERENCES

Behavior Analyst Certification Board. (2018a). BCBA/BCaBA experience standards: Monthly system. Retrieved from https://www.bacb.com/experience-standards-monthly-system

Behavior Analyst Certification Board. (2018b). *March 2018 BACB Newsletter.* Retrieved from https://www.bacb.com/wp-content/uploads/BACB_March2018_Newsletter.pdf

Behavior Analyst Certification Board. (2018c). Supervision resources. Retrieved from https://www.bacb.com/supervision-resources

BECOMING A COMPETENT SUPERVISEE

6

Gaining the Most From Your Supervision Experience

Practica coursework and fieldwork involve not only the experiences you gain from working directly with families and clients, but also the experiences you cultivate. In many ways, the trajectory of your supervision is what you, as the supervisee, make of it. The better you prepare yourself for supervision and the more you put your behaviors out there to allow your supervisor to shape them through feedback, the more you will gain from your supervised experiences. There are some fundamental differences between the supervisees who gain the most from supervision and those who meet the minimum criteria. This chapter provides some tips based on the literature on supervision as well as some of the things we have seen across our supervisees who have gained the most from their supervision experience with us.

USE YOUR SUPERVISION TIME EFFICIENTLY

To make the most out of your supervision, plan how you can use the time of your supervisor maximally. As a professional, when you obtain consultation for your clinical or organizational work, each moment of the consultation may cost you hundreds of dollars. Like consultants, lawyers' fees are time based because their time to listen, review material, and provide you with expert advice saves you money and time in the long run. You should treat your supervisor's time with the same respect given its value, even though often you are not paying for your supervision out of pocket. In Chapter 8, we provide some specific tips for preparing for your individual and group supervision meetings to help you gain the most from your supervision time. The time you get from a supervisor is a commodity. Therefore, in the following text, we outline some ways you can cultivate and take advantage of opportunities during your supervision.

Work on Your Foundational Knowledge in Behavior Analysis

The main reason the Behavior Analyst Certification Board (BACB) allows you to begin accruing your supervision hours after you have begun the appropriate coursework is because the ideal supervision experience involves you applying what you are learning in the classroom to your work setting. To apply material from your coursework, you need to have a strong foundation in theory. When you do not have a strong foundation in principles and measurement of behavior, for example, it is very hard for you or your supervisor to connect your coursework to your fieldwork. Consider Vignette 6.1.

VIGNETTE 6.1

Sally and Cris, both supervised by Nicole, work with a 12-year-old boy with autism. Both recently finished their first graduate-level course in behavior analysis, titled Principles of Applied Behavior Analysis. *Sally excelled in the class, whereas Cris struggled, but passed. During a session, right after a break and immediately before working on tasks, the client has been asking lots of questions that sometimes relate to the task and sometimes do not. Nicole has noticed that the client is not meeting his goals during these sessions and things are running longer than expected. During the supervision meeting, after observing a session, Nicole says, "It looks to me like he is asking a ton of questions; it's a clear case of negative reinforcement. I suggest you implement a differential reinforcement procedure to redirect him to work more quickly."*

Sally begins to place the client's questions on extinction by not looking his way or answering any questions until he orients and moves toward the task. She then answers his task-related questions, briefly, when he is oriented toward the task and more so as he engages with the teaching session. In contrast, Cris does not answer any of the client's questions and explains to him that he has to begin working. The client repeatedly asks Cris, "Why?" In turn, Cris responds, "You need to be working now and I am not answering questions." Needless to say, Nicole notices that during sessions with Sally, the client is making better progress than he is with Cris.

Why do you think the client is making better progress with Sally? If you said it is because the procedures she used were in line with Nicole's recommendations, your answer is correct. To implement the correct procedure, Sally had to identify that when Nicole said negative reinforcement was responsible for the client's question asking, it meant that the client is asking questions to delay, or escape, doing the task. Therefore, she provided reinforcers when he made any movements toward engaging the task and extinguished any behaviors that delayed it. Cris's answering of the client's question of "Why?" continued the delay, which maintained the problem.

In this case, Sally's supervision experience will differ from Cris's experience, even though they have the same client and the same supervisor, because Sally was fluent with the definition of the concept of negative reinforcement. She was able to identify an example of negative reinforcement and attempt to use a differential reinforcement procedure assuming escape as the reinforcer. As such, her supervisor can move to more advanced applied topics such as the procedures she used when implementing differential reinforcement or how she can alter the schedule of reinforcement based on her client's progress. Unless Cris uses the tips we have provided in Quick Reference 6.1, however, he may lose some of his supervision time as his supervisor provides examples of negative reinforcement, explains why answering the client's questions may delay the task and be negatively reinforcing, or explains how what Cris was doing is functionally similar to having answered the client's questions. In short, Cris's supervision experience is likely to become less advanced and move at a slower pace unless he spends some time reviewing his notes from course material, looking up additional examples on the Internet, and reviewing new examples in a few books to work on his foundational knowledge. It is a good idea for you to ask your supervisor for additional examples and applications of the foundational concepts, but always

---

QUICK REFERENCE 6.1   IMPROVING YOUR FOUNDATIONAL SKILLS

- Conduct a self-assessment
  - Review the BACB 5th Edition Task List, Section 1.
  - Break up the task list items that have multiple concepts.
    - For example, B-1 has three concepts: behavior, response, and response class.
  - Evaluate whether you can respond to the task list items, coherently and confidently, exclusively out loud, within 2 to 5 seconds of seeing the task list item.
    - For example, B-1 requires you to define behavior (if you said behavior is the activity of a living organism that is sensitive to reinforcement, you are correct). Then, provide an example of behavior.
- Study the terms
  - For any of the concepts you could not define accurately or fluently (rapid fashion), we recommend that you use SAFMEDS (Say All Fast, Minute Each Day, Shuffled; Graf & Auman, 2005).
    - See www.bahaviorbabe.com/safmeds/htm for some quick tips and flashcards.
  - After practicing using SAFMEDS, put yourself in a position to try to teach someone else about the concept. This is one of the best ways for you to learn the concept well, as well as to evaluate whether you can explain it accurately.
- Recruit feedback
  - Ask your supervisor if he or she would be willing to provide you with feedback if you defined and explained the term.
  - Remember that practice makes permanent, so practice with high fidelity/accuracy.

---

try to see how much you could learn on your own first, so that your supervisor is able to take you one step further than where you would have gotten on your own. Vignette 6.1 illustrates the different content that supervision may cover as well as the importance of mastering the foundational concepts. Failure to do so in coursework may potentially result in supervision focusing more on building foundational skills as opposed to their practical applications.

To use your supervisor's time efficiently, and to gain the most from supervision, you should do your best to stay on top of your course material; that way, you can reserve your supervision time for application rather than tutoring sessions. If you do not feel you have a strong grasp of the foundations, you can take the steps outlined in Quick Reference 6.1 to set yourself up for optimal learning during supervision.

Show Appreciation for Opportunities to Learn

Just as you can increase or decrease certain aspects of your client's behaviors, you can also increase or decrease your supervisor's behaviors. For example, in Vignette 6.1, Sally and Cris can thank Nicole and provide specific examples of what they appreciated. In this case, the supervisor dedicated the time not only to observe and provide recommendations to Sally and Cris, but also to give them an opportunity to problem-solve an issue. Cris and Sally can react to this opportunity in two ways. First, they could recognize it as an opportunity contrived by their supervisor to teach them a higher-level skill. By reacting with appreciation for this opportunity, they can increase the likelihood that Nicole (supervisor) will seek out and provide additional similar opportunities in the future. Alternatively, they could respond with defensiveness and tell Nicole that she should just have told them what to do. This response will likely influence Nicole to problem-solve and provide specific solutions rather than allowing her team to problem-solve with her. Although both cases result in the clinical issue being addressed, only one of them (the former) results in continued opportunities for growth beyond program implementation for the supervisees. This is very important because clinical work is not just procedural, but also involves constant problem solving. Ultimately, there is no perfect supervisor, but if you treat every moment of supervision as an opportunity to rise to the occasion and learn, you will gain much more from supervision.

Take Advantage of Opportunities That Arise

It is sad, but some individuals do not take advantage of the great opportunities that come up for them during their fieldwork. Many of the prominent figures in the field of behavior analysis established themselves by agreeing to do a lot of free work and by putting in time when and however they could. Usually, their volunteer efforts provided them with opportunities to learn as well as develop relationships that empowered them over time. Students are sometimes short-sighted, however, and they may miss the big picture of what it means to become a professional in the community. Your time in fieldwork is the ideal time to seek out opportunities you would not otherwise have, as you have access to a variety of individuals within your program and fieldwork site. Remember, supervised experience time is an investment in your future as a professional, not just a time to meet the minimum standards.

In catching up with a former student, he shared with me that he had some regrets about his internship experience at California State University, Northridge (CSUN). He explained that he had the opportunity to work at an unpaid internship site that focused on academic fluency for underprivileged individuals, his primary area of interest. Instead of taking that opportunity, he chose to work at an in-home service agency working with children with autism because he really needed the income at the time. Although both experiences would have provided him with the opportunities to meet his competencies, and he needed the income, he regretted choosing the paid opportunity because it led him down a career path outside his primary interest. In retrospect, he wished that he had found other means of generating income and interned in the area he desired to pursue after graduation.

I share this story not to discourage you, but rather to encourage you to pursue your interests during this time of your life. Do not miss out on opportunities or relationships solely because of a lack of time or money. Although time and money are realistic barriers that may interfere with your choices, you may be surprised about the number of ways you may be able to problem-solve if you recruit some help. We advise you to seek out assistance whenever you can with your decisions to forego opportunities: In the end, you may regret pushing aside your interests instead of pursuing them wholeheartedly. In some cases, a choice is unavoidable; we encourage you to consider your options and recruit help, but we also recognize that individual circumstances are different and not everyone can take advantage of all opportunities that arise.

Take Responsibility for Your Experience

We developed this handbook for the supervisee instead of the supervisor because the best supervision experiences stem from the supervisee asking, or nudging, for more from the supervisor. In addition, just as with any partnership, the supervisor–supervisee relationship takes work from both of the partners involved, not just the supervisor. Both individuals must make a commitment to the relationship, to having open communication, and to giving each other the benefit of the doubt for the relationship to work. Therefore, we recommend that you take responsibility for your experience, as the supervisee, and view yourself as a collaborator with your supervisor for your learning experiences. Oftentimes, you will need to communicate between supervisors and between the university and your fieldwork site. Taking charge of your experience will help you see all of the parties involved in your supervision as team members who are on your team to make your experiential learning as rich and memorable as possible. As a supervisee, be on the lookout for additional opportunities or experiences (e.g., helping out with an unusual assessment or a complicated case) and bring them to your supervisor to discuss how you may access them.

Medical residents, for example, are assigned daily activities during their residency and gain general practice skills by dealing with the most common reasons that patients attend their place of residency. However, residents are always on the lookout for exceptional or tough cases, even though they must volunteer time to do those in addition to their general activities. The residency model places the responsibility of gaining more than mediocre residency in the hands of the medical residents, who are often enrolled in rigorous medical school programs and juggling residency with their academic curriculum. In many ways, it is the cumulative frequency of accessing exceptional cases during residency that differentiates the career paths of physicians.

GAIN THE MOST FROM PERFORMANCE FEEDBACK

What Is Performance Feedback and Why Does It Matter?

Feedback, which is a quicker way of referring to performance feedback, has been defined as information about performance that allows a person to change his or her behavior (Daniels & Bailey, 2014). Some research evidence indicates that feedback provided by a supervisor is more likely to produce more consistent results than feedback that is self-generated (Balcazar, Hopkins, & Suarez, 1985).

That is why one of the main responsibilities of your supervisor is to evaluate and document your performance. The evaluation process is likely to be anxiety provoking for both you and your supervisor. On the one hand, you may feel some distress about being observed and eager about performing your very best. On the other hand, your supervisor may worry about your response to feedback as well as providing you with feedback that would improve your future performance. The evaluation process is extremely important in supervision, but both the supervisor and the supervisee need to prepare for it because the experience can be stressful without groundwork and trust.

All of the best practice recommendations for ethical and effective supervision emphasize effective training and delivery of performance feedback to supervisees (Sellers, Valentino, & LeBlanc, 2016; Turner, Fischer, & Luiselli, 2016). In fact, it is your supervisor's ethical responsibility to provide you with feedback (Code 5.06 of the Compliance Code). Researchers have found that effective training of performance-based skills generally consists of instructions, modeling, practice, and giving feedback until a predetermined mastery criterion is achieved. This type of hands-on training is called behavior skills training (BST; Parsons, Rollyson, & Reid, 2012). The BST approach requires that supervisors develop performance monitoring tools (PMTs) for the tasks you are to complete, find opportunities for directly observing you perform the tasks, model the correct ways to complete the tasks, and provide you with feedback until you can do the procedures correctly. Ward-Horner and Sturmey (2012) found that the feedback portion of the training was more effective than all of the other components of BST with regard to performance improvement.

Outside of training and your direct implementation of behavior programming, your supervisor can provide you with feedback on any of your behaviors that relate to your professional competence (e.g., writing skills, oral communication with clients, professional demeanor, timeliness, implementation skills) to help you improve your overall skills. There is abundant research evidence that feedback has been effective in producing changes in behavior in the desired direction for many different types of individuals (e.g., bank tellers, hockey players, children with autism) in various settings. Performance feedback is not just relevant when you are acquiring skills; it is also relevant in maintenance and generalization of those skills (DiGennaro Reed, Hirst, & Howard, 2013). That is probably why Daniels and Bailey (2014) called feedback the breakfast of the champions with regard to the tools a supervisor possesses in making behavior change. According to those authors, feedback "can make normal individuals into powerful change agents" (p. 170). However, for feedback to be effective in improving your behavior, you have to be effective in receiving and using it (see Stone & Heen, 2015, for a book on how to receive feedback).

How Can You Receive Feedback Well?

Receiving feedback well means engaging in conversation with the person who provided the feedback with a focus on how you can use the information to grow and do better in the future. Receiving feedback well doesn't mean that you are not disappointed, hurt, angry, or feeling an emotional response to the feedback. Your history with feedback will have a lot to do with how you respond to it at the beginning. It will take some time, and several new experiences with feedback, for your emotional responding to change, and an experienced supervisor will recognize that. Responding well to feedback means that you are managing your emotional triggers, and instead of placing your focus on your emotional response, you are placing your focus on what you can gain from the feedback. Consider Vignette 6.2.

VIGNETTE 6.2

Emma is a first-year graduate student providing focused treatment to a 10-year-old boy with severe aggression, in the form of kicking or punching caretakers. Over the past 2 weeks of treatment, Emma has made great progress with her client and can't wait for her supervisor, Chayanne, to see the results. During supervision, however, the client verbally refuses to comply with Emma's requests and proceeds to do his own thing instead of following through with what Emma asks him to do. At the end of the session, Chayanne provides Emma with feedback about the session. Chayanne recommends that Emma provide the client with instructions that are brief, directive, and more clear in the future. Chayanne also provides some examples of Emma's requests and explains to her how her instructions were unclear. Emma, who is emotionally drained and exhausted from the session, feels flushed in her cheeks and asks Chayanne, "Well, normally he responds really well to my instructions. He must be acting this way because you are here."

In the following, we outline some strategies you can use when you have received feedback from your supervisor.

Tip 1. Accept the Feedback

Instead of evaluating the feedback or questioning its accuracy, just accept the feedback as a recommendation from an expert. If the feedback is based on observation you feel is inaccurate, it is okay because there will be many more chances for the supervisor to observe you and form impressions of your work. Accepting the supervisor's feedback without defiance or judgment on your part demonstrates that you are open to being wrong, open to new ideas, and willing to listen. For example, in Vignette 6.2, Emma's response to Chayanne should have been focused on how she can provide better instructions instead of questioning if her instruction-giving is really the problem.

Tip 2. Restate the Feedback You Received

Try to summarize the feedback you were given when the feedback session is done. The summary should be in the form of things you understand you need to do to improve your performance in the future. This is helpful for both you and your supervisor. The process of restating the feedback puts you in a position to have to hear what the person is saying instead of emotionally responding to it. The summary you provide also helps your supervisor to identify if the supervisor got sidetracked, offered more information than necessary, or need to provide points of clarification. Finally, this process helps you to look for the golden nuggets in the feedback you receive.

Tip 3. Clarify

Ask for clarifications or specific examples so that you understand what the supervisor expects of you for improvement. Also, you can ask your supervisor for tips or techniques to practice. Butler, Godbole, and Marsh (2013) found that feedback that provides an explanation for the correct response is more likely to result in generalization of skills. Try to connect the feedback you are getting to the bigger picture of why it matters. If you have a hard time with this, ask your supervisor how the behavior you are improving may relate to the bigger picture. For example, in Emma's case, if she moved to asking questions about her instruction-giving, she may have learned more about evidence-based methods to increase compliance (which partly has to do with the way instructions are given) and the specific steps she can take to set the occasion for compliance to occur more often. Some specific questions she could have asked were, "By 'directive,' do you mean I should not use the word 'please'?" or "How would you suggest I ask him to come over to select the task we are going to work on next in a more brief manner? Should I first stick to 'come over here'?"

Tip 4. Thank the Feedback Provider

Consider the time and effort it took the individual to provide you with feedback to help you. Even if it does not sound like the feedback is coming from the right place, consider how much you can learn from it for your future success and thank the person for providing the experience. I have found, more often than not, even if I don't see value in the feedback I have been given in the moment, sometime in the future I am thankful to the person who provided the feedback because it has always helped me grow in some way. I use a pyramidal model of supervision with my students, such that senior graduate students serve as junior colleagues and provide supervision to undergraduate or newer graduate students under my supervision. I find that my supervisees' level of appreciation for my time and feedback changes dramatically after they are in a position to provide feedback to their own supervisees. Although they appreciate the feedback for its role in helping them succeed, once they give feedback they realize the time and effort that goes into giving good feedback and that brings them to a higher level of appreciation.

Tip 5. Solicit Feedback

Outside of organizational management and supervision practices, often when people ask for feedback, what they are really asking for is praise. Although I understand the importance of validating a friend or a family member and respect that not every person is seeking feedback solely for behavior improvement, this social cultural practice may confuse supervisees who are receiving feedback for the sole purpose of improving their skills for the future. This is not to say that an effective supervisor should neglect to provide ample praise or not recognize when a supervisee has made progress. In fact, effective supervisors identify the skills they want to maintain or increase in their supervisees as often as they identify the skills they need to teach or modify. As the supervisee, you want to solicit objective feedback and be approachable for impromptu feedback by smiling, nodding, and demonstrating consideration of the feedback for your own future gains.

Although as a behavior analyst I usually focus on behaviors you should emit instead of stating the don'ts, with regard to how you should receive feedback, it is extremely important that you refrain from certain behaviors to the extent that is possible. Consider the situation in Vignette 6.3.

VIGNETTE 6.3

After Chayanne explains to Emma, from Vignette 6.2, that she probably had never seen Emma give instructions to her client because he was effectively avoiding tasks by aggressing toward caregivers in the past, she goes on to explain the importance of giving clear and brief instructions. Emma then explains that she would have known to do that if she was not so focused on showing Chayanne that the client's aggression has significantly decreased. Then, Emma explains that she also did not think to give brief instructions because she was caught off guard that her client was behaving so differently, but that if she had more time to think about it, she would have given better instructions to her client.

When you have received feedback, *DON'T* engage in the following:

- *Make justifications.* Consider that there will be ample opportunities for you to show your supervisor your skills. Don't feel the need to explain why things went wrong or why you engaged in behaviors that need to be modified. In Vignette 6.3, Emma engages in unnecessary justifications.

- *Act like you already knew the feedback.* Nothing gives the message that a supervisor just wasted his or her time more than the supervisee saying he or she already knew how to engage in the correct response, but that for some reason it did not occur. First, that is usually not accurate. That is, if the correct response was not emitted, in that context and under those discriminative stimuli, the bottom line is that the supervisee did not "know" how to respond correctly in that instance. Second, saying you already knew the correct response, which Emma did in Vignette 6.3, devalues the feedback the supervisor provided. We want to clarify that refraining from saying that you already knew the correct answer is not the same as self-evaluating and identifying strategies to correct errors. Self-evaluation is an excellent quality in any professional, and we encourage you to monitor and evaluate your own performance throughout your supervisory experience and thereafter. In the case of receiving feedback, we ask that you withhold your self-evaluation unless your supervisor asks you to provide it prior to providing you with feedback. We have provided the tips here to increase the likelihood that you will engage in behaviors that encourage future feedback-giving by your supervisor.

- *Get defensive.* There is no score-keeping in giving and receiving feedback. Your supervisor is in a position to help you improve; if you already knew everything, you would not need feedback. No one knows everything or does everything correctly, so consider yourself lucky that someone cares enough to take the time to help you improve.

- *Withdraw from further discussion or engagement.* This one is easier to say and much harder to do. Sometimes if your feedback has been paired with punishers for you in the past, you may immediately withdraw in the face of corrective feedback. As noted earlier, much of your immediate response to feedback is based on your history with it. If you find yourself withdrawing, take baby steps to speak, orient yourself toward the supervisor, nod, and put any behavior out there that you can that helps you change toward more engagement and more opportunity for learning from feedback in the future.

If after giving feedback to you, your supervisor is rebuffed, argued with, dismissed, or exposed to your defensive behavior, he or she is less likely to provide you with helpful feedback in the future. Decreasing your supervisor's willingness to give corrective feedback, even if that is not your intention, is counterproductive for you and the other individuals who may not get the same level of feedback from that supervisor in the future.

The tips we have provided thus far mostly apply to vocal verbal feedback sessions. However, you may receive feedback in many other forms. You may receive feedback that is vocal and shortly after observation of you carrying out direct implantation. You may receive feedback in written form either as additional information to the vocal feedback you received during the observation or as confirmation of information you were told vocally. You may also receive written feedback on your written material, such as clinical case reports, data, or intervention plans. Sometimes the feedback you receive is graphed to help you visualize the impact of your behavior change; sometimes it is public and graphed to provide you with a social comparison. In all of these cases, we advise that you look for the golden nuggets and move toward making behavior changes that will set you on the path for success.

Effective feedback should adhere to the following guidelines (see Alvero, Bucklin, & Austin, 2001; Daniels & Bailey, 2014):

1. Specific information about behavior is given for behavior change.
2. Based on performance that is in the control of the receiver to change.
3. Immediate and right after performance or before the supervisee has to engage in the same performance.
4. Individualized so that the receiver can identify his or her contribution to making a change.
5. Delivered by the supervisor and self-monitored when possible so that the individual can begin to identify his or her own progress when the supervisor is not available.
6. Focused on behavior improvement and goals that can be achieved.
7. Graphed when possible or provided with clear standards for improvement based on either the individual's progress, the client's improvement, or peers' achievements.

Tip 6. Recognize When to Discuss Feedback

In reading the previous tips, you likely noticed that we did not suggest that you evaluate and discuss the feedback with your supervisor. However, we recognize that a percentage of the feedback you receive is flat-out wrong. Also, sometimes the feedback is confusing and you are unsure how to apply it. We suggest that, in the moment, if the recommendation is doable and is not harmful to anyone, you accept and implement the feedback. For example, if your supervisor asks you to use a more potent reinforcer by using an edible item such as pieces of a cookie for your client with diabetes, you should immediately point out that the client has diabetes. To problem-solve and demonstrate you attended to the function of the feedback, you may suggest alternative edible items the child likes, such as blueberries, grapes, roasted almonds, or popcorn. This increases the likelihood of your supervisor continuing to deliver feedback and also allows you to demonstrate your ability to take and implement feedback.

Our recommendation that you stop evaluating feedback when you receive it is not a call for you to blindly accept all of the feedback given to you; therefore, this tip is not contradictory to Tip 1. Rather, we recommend that you always take the time to review and think about the feedback given by your supervisor. It is possible that the feedback given in that moment is incorrect or that your supervisor's suggestion is not evidence based, according to what you learned from one of your professors. In those situations, give yourself 24 hours to brew over the feedback to make sure you have given yourself enough time to think about what the supervisor requested and which aspects you can take from the feedback. Then, if important portions of the feedback are unclear or appear incorrect to you, contact your supervisor and ask for a further discussion of the feedback. The best way to proceed with this discussion is to be transparent and not to present your opinion as fact, but rather to inquire about the reasoning for your supervisor's feedback and decisions.

Almost all feedback has some golden nuggets of information that you can use to become a better behavior analyst. Take these opportunities to practice your communication skills and your ability to discuss disagreements professionally in an environment where the focus is on your growth.

How to Provide Feedback to Your Supervisor

During supervision, it is likely that there will be multiple opportunities for you to provide feedback to your supervisor. First, the supervisor may solicit feedback from you as a part of his or her routine evaluation of your satisfaction with supervision. Second, the supervisor may solicit feedback to determine if something he or she is doing is working well for you. Third, the supervisor may ask why you are having difficulties meeting certain competencies and you may realize that you have had particular needs from supervision that have not been met. Fourth, your supervisor may provide you with recommendations that are inaccurate or feedback that is confusing. In all of these situations, remind yourself that how you deal with the situation itself is a reflection of your overall professionalism. It is in your best interest to give your supervisor the benefit of the doubt and refrain from jumping to conclusions. Instead, keep the communication lines open and remember to focus on behaviors, not the person. You will find that your feedback will be viewed in a more positive light if it is coming from a place intended to help rather than to pass judgment or to even out the score on an imaginary scoreboard.

We recommend that you follow a few specific steps when you are delivering feedback to your supervisor. First, prior to delivering your feedback, ensure that you have a clear understanding of what you are attempting to communicate. You can avoid misunderstandings by evaluating your statements thoroughly for clarity, tone, and rationale. Second, inquire as to the rationale or thought process of your supervisor regarding the situation or decision (don't presume it). Oftentimes, feedback revolves around the end result of decision making without accounting for the steps that were taken to get there. By asking about the thought process, your supervisor can inform you of additional information that may change your feedback. Finally, be prepared to discuss, provide solutions, and potentially help with implementing the feedback you deliver. You will want to be prepared with your solution and capable of carrying it out. As a last step, always keep in mind that supervision is a reciprocal process. Behaving in a respectful and professional manner with your supervisor in situations where you give feedback will likely result in improvements and benefit your supervisory interactions moving forward. Consider Vignette 6.4, which was provided by one of our supervisees.

VIGNETTE 6.4

One of my supervisors was implementing a program in which the child was getting a break from work after a fixed amount of time. This program was in place to reduce instances of self-injurious behavior (SIB) whenever a demand was presented at the table. I noticed that the client was still engaging in SIB when the client was at the table, and he was engaging in SIB even during his break and free play time. I was exceptionally nervous and felt much anxiety about approaching my supervisor, since I didn't know if he had some rationale as to why he was running this program, and my questioning of it would only serve to paint my lack of understanding about it.

After reading Dr. Kazemi's work, I decided to approach my supervisor and asked him if he had some time to review the client's case with me and to tell me more about why he chose to implement a fixed time escape program. My supervisor let me know he selected the program because he wanted to suppress SIB and to mimic the school setting (where most instruction and escape are contingent on fixed time and the bell ringing). I brought up my observations of SIB and how I had some reservations because I was not seeing any decrease of it. He informed me that he had introduced the program based on an interview with the mother, but that since I brought my concern to his attention, he would love to conduct a functional analysis of the SIB if I was willing to help him with a big portion of it. I was so happy to be able to help with the functional analysis because we were able to eliminate the client's SIB; I regretted letting my emotions deter me from bringing the issue up earlier with my supervisor.

Remote Supervision and Feedback

With the advent of teleconferencing technology, supervision can occur remotely from anywhere in the world. A supervisor can observe you through live, two-way audio-video via the Internet or cellular networks. Supervision through videoconferencing is highly convenient and allows your supervisor to engage in supervision with you without having to be in the same physical location. Also, this type of supervision allows both of you to save time and the costs associated with travel. For some families, travel to treatment centers is impossible; without remote supervision, they would have no access to care.

Despite the benefits of telehealth, there are a few challenges with remote supervision. First, if your supervisor is observing a session with your client, there are various Health Insurance Portability and Accountability Act (HIPAA) issues to consider to protect both your own and your client's confidentiality. Second, technical difficulties can interrupt your supervision sessions and require you to hold follow-up meetings or discussions to salvage what you may have lost in communication when the interruptions occurred. Third, without sophisticated video technology, it is hard for a supervisor to see the full context or the physical environment in which you are delivering services. It is difficult for a supervisor to be effective if he or she cannot evaluate or see all of the things that may be going on in your context. Fourth, videoconferencing may limit how much a supervisor can model. In my experience, I have found that it is helpful if your supervisor uses a doll and simulates the behavior(s) of the client when modeling the behaviors the supervisor would like for you to perform. Finally, during a high-risk situation, your supervisor cannot intervene to help you (see Florell, 2016).

If remote supervision is the primary method through which you obtain supervision, you and your supervisor need to discuss methods to support you during high-risk situations. You should have a backup plan so that an alternative supervisor can be reached and available to you if something goes wrong or if you need immediate support from a supervisor who can be available physically (Turner, Fischer, & Luiselli, 2016). If you are obtaining much of your supervision remotely, we recommend that you and your supervisor become familiar with the resources available to you regarding telehealth and remote supervision (see Grady et al., 2011; Rios, Kazemi, & Peterson, in press).

CHAPTER REVIEW

In this chapter, we discussed some of the benefits of supervision and explained how you can access them. The following two tips can help you maximize your supervision experience. First, engage in active communication with your supervisor about your experience and how supervision is progressing for you. Second, tell yourself that every event provides potential learning opportunities if you are willing to see them. By reading this book, you have already begun your journey on the right foot and taken responsibility for learning how to prepare yourself for supervision. You will do well in your journey if you continue on this path and take responsibility for your experience. Supervision passes more quickly than you might expect, so be sure that you make the most of it.

REFERENCES

Alvero, A. M., Bucklin, B. R., & Austin, J. (2001). An objective review of the effectiveness and essential characteristics of performance feedback in organizational settings (1985-1998). *Journal of Organizational Behavior Management, 21*(1), 3–29. doi:10.1300/J075v21n01_02

Balcazar, F. E., Hopkins, B. L., & Suarez, Y. (1985). A critical, objective review of performance feedback. *Journal of Organizational Behavior Management, 7*(3–4), 65–89. doi:10.1300/J075v07n03_05

Butler, A. C., Godbole, N., & Marsh, E. J. (2013). Explanation feedback is better than correct answer feedback for promoting transfer of learning. *Journal of Educational Psychology, 105*(2), 290–298. doi:10.1037/a0031026

Daniels, A. C., & Bailey, J. S. (2014). *Performance management: Changing behavior that drives organizational effectiveness.* Atlanta, GA: Aubrey Daniels International.

DiGennaro Reed, F. D., Hirst, J. M., & Howard, V. J. (2013). Empirically supported staff selection, training, and management strategies. In D. D. Reed, F. D. DiGennaro Reed, & J. K. Luiselli (Eds.), *Handbook of crisis intervention and developmental disabilities* (pp. 71–85). New York, NY: Springer Science + Business Media. doi:10.1007/978-1-4614-6531-7_5

Florell, D. (2016). Web-based training and supervision. In J. K. Luiselli & A. J. Fischer (Eds.), *Computer-assisted and web-based innovations in psychology, special education, and health* (pp. 313–338). New York, NY: Academic Press/Elsevier.

Grady, B., Myers, K. M., Nelson, E., Belz, N., Bennett, L., Carnahan, L., . . . Voyles, D. (2011). Evidence-based practice for telemental health. *Telemedicine and e-Health, 17*(2), 131–148. doi:10.1089/tmj.2010.0158

Graf, S. A., & Auman, J. (2005). SAFMEDS: A tool to build fluency. Retrieved from https://static1.squarespace.com/static/52f9aba6e4b0a0539a453ec0/t/53192ce6e4b0fa5080ab3661/1394158822332/SAFMEDS.Tool.06.pdf

Lundstrom, K., & Baker, W. (2009). To give is better than to receive: The benefits of peer review to the reviewer's own writing. *Journal of Second Language Writing, 18*(1), 30–43. doi:10.1016/j.jslw.2008.06.002

Parsons, M. B., Rollyson, J. H., & Reid, D. H. (2012). Evidence-based staff training: A guide for practitioners. *Behavior Analysis in Practice, 5*(2), 2–11. doi:10.1007/BF03391819

Rios, D., Kazemi, E., & Peterson, S. (in press). Best practices and considerations for effective service provision via remote technology. *Behavior Analysis in Practice.*

Sellers, T. P., Valentino, A. L., & LeBlanc, L. A. (2016). Recommended practices for individual supervision of aspiring behavior analysts. *Behavior Analysis in Practice, 9*(4), 274–286. doi:10.1007/s40617-016-0110-7

Stone, D., & Heen, S. (2015). *Thanks for the feedback: The science and art of receiving feedback well (even when it is off base, unfair, poorly delivered, and frankly, you're not in the mood).* London, UK: Penguin.

Turner, L. B., Fischer, A. J., & Luiselli, J. K. (2016). Towards a competency-based, ethical, and socially valid approach to the supervision of applied behavior analytic trainees. *Behavior Analysis in Practice, 9*(4), 287–298. doi:10.1007/s40617-016-0121-4

Van Zundert, M., Sluijsmans, D., & Van Merriënboer, J. (2010). Effective peer assessment processes: Research findings and future directions. *Learning and Instruction, 20*(4), 270–279. doi:10.1016/j.learninstruc.2009.08.004

Ward-Horner, J., & Sturmey, P. (2012). Component analysis of behavior skills training in functional analysis. *Behavioral Interventions, 27*(2), 75–92. doi:10.1002/bin.1339

7

Putting Time and Effort Into Increasing Your Pivotal Skills

One of the most challenging aspects of professional training in human service professions, such as applied behavior analysis, is that the skills that supervisees need to become competent professionals encompass much more than understanding the core principles, the science, and the procedures for practice. For example, the skills to greet a client appropriately to begin a session on a pleasant note are just as necessary in the applied setting for behavior analysts as implementing behavior procedures with high fidelity, but cannot be practiced and trained to mastery in university coursework (see Friman, 2015). Furthermore, other skills. such as how you communicate about your decisions at work, network with colleagues and influential stakeholders, sustain work efforts during tough times, and juggle different demands of your time. are just as important as your competence in behavior analysis. If a professional is skilled in presenting himself or herself well, but not competent in behavior analysis, it is unlikely that he or she will be successful in behavior analysis.

One way to look at this is to picture opening a box of your favorite chocolates, only to find those little paper holders without any chocolate. The empty box of chocolates is a metaphor for the behavior analyst who presents himself or herself well but lacks competence. People will be excited about the potential of this person but, when it comes to starting the work, the end result will be unsatisfying because there is no substance to effect change. To paraphrase the movie *Forrest Gump*, "People are like a box of chocolates, sometimes full of variety but sometimes full of emptiness and disappointment."

Alternatively, if a professional is skilled in behavior analysis, but lacks the skills to collaborate and be liked by other professionals on the treatment team, it is unlikely that his or her treatment recommendations will be adopted or implemented. If we apply the earlier analogy to this person, he or she would be like the world's best artisanal chocolates, but wrapped in a box that looks like it has been crushed, is smeared with mud, and is sitting in a gutter. No matter how amazing the contents of the box, no one would take the time to pick it up and see if anything of value is inside.

In this chapter, we refer to these skills as "pivotal" because they are crucial in your success as a behavior analyst and deemed important by all professionals.

TIME MANAGEMENT SKILLS

I have found that supervisees' timely submission of course assignments and the quality of their classwork are correlated with their timely submission of clinical reports and the quality of their fieldwork. This correlation leads me to believe that much of the difficulties I see in late submission of work, or submission of material that is not well thought out or edited, are symptoms of poor time management skills. Although not a part of the competencies outlined in the BACB task list, your success in a fieldwork setting and graduate program hinges on managing the various requirements of your position(s). If you find yourself lacking a method for organizing and ordering deadlines for assignments and responsibilities, reach out to your supervisor for support. Your development of time management skills will likely make or break the success of your supervision experience as well as your professional career.

As a supervisee and as a practicing behavior analyst, there will always be more work to be done, more cases to see, more articles to read, more reports to write, more opportunities to access, and more friends and family to satisfy. The key to juggling all of these exciting, but time-consuming, prospects in life is to be selective about what you do daily and to make progress toward each goal daily rather than cramming to meet each deadline.

Effective time management involves recognizing that all of the tasks you have will not be accomplished at once. You need to carve out time for yourself to plan out your deadlines and prioritize your daily activities. To do this, you need to invest in a calendar or a planner that works for you. If you find you have adopted planners but then stop using them after a few months, consider getting a different type of planner. There could be two reasons why your use of the planner may have been extinguished. First, you may have placed a few deadlines on the planner for which there were several other prompts (e.g., peers reminding you of the date or the supervisor sending you reminders), which made the planner less valuable. Second, you may have gotten a fancy planner that was not easy to take everywhere and inaccessible when something came up that you needed to jot down. Another explanation for why previous planners may not have been helpful is that you placed your wish list (e.g., scholarships or fellowships you wish to obtain) in your planner and ignored the deadlines when you realized you had gotten too ambitious with your time. You need to prioritize what you place in your planner and color-code things to assure important deadlines are salient in your planner. Finally, you probably did not come into contact with your planner daily to access reinforcers for adhering to a preset schedule.

If you create a system so that you place your important deadlines (things that matter to you) in your planner and give yourself self-imposed deadlines to work toward the deadline and honor them, your planner will become the most precious tool in your professional life. For example, suppose you plan to attend a symposium on a topic of interest to you. What you should place in your planner is the date of the symposium as well as the registration deadline (always give yourself some wiggle room), the deadline for reserving the hotel or travel, the deadline for reviewing the materials you need to read to gain the most from the symposium, the deadline for informing your workplace that you will be taking the day off to attend the symposium, and anything else that is directly relevant to the event for you. If you place all of those items in the planner along with the symposium date, you are much more likely to be prepared and meet your goal of attending the symposium. As a rule of thumb, for every hard deadline for any written work, place a deadline for submitting your best draft for review and give yourself time to make revisions based on that feedback. Your daily activities should not be controlled by the hard deadlines, but rather by the deadlines you preplanned to meet the hard deadline successfully.

At its essence, time management is an exercise in prioritization and sacrifice. Taking the time and putting forth the effort to assign deadlines will highlight the things you need to sacrifice to meet your goals. For example, if you have a report deadline set for tomorrow, it is likely that you will have to sacrifice going out with friends that night if you are to accomplish your task.

For more tips about good time management skills, we recommend that you read the chapter on time management in Bailey and Burch's (2010) *25 Essential Skills and Strategies for the Professional Behavior Analyst*. Also, place *The 7 Habits of Highly Effective People* by Covey (1991) on your summer list of must-reads!

SELF-CARE SKILLS

Like time management, self-care is a pivotal skill that every professional, but especially individuals in human care services, needs to be successful. Helping professionals, such as teachers, physicians, nurses, social workers, and behavior analysts, work in highly demanding fields and deal with many day-to-day challenges. Therefore, these professionals are at greater risk for burnout, fatigue, and stress-related health problems. Typically, individuals drawn to these professions wish to help people, but their desire to be helpful sometimes results in them attending to their clients' well-being more than their own. Therefore, it is essential for professionals in the helping professions to learn to balance attending to their own needs with the needs of their clients. To combat burnout, you will need to use certain strategies and practice using them as a part of your professional development. We highly recommend that you read *The Resilient Practitioner: Burnout and Compassion Fatigue Prevention and Self-Care Strategies for the Helping Professions* (Skovholt & Trotter-Mathison, 2016) and discuss how to implement these strategies with your supervisor. The authors of this book provide great case examples and highly practical strategies.

In general, self-care refers to activities and strategies that support your overall well-being, health, and happiness so that you can meet your commitments to helping others. Some primary self-care activities include having a well-balanced diet, go to bed early enough to get an average of 8 hours of sleep, hydrating your body, and exercising regularly. Also, research evidence shows that you can decrease your stress by spending some of your leisure time (as few as 10 minutes a day) on activities that enable you to relax and not think about things that are stressful (e.g., daily meditation). Neglecting to take care of yourself is a reflection of your poor time management skills. Covey (1991), the author of *The 7 Habits of Highly Effective People*, provides some great examples of how people get into vicious life cycles that cause their health and well-being to deteriorate over time, which chips away at their overall goals and happiness. For example, he tells the story of a woodcutter who cuts down an impressive number of trees each day and is highly committed to doing an excellent job. After some time, he puts in overtime to cut more trees. As time passes, instead of maintaining his impressive numbers, he begins slowing down, feels more tired, and has to put in more hours to get his job done. Then, the author reveals that the woodcutter had not sharpened his saw because he had been too busy. This story elucidates the importance of taking care of your tools, which in your case are your body and mind. We are no good to clients, colleagues, or family members if we burn out. Quick Reference 7.1 is a checklist you can use to ensure you are taking care of yourself.

QUICK REFERENCE 7.1   SELF-CARE CHECKLIST

Your environment

- ❏ Remove all distracting items from the site (e.g., television, tablets, smartphones)
- ❏ Keep your workspace clean
- ❏ Make your workspace safe and comfortable
- ❏ Organize your workspace to work for you

Your rewards

- ❏ Review the rewards of your profession
- ❏ Identify new, more immediate, rewards to gain through completion of work
- ❏ Engage in a few tasks that will access rewards quickly, and simultaneously engage in tasks that will pay off much later
- ❏ Identify a few people you trust and nurture your support system so that you can depend on them in the times you feel stressed or confused

Your body

- ❏ Identify the tasks causing you stress; instead of avoiding them, arrange to access rewards right after you approach the task for short periods of time
- ❏ Take breaks that involve activities unrelated to your work and away from your workspace on a fixed schedule
- ❏ Keep water and healthy snacks nearby, in your bag, at work, and in other areas that make them accessible to you
- ❏ Ask for help way before you find you are in trouble to prevent big fires for yourself
- ❏ No matter how much you have on your plate, get enough sleep and physical activity

COMMUNICATION SKILLS

Written Communication

We frequently host a professional panel of clinical directors and employers for our graduate students and alumni at California State University, Northridge (CSUN). When we ask employers which pivotal skills they need a professional behavior analyst to possess, they say better writing and time management skills. I mention this because these two skills are interrelated: Good writing involves editing, which involves managing your time well to leave room for editing. However, in addition to having time to edit to avoid gross spelling or grammatical errors, you would benefit from learning to write with more clarity and brevity during your internship. The best way to do this is to solicit feedback on your writing skills and to apply that feedback to new material you write. In other words, the best way to improve your writing skills is to select a few key components of your writing that need improvement and to work on them. As an example, you might set up a writing appointment with your supervisor to solicit feedback on work you have completed. Writing meetings via teleconferencing software (e.g., Skype, Zoom, GoToMeeting, WebEx) allow you to share screens so that you can see how your supervisor reviews your written work and discuss the feedback. Shared documents, such as Google docs, can meet this function as well. Also, when you are producing written work in graduate school, we encourage you to use software that helps you identify grammatical errors (e.g., Grammarly, Whitesmoke) so that you become familiar with using the software and learn to write with this type of tool from the beginning of your professional career.

Oral Communication

Albert Einstein once said, "If you can't explain it simply, you don't understand it well enough." In the human care professions, your skills for communicating with your clients about their treatment plan, sometimes referred to as your bedside manner, are extremely important. For example, it is ultimately the manner in which you explain the intervention plan that can put families at ease when their child's problem behavior has caused them a great deal of suffering. Similarly, it is how you explain the assessment and treatment plans that can help you get buy-in from a teacher who feels she has tried every trick in the industry and yet nothing seems to prevent her student from harming others in the classroom. To be able to explain things well to others, first, as Einstein noted, you have to understand the concept and procedures well. But understanding it is not enough: To explain it well, you have to practice explaining it orally. That is why in this book we inserted a few exercises to have you engage in role-play and practice saying things out loud. Your supervision meetings may provide you with fantastic opportunities to practice talking about your assessment or intervention plans and to solicit feedback. You will find that the first few times you describe a procedure, you may provide too much detail or use jargon. With practice, you are more likely to hit your key points and provide just enough detail that the listener can understand and ask questions.

PROFESSIONAL SKILLS

In clinical practice, how you dress, how you interact with others, and your overall professional demeanor are very important in how you represent the field and the impression you make on your clients (see Baily & Burch, 2010). It is important that you are open to receiving feedback from your supervisor about your professional demeanor and make a commitment to work on becoming a strong representative of the field of behavior analysis through possessing excellent professional skills. In addition to encouraging you to target your professional skills for improvement during supervision, we outline some tips from Dale Carnegie's (1998) book *How to Win Friends and Influence People*, which is very well known in the business and professional world. Although some of these steps seem like common sense, the truth is that many people don't do them. If you commit yourself to doing these things more often, you are likely to find that there is a reason why gurus in business etiquettes still refer to this book.

Tip 1. Become genuinely interested in other people and get them to talk about themselves. People love to talk about themselves, so if you want people to like you, then you should listen to them tell you about themselves. Over time, people will like you because they feel like you know them.

Tip 2. Let the other person feel that the idea is his or hers. Carnegie said, "It is amazing how much you can accomplish if you allow other people to get credit for it." This is especially true if you are in a position of leadership. The secret is for you to provide general ideas or seed the ideas, but to allow your team to take ownership of it. You want your team to feel that they will be credited for their work. With regard to your clients, you want the family, teacher, or client to feel as if they contributed to the intervention plan. For example, Brian Rice was working with a child who engaged in stereotypic hand flapping. He felt that the family would be resistant to the treatment plan he wanted to propose. Therefore, rather than informing the family of his treatment plan of choice, he provided the family with three different treatment options, one of which was the intervention he would have proposed. He left the written intervention plans with the family for a week and allowed them to take the time to review each plan on its own merit. This approach made the family feel much more involved in the decision making, and the family actually chose the intervention that Brian would have proposed initially.

Tip 3. Talk about your own mistakes before criticizing the other person. If you share something vulnerable about yourself, people will be less intimidated and feel less judged. When you provide peers with corrective feedback or make recommendations for change to your family, this could be a very handy tip. If you want to be able to provide constructive feedback that effectively changes behavior, the person needs to feel that your feedback is not a judgment of him or her.

Tip 4. Dramatize your ideas and get out of the standard narrative if and when you want to be heard. Think of some of the greatest ideas you have heard: The ones that got your attention were probably those that were dramatic and stood out. For example, Immortal Technique's song, "Dance with the Devil," is profound and thought provoking. The rapper shares a story about a guy who joins a gang that has him attack and rape a woman for initiation. After he and his friends rape and kill the woman, he reveals her face and learns that it was his mother. The narrative is unique not just because of the terrifying unveiling at the end, but also because of the way the rapper tells the story from the very beginning. If he had discussed gang violence and its effect on families, or if he had just shared the golden rule of "Do unto others as you would have them do unto you," his song would have never gotten the same effect. This is a great tip for when you present your work at conferences, write research grants or fellowships, or present your clinical outcomes to stakeholders.

Tip 5. Talk in terms of the listeners' interests. Listeners are wondering, "What's in it for me?" when they are across from a speaker. This is what everyone is wondering when they hear you speak, when they surf the web, or when they read something. This is not to say people are not altruistic; instead, they are being efficient in looking for the relevant information when presented with several things. So, when you are given the floor to speak, talk in terms of what is in it for the listener.

Tip 6. Get the other person to say "yes" before asking for something bigger. This is in line with the concept of behavioral momentum. If you need someone to do something for you that requires effort, and you know that the person may say no, start by asking the person to do a few things to which he or she will most likely agree.

Tip 7. Give honest and sincere appreciation. There is a big difference between flattery and appreciation. If you say "thank you," for example, explain exactly what you are thanking someone for. You don't have to be dramatic;, less is more in the case of appreciation with regard to what you say. However, it is important that you make statements of appreciation at least once a day or once during each interaction. For example, after a symposium or an invited talk, you can thank the speaker for his or her efforts and say, "I noticed the room lit up when you gave that example of...."

Tip 8. Give the other person a fine reputation to live up to. For example, if you see that a parent is struggling with the intervention plan, you might say, "I see how many things you are doing and how much you want to do for [child's name]. It is unlike you to not follow through with something that is good for [child's name]. So, I can only imagine that there have been serious impediments in your way. I am highly optimistic that you have got this. Let's take a look and see if there are things we need to revisit or change so that you can be successful with this intervention." All of us want to be more than we are today and at this time. Giving other people a goal and a standard to reach will make them feel that you believe in them and provide them with a target to move toward.

Tip 9. Know the power of your own identity and recognize that you build your identity through words. The two most important words in the English language are "I" and "am." Some damaging versions of the use of *I am* would be "I am too scared to try something I don't know," "I am inexperienced with children," "I am not trained enough," and "I am horrible at making friends." Alternatively, some examples of the use of the words *I am* to build a good impression would be "I am able to accomplish anything I set my mind to," "I am excited by new learning opportunities," and "I am not the type of person who shies away from a new challenge."

Tip 10. Work on remembering people's names and saying those names when you are speaking with them. It is easier to avoid asking for people's names or pronunciations, especially if you are unsure if you are saying names correctly, but the effort is worthwhile. People feel you know them well when you remember their names and use it in conversations (this includes the names of their partners, their children, and even the names of their pets). There is a big difference between me saying to Brian Rice, "I wish you and your family a happy Thanksgiving" versus "I hope you have a wonderful Thanksgiving, Brian, and say hello to Ashley [Brian's wife], Jossalyn [daughter, 6 years old], and Charlie [daughter, 3 years old]." I am willing to bet that even for you, as the reader of this text, the personalization of Brian's family members made you feel just a bit closer to him as the coauthor of this book.

CHAPTER REVIEW

In this chapter, we discussed some of the pivotal skills all professionals need to succeed in practicing their craft. Reviewing the tips we outlined in this chapter is a great place to start working toward improving your skills. Furthermore, we encourage you to target these skills during your supervision experience and solicit feedback from your supervisor in areas you feel you could grow as a professional. Many of these skills take a very long time to improve. Taking the opportunity to target them when you can obtain honest feedback from your supervisor may be the main ingredient in your professional success.

REFERENCES

Bailey, J. S., & Burch, M. R. (2010). *25 essential skills and strategies for the professional behavior analyst: Expert tips for maximizing consulting effectiveness.* New York, NY: Taylor & Francis.

Carnegie, D. (1998). *How to win friends and influence people.* New York, NY: Pocket Books.

Covey, S. R. (1991). *The 7 habits of highly effective people.* New York, NY: Simon & Schuster.

Friman, P. C. (2015). My heroes have always been cowboys. *Behavior Analysis in Practice, 8*(2), 138–139.

Skovholt, T. M., & Trotter-Mathison, M. (2016). *The resilient practitioner: Burnout and compassion fatigue prevention and self-care strategies for the helping professions.* New York, NY: Routledge.

8

Knowing What to Expect From Individual Versus Group Supervision Meetings

As you may recall from Chapter 1, the function of supervision is for you to gain the skills you need to become an ethical, competent behavior analyst. Supervision occurs in the context of both individual and group meetings. Typically, your graduate degree program as well as your credentialing board(s) have certain requirements for the amount of individual versus group supervision you receive to assure that an adequate portion of your supervision is individualized. During supervision meetings, the activities in which you engage, the structure, and the format can highly impact your learning experience. Whether your group supervision is a part of your academic practicum, your fieldwork supervision, or both, much of the experience is likely to be very similar. In this chapter, we begin by outlining the Behavior Analyst Certification Board (BACB) requirements. Then, we discuss what your individual and/or group supervision meetings are likely to entail and provide an in-depth description of each type of supervision.

BACB REQUIREMENTS OF SUPERVISION MEETINGS

Currently, for all categories of supervision (i.e., university-based practica versus independent fieldwork experience), you are expected to work no fewer than 10 hours, but no more than 30 hours, per week; this time includes your supervision hours. By January 2022, this requirement will change for candidates accruing supervision hours under the Concentrated Supervised Fieldwork Option (see October 2017 BACB Newsletter) to a minimum of 15 hours, but no more than 30 hours, per week. Only allowable activities may count toward your experience requirements. This is important because a portion of your supervision meetings may be spent on administrative activities such as scheduling, billing, record keeping, discussing crisis management such as CPR, and clients' diagnostic assessments. You should track all of these administrative hours, but you cannot count them toward your supervision experience. In addition, the BACB restricts the total hours you can accrue from delivering instruction or implementing treatment to no more than 50% of your total experience. This restriction is intended to protect you, the supervisee, from working full time as a direct implementer during your supervision experience and not gaining the experiences you need to become an independent practitioner. The following activities are deemed much more in line with the kind of work you would be doing as an independent practitioner, so the hours you accrue engaging in these activities are unrestricted by BACB. You can count the hours you spend in the following activities:

- Reviewing or obtaining feedback on work toward conducting behavioral assessments
- Designing, implementing, and monitoring behavioral programs
- Writing behavior plans, progress summaries, and clinical notes
- Overseeing the implementation of behavior analytic programs by others
- Training and performance management of others
- Communicating effectively with caregivers and other professionals
- Working on various applied writing activities
- Developing communication skills to work effectively with consumers, supervisors, families, and others
- Implementing behavior programs
- Other activities deemed behavior analytic and appropriate by your supervisor, such as summarizing literature relevant to client programming

If you are unsure whether a specific activity counts, seek out your supervisor's opinion prior to counting the hours for that activity toward your total supervision hours. Be aware that all of your supervision activities must be approved by your supervisor.

According to the BACB, no more than 50% of your total supervised experience hours may be conducted in small groups during each supervisory period. Small groups are interactive meetings of 2 to 10 supervisees who share similar experiences in the supervision activities. The number of supervisees in your group meetings may not exceed 10 at any time, regardless of the number of Board Certified Behavior Analysts (BCBAs) in the meeting. If non-supervisees are present, their presence must not interrupt or inhibit behavior-analytic discussions, and they may not participate. Remember, the amount of small-group supervision you receive may not exceed the amount of individual supervision you must have within any given supervisory period.

PRACTICUM VERSUS FIELDWORK

Depending on your university program, enrollment in a practica course may be mandatory, optional, or not available. Although all supervisors are likely to work on similar skills with you, specific differences may emerge in your individual and group supervision meetings depending on your experience setting. For example, if you are enrolled in practicum, your supervision contract with your practicum instructor is likely to be your syllabus. Therefore, some instructors ask that you review and sign the syllabus at the beginning of each practicum course. Fieldwork sites, in contrast, typically provide you with a standard contract related specifically to supervision at the site.

Another example of how practica meetings may differ from fieldwork meetings with your supervisors is that practica are likely to be restricted to supervisory discussion of specific skills and peer work samples with limited (or no) instances of direct in-field observation of your skills. Fieldwork supervision, however, most often balances supervisory discussion with in-field observations of your work with clients.

Lastly, the purpose of supervision in each setting may differ slightly. Your practicum supervision likely focuses primarily on the acquisition of behavior-analytic skills and assessing your competency in each targeted skill area. In contrast, your fieldwork supervision is likely to devote more time to specific case discussions and client services. These client discussions are imperative to the fieldwork supervision process but may result in less time being spent on the application of specific competencies in the fieldwork supervision setting.

ACTIVITIES DURING SUPERVISION MEETINGS

Your activities during your individual versus group supervision meetings are likely to be similar. The goal of these meetings is to help you improve your skills to become an ethical, professional behavior analyst, which includes your skills in communicating about your work with clients, families, and other stakeholders. Therefore, with informed consent both from the individuals you serve and from your fieldwork setting, you can use any of the following techniques during supervision meetings to gain insight from your supervisor regarding your performance as an aspiring behavior analyst.

Audio or Video Recordings

You can bring in samples of your work to your supervision meetings to show your progress, receive feedback, and obtain guidance on future directions with the case. Usually, you need to provide some context, such as the referral problem, case history, and any assessment or treatment outcome data that are available. If you take audio or video recordings to your supervision meeting, it is likely that you will review the material together with your supervisor. Using this format, your supervisor may provide feedback on your performance after asking you to self-reflect and comment on what you hear or see. Also, it is likely that your supervisor will request additional recordings to see how you implement the feedback.

Clinical Records

You can bring in samples of your clinical records, such as data sheets, graphs, progress reports, intervention protocols, or behavioral assessment reports, to supervision meetings for feedback. During review of your work, you may obtain feedback on a number of things, including the accuracy of your data, your case conceptualization, problem solving with regard to outcomes, assessment approach, presentation and interpretation of assessment results, and much more. Also, you may use supervision time for formal case presentation, during which you would present everything you have on a case and recruit feedback for future direction.

Role-Play

Your supervisor may find various opportunities for you to role-play during supervision. Sometimes you will role-play with your supervisor alone. For example, you may play the role of you, as the intern, and your supervisor may play the role of the caregiver and ask you to justify the procedures of the treatment you want to implement. During such role-play, the supervisor will have the opportunity to observe and evaluate your skills, provide you with performance feedback, and observe you implement the feedback until you have achieved mastery. Alternatively, you may role-play with peers, during group supervision, and receive feedback from the supervisor or your peers.

Professional and Personal Support

Supervision is not solely limited to your clinical competencies or the specific work skills you need to gain. Your supervisor will check in with you to make sure you are on task, managing your time well, engaged during supervision, and progressing on your competencies. You will want to use supervision time to discuss rapport building with clients, family, staff, and coworkers and obtain guidance if you are having difficulty in any of these areas. You will also want to discuss with your supervisor any personal or health issues that may be impacting your fieldwork and seek guidance during individual supervision.

INDIVIDUAL SUPERVISION

Benefits

Individual supervision makes up at least 50% of your total supervised experience but, in many cases, it may be your primary method of accessing supervision hours.

This type of supervision focuses exclusively on your development and allows for your supervisor to individualize activities, discussions, and assignments specifically to address your area(s) of weakness or interest. This experience allows for a deepening of the supervisory relationship through in-depth discussions of not only case-related information, but also the experiences of your supervisor. Because you will have exclusive access to your supervisor during this type of supervision experience, we recommend that you work on putting your behavior out there. The term "putting your behavior out there" means to do the best that you can under the circumstances and to forget that your supervisor is watching so that you are not influenced by how you feel about corrective feedback. It is much easier, as a supervisor, to provide accurate and relevant feedback to an individual when he or she actively engages in tasks and provides multiple samples of their performance. The more you behave as a supervisee, the more samples your supervisor will obtain, and the more opportunities there will be for your supervisor to work on improving your skills.

For example, if you are asked to develop a progress report, it is in your best interest to develop several versions of your tables or graphs to summarize your data, instead of just one, so that your supervisor can (a) see how you apply your skills, (b) provide feedback on which graphs or tables best represent the data, and (c) get a sense of what you can produce independently. If you produce just one table or graph, it is much more difficult for your supervisor to identify how much thought you gave the assignment and how much the product is a reflection of your efforts versus your current skill set. Great supervisors conduct Can't Do versus Don't Do assessments (i.e., they assess if the issue is a motivation problem or a skill deficit) of their supervisee's skills frequently. If you produce multiple versions of things, or if you provide your supervisor with multiple samples of your behavior, you eliminate lack of effort or motivation on your part as potential explanations for the results you have produced.

Observation and Performance Feedback

A large proportion of your individual supervision meetings will involve your supervisor overlapping time with you to observe your work with the clients. For these observation periods, we recommend that you confirm the date, time, and location of the meeting at least one day in advance. In situations where you are not informed beforehand of a supervisory visit, be sure to prepare in advance of the session for what you would want addressed in the event your supervisor arrives at the session. Also, be sure to pose any questions you have (e.g., about the intervention plan, the structure of supervision for that day, the performance monitoring tools being utilized by your supervisor) ahead of time, ideally in the time before the session begins.

It is normal to feel a bit nervous when your supervisor is observing you. During your observation sessions, you should try to be yourself and behave as you usually would, so that your supervisor can obtain a good sample of your typical performance. The more times you are observed and benefit from the feedback your supervisor provides, the more you will establish trust with your supervisor, and the less nervous you will be over time (see Sellers, Valentino, & LeBlanc, 2016, for some recommended practices for individual supervision of aspiring behavior analysts). You can gain the most from this type of supervision by reviewing the feedback your supervisor provides to you after the observation (this could be right after the session or at a meeting after the session), practicing or rehearsing the suggestions, asking clarifying questions, and implementing the feedback. We recommend that you have your supervision form ready, prefilled when applicable, to facilitate the feedback-giving and record-keeping process. In addition, we recommend that you keep running notes of your supervision meetings so that you can track the feedback you receive and the impact of that feedback on your behavior.

Individual Meetings

As noted in previous chapters, preparation for supervision is paramount. Come to your scheduled supervision meetings ready with your questions about client performance and programming, areas of your coursework you are struggling with, completed assignments or projects due to your supervisor, and any other areas in which you'd like to receive guidance. If you take the time to prepare, you will find that supervision meetings run more smoothly and efficiently. See Quick Reference 8.1 for tips on preparing for these meetings.

QUICK REFERENCE 8.1   TIPS FOR HOLDING EFFECTIVE INDIVIDUAL SUPERVISION MEETINGS

- Before your meetings (usually 24 hours before would be best)
  - Confirm the meeting time and location with your supervisor (email or, ideally, send a calendar invite).
  - Send your agenda for the meeting.
    - The agenda should contain specific updates and work you are going to show to solicit feedback, or if you faced an ethical or professional issue, what you'd like to discuss.
    - Prioritize your agenda items to begin with the quickest things first.
    - Consider the amount of time that each agenda topic will take, and provide an estimated duration next to each agenda item, so that you have an agenda that can be accomplished within the supervision meeting time frame.
  - Send the documents that you plan to review during the meeting with your agenda to save time during supervision as well as to allow the supervisor to decide how much of the feedback can be in written form.

(continued)

QUICK REFERENCE 8.1   TIPS FOR HOLDING EFFECTIVE INDIVIDUAL SUPERVISION MEETINGS (*continued*)

- During the individual meeting
  - Set a timer for yourself so you can end your meeting about 5 minutes before the scheduled time.
  - Begin the supervision meeting by giving a quick summary of your agenda items.
  - State the agenda item and the estimated time as you tackle each during the meeting.
    - Example: I'd love to give you an update regarding X; I estimated this would be 5 minutes today.
  - Note, for yourself, the time it took to have each discussion to help you develop agendas more realistically in the future (or to prioritize better).
  - End the supervision meeting by confirming your action items or "To Do" activities and deadlines, based on the meeting.
- Have your supervision form ready, with prefilled fields where applicable, if the individual meeting is the end of your supervision period.

GROUP SUPERVISION

Bernard and Goodyear (2009) have defined group supervision as the regular meeting of a group of supervisees with a designated supervisor, or supervisors, to monitor the quality of their work. In addition, the function of the group meetings is to further supervisees' understanding of themselves as practitioners, of the clients with whom they work, and of the service delivery system. Usually, the supervisor is responsible for determining the group's purpose, its goals, and the format of discussions. In group supervision, the supervisor also evaluates the supervisees' team skills, dependability, and professional skills. To date, much of the research on the effects of group supervision has been based on self-reports, and the field of behavior analysis would benefit from more research on effective group supervision practices. However, there are several discussion papers and books on supervision, which we reviewed when writing this book. Proponents of group supervision argue that it is more time-efficient because the supervisor is not in a position to say the same things, or provide the same instructions, over and over again across individual supervisees. Therefore, it is clear that in terms of time and money, group supervision is efficient.

Benefits

Group supervision could potentially have many more benefits than efficiency for the supervisor. For example, the supervisor's power and authority are likely to be diffused in group supervision, which provides you with more opportunities to ask clarifying questions, admit when certain expectations are set too high, and participate in problem solving with a group. In addition, you are likely to be exposed to a greater breadth of contexts of treatment (e.g., school versus home), client characteristics (e.g., culture, gender, and diagnosis), caregiver and family dynamics (e.g., sibling relations), problem behaviors, and treatment protocols. Group supervision can encourage team building and networking with your peers. This is important because you will have a team of professionals in the future whom you can depend on for support, consult, and professional networking. Very often, in our experience, you will continue to rely on this group for support and collaboration even after you have left your graduate program.

The group context, when moderated well by a supervisor, also has other advantages for individual supervision (see Valentino, LeBlanc, & Sellers, 2016, for tips on holding productive supervision meetings). The group provides you with multiple listeners, which can be very beneficial for honing your speaking skills. If, for example, you have a hard time providing context before discussing details of a case, your peers will not have the information they need to help you with the case and will have to ask many follow-up questions about the context and background. The questions themselves serve as great feedback that information was missing and needed, which should shape how you present information in the future. Along the same lines, group supervision meetings are a fantastic context for practicing your presentation and group training skills. As a behavior analyst, you are likely to be in a position to present your case to a committee or stakeholders at a school. You may conduct research (whether in the field or at the university) and present your results at a professional conference. You may also pick up additional group training and teaching roles as you grow as a professional. In all of these cases, you need to practice public speaking and presenting. Group supervision meetings are an excellent forum for this because they are a safe environment that provides you with opportunities to receive feedback and grow. Friman (2014) provided a 15-step tutorial for public speaking that is a must-read for every behavior analyst. Group supervision is the perfect location to implement his recommendations and improve your public speaking, as you have not only a captive audience, but also an audience that will be willing to provide you with constructive feedback.

Another benefit of group supervision is that it provides you with social comparisons so that you can determine where you stand with regard to your ethics, competencies, and professional skills compared to your peers. Although the social comparison can give you a realistic goal, anytime a group of individuals have the common goal of learning with each other, there is also a potential for judgment, conflict, competition, shame, and feelings of incompetence. These disadvantages can be mitigated if you bring any of these issues to your group supervisor's attention. It is sometimes easy to assume that because you are all in graduate school, the members of the group will be professional and that differences in opinion, or multicultural differences, will not occasionally conflict. However, many differences can impact group cohesion, including gender identity, ethnicity, race, age, religion, and disability. These differences can actually enhance the group experience if you view them as learning opportunities and remain open to hearing others' perspectives. Other ways you can improve your group's dynamics is by engaging in self-awareness exercises and holding open discussions about how cultural differences impact each client whom you discuss.

Group Dynamics and Rules

Group supervisions can have different structures and formats, depending on your supervisor's preference and whether you are enrolled in practica. The most common form for group supervision is for supervisees to take turns presenting material to the group and receiving feedback. Other members may ask questions, make suggestions, and offer potential solutions. Therefore, another benefit of group supervision is that you are afforded the opportunity to practice giving feedback to your peers. Feedback giving and receiving from peers can be very valuable because it gives you the opportunity to gain a range of skills that are important in your development, including meaningful professional interactions with your peers, greater exposure to ideas, and new perspectives (see Lundstrom & Baker, 2009, for details on peer review of written work). Peer feedback sessions are typically moderated by your practica instructor or supervisor. Until now, you may not have had many opportunities to hone your skills in giving feedback to peers and may need coaching from the practica instructor. In fact, researchers have found that peer assessment and feedback are improved through training and experience with giving feedback (Van Zundert, Sluijsmans, & Van Merrienboer, 2010).

We recommend that you adhere to the guidelines given in Chapter 6 on how to provide effective feedback. Those guidelines apply when you provide feedback to a supervisee, a peer, or a supervisor. For example, peer feedback should focus on concrete behaviors, be descriptive rather than judgmental, focus on the behaviors of the individual rather than personal characteristics, and be balanced between things to keep and things to discard. Also, when you are giving feedback, you want to be selective and prioritize things that make a big difference rather than providing a laundry list. What really differs in providing feedback in group settings or to peers is how you phrase the feedback. Particularly in group settings, you want to refrain from sounding like a "know-it-all." We recommend that you phrase feedback in the form of tentative statements, rather than making authoritative conclusions. For example, instead of saying, "The grammatical errors in this sentence make it hard for me to understand what you are trying to convey to the reader," you might say, "I felt you are trying to say something very important in this sentence, but I am having a hard time grasping what you would like for me, as the reader, to understand."

It usually takes a bit of time for the supervision group to form, and for you and your peers to become accustomed to working with each other. At the beginning of the group, there may be some differences in your viewpoints, models, and attitudes. For the team to become cohesive, safe, and productive, there need to be some rules about how you participate, provide feedback to each other, and resolve problems. In Quick Reference 8.2, we suggest some pertinent rules.

QUICK REFERENCE 8.2   RULES TO ENCOURAGE SAFE AND PRODUCTIVE GROUP MEETINGS

- Arrive at least 5 to 10 minutes before the meeting time.
- Complete assignments on time and prepare to share your work with peers before the meeting.
- Be open to hearing different viewpoints and be respectful of their differences.
- Own your own opinions and avoid giving advice.
- Keep information about your peers, and their work, confidential and within the group.
- Participate actively, by asking questions, adding to comments that are shared during a discussion, or answering questions to show engagement and be open to sharing information.
- Attend and listen to all peers when they speak, and not just to information that seems immediately important to you.
- Avoid talking over other individuals by waiting your turn to speak, raising your hand, or looking for a period of silence.
- Avoid distractions by staying on topic and saving new items for discussion as future agenda items.
- Assign a timekeeper to help members stick to a predetermined allocation of time based on the group's agenda.
- Assign a notetaker for each meeting to take notes of major tasks, decisions, action items, and activities. This would help you avoid discussing the same things repeatedly, and your action items will create accountability.
- If you agree with something said during the meeting, state that you do. because lack of disagreement is not the same thing as group agreement or cohesion.

FIGURE 8.1   Stages of the team development process.

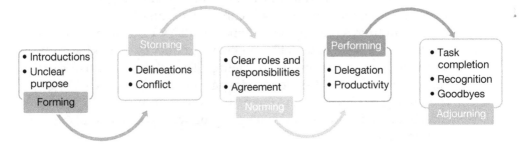

Supervisors usually work on team development and the group's ability to work together to achieve common goals. Your supervision group is likely to undergo certain stages as you spend more time with members of the group and become acclimated with each other. Tuckman first proposed a series of stages of group development in the late 1960s, which has since become the most widely recognized model of group dynamics in the organizational literature (Tuckman & Jensen, 1977). Although the empirical literature supporting this model lags behind, the model provides us with a simple means of discussing team dynamics. Figure 8.1 illustrates the key components of each stage so that you can get a sense of your group's dynamics.

In Tuckman's model, the first stage of the team development process is called Forming. In this stage, the team members are getting to know each other, exploring, and becoming oriented to the group as a whole. This initial stage can be stressful, as members attempt to learn more about each other, what is expected of them, and what their role in the group is. The second stage of team development is Storming, during which group members attempt to delineate exactly what each member's specific role will be. In this stage, Tuckman explained, members worry they may not be heard and there is conflict as members assert their different roles on the team. Norming is the third stage of the development; it is characterized by agreement among the team members. During this stage, the members have figured out each other's roles and feel heard by other members on the team. Performing, the fourth stage of team development, is characterized by solving organizational problems and meeting the tasks assigned. Tucker noted that this is the stage at which the group becomes productive and begins to access reinforcers for their productivity. By the last stage, Adjourning, the team has met all of its goals and is moving toward saying its goodbyes. Team members may feel a sense of loss, as membership on a team is often rewarding after the initial stages of ambivalence.

Group Supervision in Practicum Versus Fieldwork

Practicum meetings are group supervision meetings, and you can record them as such in your experience form if the practicum format and activities are aligned with the BACB requirements (e.g., 10 or fewer supervisees). Unlike group supervision meetings at your fieldwork, practicum groups are usually made up of your peers in graduate school. Although the group makeup is homogenous with regard to your graduate school training, it is likely that your peers in practicum will work in different contexts and with different client populations. These differences do not deter from learning: Most often they enrich it. As an example, in a discussion of operational definitions, a group member working in an autism clinic may bring definitions regarding specific problem behaviors (e.g., self-injury, stereotypy), while a group member working with a geriatric population may bring definitions regarding medication compliance and physical activity. Bringing together different experiences not only allows for richer discussions, but also provides generalization opportunities typically unavailable when meeting with other individuals at a single site or with a single population.

During practicum, you usually bring de-identified components of your case for review and feedback. Therefore, the fieldwork agency and the clients need to be informed at the outset that other individuals will be reviewing their cases for group supervision purposes, and you must obtain their informed consent to share their information.

Also, your practicum supervisor, in many cases, is not the person who supervises your fieldwork. Therefore, prearrangements need to be made to ensure that the learning experience does not interrupt the client's services. Specifically, in some practica arrangements, your practica supervisor may conduct field visits. If this is the case for your program, it is your responsibility to ensure that permission has been granted by both the client (and the client's family, if applicable) and your fieldwork supervisor. In addition, any discrepancies between recommendations that arise in practicum must be communicated with the field supervisor. Ultimately, the fieldwork supervisor is the one conducting infield observations of the case and the person responsible for service provision. As such, the course of action recommended by your field supervisor will take precedence over the recommendations made by your practica supervisor.

If you have group supervision meetings at your internship site, the group is likely to be homogenous with respect to the fieldwork setting policies and general clients. However, you are likely to be in a group with supervisees at different stages of supervision and in different university degree programs. These differences may either enhance group discussions or hinder them, depending on the nature of the differences, which makes group productivity for supervision a bit more challenging. Due to the varying emphases of degree programs and the differences in skill levels, such groups may focus on tasks set for the average group member as opposed to focusing on the most applicable area for the group as a whole. Also, infield group supervision is at higher risk than practica group supervision to lose time to administrative tasks and schedule conflicts. This tendency occurs because members of the group are coworkers and may have a hard time scheduling time to meet. In addition to scheduling issues, work sites typically have specific agenda items to be addressed with their teams, such as productivity reports, mandatory trainings, and administrative tasks. Therefore, a large proportion of group supervision time may be spent on administrative and logistical issues, which do not count as supervision hours. If you find this is occurring relatively often in your group supervision meetings, take charge of your supervision by setting aside some time to meet with your group supervisor to discuss this issue. As with any feedback delivered to a supervisor, be prepared to discuss the issues in an objective manner and be ready with possible solutions to be discussed during the interaction.

CHAPTER REVIEW

Supervision is intended to help you gain the skills you need to become an ethical, competent behavior analyst. The process by which you gain these skills, however, can vary drastically—not only between programs or work sites, but also across supervisors. In this chapter, we outlined how you should prepare yourself to gain the most from your individual as well as group supervision meetings. We also provided tips on working collaboratively with your peers during group supervision. Although the majority of this chapter focused on the structure of supervision, the key take-home message is that in all situations it is in your best interest to put your behavior out there to be shaped by your supervisor. Supervision is only as effective as you make it. Regardless of the structure of supervision, embrace the process of being evaluated and growing from performance feedback with the support of your supervisor and your peers.

REFERENCES

Bernard, J. M., & Goodyear, R. K. (2009). *Fundamentals of clinical supervision* (4th ed.). Upper Saddle River, NJ: Pearson.

Friman, P. C. (2014). Behavior analysts to the front! A 15-step tutorial on public speaking. *The Behavior Analyst, 37*(2), 109–118. doi:10.1007/s40614-014-0009-y

Lundstrom, K., & Baker, W. (2009). To give is better than to receive: The benefits of peer review to the reviewer's own writing. *Journal of Second Language Writing, 18*(1), 30–43. doi:10.1016/j.jslw.2008.06.002

Sellers, T. P., Valentino, A. L., & LeBlanc, L. A. (2016). Recommended practices for individual supervision of aspiring behavior analysts. *Behavior Analysis in Practice, 9*(4), 274–286. doi:10.1007/s40617-016-0110-7

Tuckman, B. W., & Jensen, M. A. C. (1977). Stages of small-group development revisited. *Group & Organization Studies, 2*(4), 419–427. doi:10.1177/105960117700200404

Valentino, A. L., LeBlanc, L. A., & Sellers, T. P. (2016). The benefits of group supervision and a recommended structure for implementation. *Behavior Analysis in Practice, 9*(4), 320–328. doi:10.1007/s40617-016-0138-8

Van Zundert, M., Sluijsmans, D., & Van Merriënboer, J. (2010). Effective peer assessment processes: Research findings and future directions. *Learning and Instruction, 20*(4), 270–279. doi:10.1016/j.learninstruc.2009.08.004

EVIDENCE-BASED STRATEGIES FOR DEVELOPING COMPETENCE THROUGH SUPERVISION

9

Evidence- and Competency-Based Supervision

Competence means the skills to do something successfully. A competent behavior analyst is someone who has the skills to carry out the role and duties of a behavior analyst successfully. The Behavior Analyst Certification Board (BACB) has established a task list of knowledge and skills that it believes every Board Certified Behavior Analyst (BCBA) should possess. Although the task list serves as the foundation of the BCBA and Board Certification at the Assistant Level (BCaBA), the emphasis of the BACB examination is on your knowledge, which is assessed through a multiple-choice test of your ability to answer questions related to the task list. As a practitioner, you need to be able to perform the skills outlined in the task list. Performance-based assessment of your skills would require that you actively perform the specific responses you have been trained to carry out. This is where effective supervision is crucial. Evidence-based training strategies to improve your performance go beyond classroom lectures and reading to the actual performance of the skills.

To improve your performance, your supervisor will need to use behavior skills training (BST; Sarokoff & Sturmey, 2004), which includes instruction, modeling, rehearsal, and feedback. This approach to training requires data-based decision making as the trainer provides you with opportunities to practice (i.e., rehearse or role-play) your skills and provides you with performance feedback to help you improve. Competency-based training means that your supervisor will continue to train you in this manner until you perform the skills at a level your trainer deems as competent (Parsons, Rollyson, & Reid, 2012). To identify when your skills have reached competence, your supervisor will need to have established mastery criteria for the skills you will be asked to perform. These criteria can be based on well-established literature, your supervisor's previous and current supervisees' performances, your previous performance, or a combination of any of these.

THE NEXT SECTIONS OF THIS BOOK

We have provided you with several tools in this book to facilitate the supervision process and performance review of your skills. Based on our many years of experience supervising aspiring behavior analysts, we established a total of 10 general skills that we feel every behavior analyst should possess. In Table 9.1, we have outlined how our 10 competencies align with Section 2 of the BACB Fifth Edition Task List (i.e., task list items related to the application of behavior analysis).

TABLE 9.1   List of Competencies as They Align With the BACB Fifth Edition Task List

COMPETENCIES	BACB FIFTH EDITION TASK LIST SECTION 2
1. Adhere to legal, professional, and ethical guidelines	Section E. Ethics
2. Develop and use behavior measurement methods and record and analyze data	Section F. Behavior Assessment
3. Conduct behavior assessments (e.g., Functional Behavior Assessment, Preference Assessment, Reinforcer Assessment)	
4. Evaluate and develop evidence-based intervention plans	Section H. Selecting and Implementing Interventions
5. Design and implement skill acquisition procedures based on initial assessment (e.g., design a language acquisition program based on VB-MAPP results)	Section G. Behavior-Change Procedures
6. Design and implement behavior reduction procedures	
7. Program and probe for generalization and maintenance	
8. Conduct experimental evaluations and ongoing assessments of interventions	Section H. Selecting and Implementing Interventions
9. Train another individual to conduct a procedure	Section I. Personnel Supervision and Management
10. Represent and disseminate the field of behavior analysis	Section H. Selecting and Implementing Interventions. Also Sections E and G.

VB-MAPP, Verbal Behavior Milestones Assessment and Placement Program.

There are several steps you need to complete to have advanced skills and reach mastery for each competency. To facilitate your self-evaluation as well as your performance review, we have provided you and your supervisor with a developmental chart, a diagram, in which we used a 3-point scale (i.e., elementary, intermediate, and advanced) to gauge your skill development. Your supervisor can determine that your skills have reached competence when you are performing the skills at the advanced level. In this book, we have broken down each overarching competency into smaller steps, what we consider to be the component skills that you need to accomplish to master each competency. To help you and your supervisor, for each competency, we have provided a diagram depicting the different skill levels as well as a case example of how a supervisor may work on your skills. For each case example, we have provided guidelines on the prerequisite skills you will need to have at baseline for your supervisor to work on the particular skill. We have also provided some example tools (e.g., worksheets, performance monitoring checklists) to help you work toward building the necessary skills. Finally, we outline a task list for each major component of each competency to help you initiate and keep track of your activities during supervision. For each competency, we end with additional references and resources your supervisor may wish for you to review.

REFERENCES

Parsons, M. B., Rollyson, J. H., & Reid, D. H. (2012). Evidence-based staff training: A guide for practitioners. *Behavior Analysis in Practice*, 5(2), 2–11. doi:10.1007/BF03391819

Sarokoff, R. A., & Sturmey, P. (2004). The effects of behavioral skills training on staff implementation of discrete-trial teaching. *Journal of Applied Behavior Analysis*, 37(4), 535–538. doi:10.1901/jaba.2004.37-535

COMPETENCY 1. ADHERE TO LEGAL, PROFESSIONAL, AND ETHICAL GUIDELINES

The first competency every professional behavior analyst must possess is how to behave in accordance with the behavior analysts' professional and ethical code of conduct as well as the state and federal laws that apply to behavior-analytic practice. This competency applies to every aspect of a behavior analyst's job duties. Therefore, you are likely to work on this competency throughout your supervision experience and alongside other competencies. We believe that the best way for you to gain skills in making ethical decisions when you are facing challenges in your role as a behavior analyst is to have ongoing conversations about your decisions with your supervisor.

For this competency, we outlined activities for you to complete with your supervisor to (a) demonstrate your knowledge of ethical, responsible, professional, and disciplinary guidelines and (b) demonstrate your knowledge of state and federal laws such as the Health Insurance Portability and Accountability Act (HIPAA) and confidentiality rules (see Competency Task Lists 1.1 and 1.2). In Diagram 9.1.1, we provide you with benchmarks to help you gauge your skill development in this competency.

DIAGRAM 9.1.1 Competency benchmarks for legal, professional, and ethical conduct.

Elementary Skills

- Can explain the purpose of the code of conduct
  - Can explain ethical violations (e.g., dual relationships, conflict of interest)
- Can explain the disciplinary actions that could be taken if a certified behavior analyst violates the code of conduct and state and/or federal laws
- Can explain the purpose of HIPAA
- Can explain what is informed consent and why it is important
- Can explain the role of a mandated reporter

Intermediate Skills

- Can discriminate the difference between legal and ethical violation (e.g., falsifying billing vs. intervention data)
- Can detect legal and ethical violations and can discriminate which code or law applies to the given situation
- Can follow HIPAA guidelines by securing client identifying information
- Can describe and follow the steps for filing a child or elderly abuse report
- Can seek supervision when faced with possible ethical or legal violations

Advanced Skills

- Can follow ethical and legal guidelines and ensure that supervisees are adhering to them
- Can explain the ethical and legal guidelines governing the role of a behavior analyst to parents, teachers, and other stakeholders
- Can be proactive by setting specific expectations with parents, teachers, and other stakeholders, at the onset of the intervention, to minimize or avoid ethical and legal violations
- Can make decisions about the steps to take to minimize harm to clients when faced with ethical or legal violation (e.g., following disciplinary actions if a fellow behavior analyst is in violation of an ethical guideline and no resolution has been achieved)

Continuing Education & Professional Development

To gain advanced skills in Competency 1, you are likely to engage in several activities that require you to detect an ethical or legal violation and to problem-solve by explaining the exact steps you would take to mitigate harm to your client. Next, we provide one example of how you and your supervisor can work on your skills. We also outline the prerequisite skills you need to have for your supervisor to be able to work on this skill with you. In this example, the supervisor would have the supervisee complete a risk–benefit analysis (see Worksheets 9.1.1, 9.1.2, and 9.1.3). Therefore, with the example, we provide risk–benefit analysis worksheets.

Competency 1. Example Case Scenario 9.1.1. Teaching Ethical Conduct

(1) *Readiness for practicum (prerequisite skills)*

   a. Supervisee would have read the BACB's Professional and Ethical Compliance Code (PECC)

      i. www.bacb.com/ethics/ethics-code

   b. Supervisee would have read *Ethics for Behavior Analysts,* third edition, by Jon Bailey and Mary Burch.

      i. Bailey, J., & Burch, M. (2013). *Ethics for behavior analysts* (3rd ed.). Abingdon, UK: Routledge.

   c. Supervisee would have done at least one of the following to demonstrate fluency with the PECC:

      i. Completion of SAFMEDS (Say All Facts one Minute Every Day Shuffled) for PECC numbers and ascribed labels and any applicable legal standards

      ii. Definition of specific PECC items when given the label assigned to the specific code or legal standard (e.g., 5.02 Supervisory Volume)

      iii. Identification of relevant ethical codes and applicable legal standards to set criteria when presented with vignettes of situations (e.g., vignettes presented in Bailey & Burch, 2013).

(2) *Baseline assessment of your skills*

   a. Your supervisor would provide you with a vignette for an ethical scenario that you might encounter in your specific practice setting:

      i. Example:

         1. *You have been assigned an assessment with a 21-year-old male participant with a diagnosis of mild intellectual disability. Prior to entering the home, you are informed that the participant is not conserved (i.e., the participant has full rights as an adult in terms of decision making and confidentiality). Upon entering the home, the participant's mother (who lives with him) welcomes you and proceeds to explain how excited she is to tell you about the things she wants you to target with her son. When you meet your participant, he greets you and, as part of your conversation, asks if his mother has to be involved in the process. He states that he is not comfortable sharing certain things in front of his mother. How do you proceed?*

b. Your supervisor would provide you with a copy of a risk–benefit analysis sheet (see Bailey & Burch, 2013).

   i. You would complete all sections of the form.

   ii. Your supervisor would review your form and discuss the content with you.

c. Moving from baseline to either training or generalization would be determined based on the criteria set by your supervisor.

(3) *Training*

a. Instruction and modeling

   i. Your supervisor would present you with a series of vignettes with applicable ethical codes embedded in scenarios.

   ii. Your supervisor would allow you to choose one of the vignettes for review.

      1. You would then present the following questions to your supervisor:

         a. What ethical codes do you see as being relevant in this situation?

         b. Why are they relevant (what in the scenario indicates they are relevant)?

         c. What action would/could you take to address this ethical code?

         d. What would be the potential consequences (good/bad) you would expect given _____ action?

         e. What steps would you take given those potential consequences?

      2. Your supervisor would answer these questions, at the same time modeling for you how to fill out the risk–benefit analysis.

      3. Your supervisor would then explain how he or she would proceed in this given situation and provide you with the rationale.

   iii. This process would repeat as often as your supervisor believes would be necessary prior to role-playing with you.

      1. This is an opportunity to practice decision making with your supervisor's guidance.

b. Rehearsal

c. Your supervisor would provide you with a vignette for an ethical scenario that you might encounter in your specific practice setting.

   i. Example:

      1. *You have been working with a family with a 3-year-old with autism for the past 3 months. The father approaches you after the session to inform you that they are planning to begin the following interventions: B_{12} shots, gluten–casein-free diet, and sensory integration therapy. The father asks you for your opinion of these therapies and enquires whether you would be willing to continue your service when the family obtains these other services. How do you respond to this parent?*

    d. Your supervisor would provide you with a copy of a risk–benefit analysis sheet (Bailey & Burch, 2013).

       i. You would complete all sections of the form.

      ii. Your supervisor would compare your form to a completed form and discuss the content with you.

    e. Moving from baseline to either training or generalization would be determined based on the criteria set by your supervisor.

(4) *Generalization*

    a. Your supervisor would ask you to create at least two specific vignettes of ethical issues based on your current caseload.

    b. You would be responsible for:

       i. Writing the scenario in a format appropriate for training purposes.

      ii. Identifying the specific issues presented in the scenario.

     iii. Completing the risk–benefit analysis with all possible ethical codes and responses.

     iv. Proposing solutions to be implemented.

      v. Documenting the scenario and developing a library of scenarios for future use in trainings.

WORKSHEET 9.1.1   RISK–BENEFIT ANALYSIS TEMPLATE MODIFIED FROM BAILEY AND BURCH (2016)

Situation:

Decision:

Risks	Notes/Analysis
(1)	
(2)	
(3)	
(4)	
(5)	
Benefits	Notes/Analysis
(1)	
(2)	
(3)	
(4)	
(5)	

Summary of risks versus benefits for decision:

Source: Bailey, J., & Burch, M. (2016). *Ethics for behavior analysis* (3rd ed.). New York, NY: Routledge.

WORKSHEET 9.1.2   COMPLETED RISK–BENEFIT ANALYSIS WORKSHEET CONSIDERING CASE SCENARIO 9.1.1 AND GOING ALONG WITH ALTERNATIVE TREATMENTS

Situation: Parents want to include alternative treatments (diets, vitamins, and facilitated communication) as part of treatment plan for client.

Decision: Go along with parents' plan; provide great services and hope they change their mind.

Risks	Notes/Analysis
(1) Other treatments could result in lower-quality services	These treatment options could interfere with the current programming and inhibit the progress of the client.
(2) Any gains could be wrongly attributed to alternative treatments	This could result in the family discontinuing ABA services, resulting in potential harm to the client's development and false hope for the family.
(3) Fail to meet ethical standards	This could be a violation of ethical codes 1.01, 2.09, and 6.01.
(4) If these alternative treatments fail, parents may pursue other, riskier options	This could result in client harm (if specific treatments are used) and could inhibit the success of the program.
(5) Family may ask me to implement the alternative treatments.	I would have to refuse and risk conflict with the family or go along and violate my ethical standards.

Benefits	Notes/Analysis
(1) Parents will definitely allow us to continue services	No risk of family leaving because I am agreeing with their course of action.
(2) It is possible that the alternative treatments will result in positive change	Some of the research on these items indicates that they can work in some situations. Probability and evidence are low but are potentially nonzero.
(3) Minimizes conflict with the family	If I don't disagree, there is no discussion of other options that might be aversive to parents.
(4) Parents are pursuing anything to help their child	Commitment to my treatment methods may be better because they are willing to go to any cost.

Summary of risks versus benefits for decision: The primary benefit of this decision is the elimination of conflict between myself and the parents. Given that none of the treatment options are empirically validated, the likelihood of success is low, especially as compared to ABA treatment options. If my treatment options are effective, there is a strong likelihood that the gains will be attributed to the other treatments (since previous ABA was not effective), thereby lessening my involvement and increasing the likelihood that the family will focus on these treatment options.

ABA, applied behavior analysis.

WORKSHEET 9.1.3 COMPLETED RISK–BENEFIT ANALYSIS WORKSHEET CONSIDERING CASE SCENARIO 9.1.1 BY PROVIDING EVIDENCE FOR ABA AS SUPERIOR TO NON-EVIDENCE-BASED TREATMENTS

Situation: Parents want to include alternative treatments (diets, vitamins, and facilitated communication) as part of the treatment plan for the client.

Decision: Present the evidence for ABA and against the other treatments and allow them to make their decision.

Risks	Notes/Analysis
(1) Family could fire me	Given that we are going to be in disagreement, the family may ask for my removal from the case or to leave our agency. This will look bad for me.
(2) Family may not accept my evidence and pursue treatments anyway	I cannot force them into a decision. However, I can set up data-gathering methods to control for the targeted areas. I can target different items than those the alternative treatments evaluate and obtain data on the change based on my programs and those of the alternative treatments. Data might be more convincing.
(3) May lose buy-in from family	The work I have done to get the family on board may be lost and I may have to restart. Given their history, this may be a very difficult task.
(4) I might not be able to find convincing evidence and will look like I don't know what I am talking about	I have never evaluated these treatments. I don't know where to look, so I would need assistance from someone more familiar with this research.
(5) I am wrong	The alternative treatments are efficacious for this client.
Benefits	Notes/Analysis
(1) I am adhering to my ethical standards	I will not be at risk for violating standards because I am advocating for the most evidence-based decision.
(2) This process could convince the family to avoid these alternative treatments or, at worst, allow for an objective evaluation of them	I can provide additional evidence that these treatments don't work and the family might decide to hold off on implementing them. Also, if they pursue the treatments, I can at the very least teach them about evaluating options and show the effects of the decision.
(3) I will learn how to best evaluate the evidence for a specific case	There is research (Kay & Vyse, 2005; Schreck & Miller, 2010) to guide me in how to complete this process.

(continued)

100

WORKSHEET 9.1.3 *(continued)*

Situation: Parents want to include alternative treatments (diets, vitamins, and facilitated communication) as part of the treatment plan for the client.

---

(4) This decision could potentially result in the greatest level of client improvement and parent knowledge in the long term	If (2) is effective, then the client will show progression in the areas on which I am working and not miss out on services (as in the case where I terminate). I can also potentially increase buy-in through honest discussion and proof of process.

Summary of risks versus benefits for decision: The benefits of this decision primarily involve utilizing the principles of science to evaluate the treatment. ABA treatment continues and the data are used to evaluate efficacy. At worst, the client does not improve in areas targeted by the alternative treatments and the parents learn how to better evaluate treatments. At best, they choose to stick with evidence-based treatments. The risks are primarily on my end in terms of having to deal with a conflict or failing to convince the family to change. There are more avenues to deal with the risks, however, than I had initially thought.

Competency 1. Possible Group Supervision Activities

Case Scenario 9.1.1 is one example of how your supervisor may choose to work with you on this competency, which he or she could do during individual or group supervision activities. In addition, to work on your professional skills for Competency 1, your supervisor may require that you read specific chapters from Bailey and Burch (2016) and be prepared for group discussions about how and why first impressions matter and what tips you can give each other, in the group, for making better first impressions. Your supervisor may also ask you to work on activities that emphasize your time management skills, such as having you bring your calendar to your group meeting to learn how to schedule blocks of time for your internships activities, coursework activities, and upcoming deadlines, while simultaneously considering the time you need for peer review and editing. Other group activities may include discussions about when you should seek a supervisor's help and how to respond to feedback. For Competency 1, it is especially important that you discuss when you should reach out for supervision and when to seek help because you are learning about mandated and special incidents reporting.

Competency 1. Specific Task Lists and Additional Resources

In addition to the case scenario and suggestions for group supervision activities, we believe you need to accomplish certain tasks to meet each component skill in Competency 1. Competency Task Lists 9.1.1 and 9.1.2 are intended to help you initiate tasks and select activities to complete. We encourage you to hold conversations with your supervisor to determine which of these tasks are appropriate for you and whether the supervisor believes you must accomplish additional tasks to meet this competency.

COMPETENCY TASK LIST 9.1.1   CONSIDER INITIATING AND COMPLETING THE FOLLOWING TASKS WITH YOUR SUPERVISOR

	(Mark done or record benchmark)
I. Review BACB ethical guidelines	
A. Review and discuss with supervisor • Responsible conduct of a behavior analyst • The behavior analyst's responsibility to clients • The behavior analyst as teacher and/or supervisor • The behavior analyst and the workplace • The behavior analyst's ethical responsibility to the field of behavior analysis • The behavior analyst's responsibility to colleagues • The behavior analyst's ethical responsibility to society • The behavior analyst and research • Review state-specific laws with regard to behavior-analytic services	
II. Review BACB Task List, Fifth Edition	
A. Use suggested readings to learn • How the BACB Task List is formulated • The history of the training and BACB certification • The difference between licensure and certification • The importance of maintaining the integrity and future of BCBA certification	
III. Review BACB Disciplinary Actions	
A. Review the BACB disciplinary actions • Steps you should take when you find a colleague is not adhering to legal, professional, and ethical codes • The ramifications of violating ethical guidelines	
IV. Review Ethical Code of Conduct for Researchers	
A. National Institutes of Health's online ethics training https://researchethics.od.nih.gov/CourseIndex.aspx	

COMPETENCY TASK LIST 9.1.2   CONSIDER INITIATING AND COMPLETING THE FOLLOWING TASKS WITH YOUR SUPERVISOR

	(Mark done or record benchmark)
I. Review BACB ethical guidelines	
A. Review and discuss with supervisor • The behavior analyst's responsibility to clients	
II. HIPAA and confidentiality	
A. Obtain information regarding HIPAA guidelines and confidentiality that pertain to the state in which you will complete your supervised BACB competences	
B. Obtain information regarding HIPAA guidelines and confidentiality that pertain to your current place of work	

C. Discuss with supervisor:
  • Record keeping
  • Email and any electronic transmission of confidential information
  • Use of smartphones and protection of electronic files	

III. Consent	
A. Discuss with supervisor: • Informed, surrogate, guardian, and conservator consent	
B. Discuss with supervisor the difference between consent and assent; discuss when consent and assent should be used	
C. Obtain and review consent and assent forms used at your current place of employment or internship	
D. Keep a sample of the consent and assent forms for your records for this competency	
IV. Obtain informed consent	

A. Before your first use of the *consent procedure*
  a. Role-play with the supervisor the following:
    i.   Introducing the forms
    ii. Explaining the forms using nontechnical verbal behavior
    iii. Obtaining a signature from the client(s)	

B. Obtain immediate feedback and practice until you meet the criteria set by the supervisor	
V. Review mandated reporting training and videos	
A. Complete this online mandated reporter module: http://educators.mandatedreporterca.com	
B. Review this video for reporting elder or adult dependent abuse: https://www.youtube.com/watch?v=810mV4zwA6Y	
C. Review this video for mandated reporting of child abuse or neglect: https://www.youtube.com/watch?v=WunricaVsLo	

Additional Resources to Consider

Bailey, J., & Burch, M. (2016). *Ethics for behavior analysis* (3rd ed.). New York, NY: Routledge.

Bailey, J. S., & Burch, M. R. (2009). *25 essential skills and strategies for the professional behavior analyst: Expert tips for maximizing consulting effectiveness.* New York, NY: Routledge.

Brodhead, M. T., & Higbee, T. S. (2012). Teaching and maintaining ethical behavior in a professional organization. *Behavior Analysis in Practice, 5,* 82–88. doi:10.1007/BF033

Kay, S., & Vyse, S. (2005). Helping parents separate the wheat from the chaff: Putting autism treatments to the test. In J. W. Jacobson, R. M. Foxx, & J. A. Mulick (Eds.), *Controversial therapies for developmental disabilities: Fad, fashion, and science in professional practice* (pp. 265–277). Mahwah, NJ: Lawrence Erlbaum.

Newman, B., Reinecke, D. R., & Kurtz, A. L. (1996). Why be moral: Humanist and behavioral perspectives. *The Behavior Analyst, 19,* 273–280. doi:10.1007/BF033

Schreck, K. A., & Miller, V. A. (2010). How to behave ethically in a world of fads. *Behavioral Interventions, 25*(4), 307–324. doi:10.1002/bin.305

Shook, G., & Neisworth, J. (2005). Ensuring appropriate qualifications for applied behavior analyst professionals: The Behavior Analyst Certification Board. *Exceptionality, 13,* 3–10. doi:10.1207/s15327035ex1301_2

Shook, G. L., Ala'i-Rosales, S., & Glenn, S. (2002). Certification and training of behavior analyst professionals. *Behavior Modification, 26,* 27–48.

Shook, G. L., & Favell, J. E. (2008). The Behavior Analyst Certification Board and the profession of behavior analysis. *Behavior Analysis in Practice, 1,* 44–48. doi:10.1007/BF033

Shook, G. L., Johnston, J. M., & Melichamp, F. (2004). Determining essential content for applied behavior analyst practitioners. *The Behavior Analyst, 27,* 67–94. doi.org/10.1007/BF033

COMPETENCY 2. DEVELOP AND USE BEHAVIOR MEASUREMENT METHODS AND RECORD AND ANALYZE DATA

The second competency is the heart and soul of a behavior analyst, in that behavior analysis is distinguishable from other disciplines interested in behavior because of its emphasis on direct observation and measurement of behavior. The skills to measure, record, and analyze dimensions of behavior are integral for a behavior analyst and prerequisites for behavior assessment and behavior change procedures. Therefore, the BACB Task List includes this skill in Section 1. Foundations. We, however, include it in our list of competencies because we have found that our supervisees require multiple practice and performance feedback opportunities to capture dimensions of behavior reliably and accurately.

For this competency, we have identified four component skills: (a) select and define target behavior for change, (b) measure target behaviors using various direct observation measurement methods, (c) assess quality of behavioral measurement (i.e., accuracy and reliability), and (d) graph and analyze the information gathered. Diagram 9.2.1 provides some benchmarks to help you gauge your skill development in this competency.

DIAGRAM 9.2.1 Competency benchmarks for conducting behavior measurement.

Elementary Skills

- **Establish operational definitions of behavior**
  - Can say/write the definition of behavior
  - Can explain Dead Man's test and discriminate between observable and not observable behaviors
  - Can explain the difference between topographical and functional definitions of behavior
  - Can discriminate between topographical and functional definitions of behavior
- **Measurement**
  - Can describe the procedures for collecting data using count, frequency/rate, duration, latency, inter-response time
  - Can describe the procedures for collecting data using partial- and whole-interval recording and momentary time sampling
  - Can describe how to collect percentage and trials to criterion data
- **Evaluate the validity and reliability of measurement procedures**
  - Can explain the purpose of using interobserver agreement (IOA)
  - Can discriminate between accurate and inaccurate data by examining the IOAs and samples of continuous observations of behavior
  - Can describe how to collect IOA
  - Can calculate IOA for data collected using various data collection methods (e.g., partial interval, frequency/rate, duration)
- **Data display**
  - Can summarize data that has been visually depicted

(continued)

DIAGRAM 9.2.1   (*continued*)

<u>**Intermediate Skills**</u>

■ **Establish operational definitions of behavior**
- Can define problem behaviors using topographical and functional definitions
- Can define behaviors targeted for increase using topographical and functional definitions
- Can give examples of behaviors that could be defined topographically or functionally

■ **Measurement**
- Using given operation definition(s), can collect accurate data using:
  - Continuous measures (e.g., frequency/rate, duration, latency, inter-response time)
  - Discontinuous measures (e.g., partial- and whole-interval recording and momentary time sampling)
  - Percentage and trials to criterion
- Can accurately record data using given data sheets
- Can explain the strengths and weaknesses of various data collection methods (e.g., rate, duration, partial and whole interval, and momentary time sampling)
- Can give examples of behaviors that can be accurately measured by specific measures (e.g., discrete aggression could be measured by frequency/rate)

■ **Evaluate the validity and reliability of measurement procedures**
- Can select the correct method of calculating IOA for data collected using different measurement methods (e.g., interval by interval for data collected using partial interval data collection)
- Can list variables that affect accuracy of data collection and low IOAs

■ **Data display**
- Can select an appropriate type of graph to use given a data set
- Can graphically display data using variations of line graphs (e.g., two or more dimensions of the same behavior or two or more different behaviors on the same graph), bar graphs, and scatterplots
- Can generate graphs that include all elements of graphs (e.g., phase lines, condition labels, figure caption) and have correctly scaled and labeled vertical and horizontal axes
- Can graph given data using Standard Celeration Charts

■ **Interpretation of data**
- Can draw level and trend lines for stable and variable data paths
- Can discriminate between variable and stable data paths
- Can conduct visual analysis between and within conditions (e.g., effects of intervention on behavior)
- Can use baseline logic to evaluate presence of functional relationship between the IV and DV when visually inspecting graphs from research articles
- Can define and calculate effect size

(*continued*)

DIAGRAM 9.2.1 (*continued*)

<u>**Advanced Skills**</u>

■ **Establish operational definitions of behavior**
- Can pinpoint target behaviors to decrease and increase using information obtained from indirect assessment and direct observations
- Can generate clear and parsimonious operational definitions for the selected target behaviors using topographical or functional definitions

■ **Measurement**
- Can select appropriate measurement method to collect baseline and intervention data for target behaviors
- Can create a data sheet that represents the selected data collection method
- Use BST to teach others how to collect and record data on target behavior(s) using the developed data sheets and various data collection methods (e.g., rate, duration, partial- and whole-interval recording and momentary time sampling)

■ **Evaluate the validity and reliability of measurement procedures**
- Can monitor accuracy of data collection by others by collecting IOA data for various data collection methods
- Can pinpoint and correct the variables that could have resulted in low IOAs (e.g., complex operational definition)
- Can use BST to teach others how to collect and calculate IOA data

■ **Data display**
- Can select an appropriate type of graph to use when graphing assessment and intervention data for each client
- Can generate and incorporate graphs into reports to funding entities that include all elements of graphs (e.g., phase lines, condition labels, figure caption) and have correctly scaled and labeled vertical and horizontal axes

■ **Interpretation of data**
- Can make clinical decisions after conducting visual analysis between and within conditions (e.g., effects of intervention on behavior) of client data
- Can use baseline logic to evaluate presence of functional relationship between the IV and DV when visually inspecting graphs based on client's data
- Can calculate effect size and make clinical decisions based on the calculated effect size

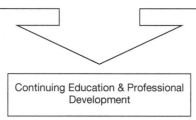

Continuing Education & Professional Development

To gain advanced skills in Competency 2, you are likely to engage in several activities that require you to observe sessions and record and interpret behavioral data. It is also likely that you will be asked to watch videos or bring in sample cases to discuss how you would prioritize which target behaviors to address. To measure behavior, you will develop behavior measurement tools and be asked to use those tools to observe and record behavior. You will also be asked to justify the reliability and accuracy of your behavior measurement method. Next, we provide one example of how you and your supervisor may work on this competency.

Competency 2. Example Case Scenario 9.2.1. Teaching Continuous Behavior Measurement Methods

(1) *Prerequisites*

    a. Complete a chart detailing the specifics of each continuous measurement method.

        i. This chart includes:

            1. Measurable dimension of behavior

            2. Procedure for collecting data

            3. y-Axis label for graphing

            4. Advantages

            5. Disadvantages

            6. Behaviors appropriate for this measure

    b. Show competency in verbal description of information from the measurement chart.

        i. Your supervisor would provide you with a continuous measure and, without the aid of the chart, ask for specific information about the measures.

            1. Example: "Tell me which measure you would use if you were attempting to increase a child's attending (defined as eyes oriented toward teacher during instructional periods)."

            2. Example 2: "What measurement methods measure temporal locus?"

        ii. The number of questions asked would depend on your supervisor's criteria for demonstrating competency in this area.

(2) *Baseline assessment of your skills*

    a. Your supervisor would provide you with an opportunity to gather data on target behaviors from participant or online videos.

        i. Note: Your supervisor may choose to conduct the baseline in vivo interaction with a client.

    b. Your supervisor would provide you with:

        i. Operational definition(s) of the behavior(s)

        ii. Data sheet(s) for behavior(s)

        iii. Measurement method to be utilized

    c. To demonstrate competency, you would need to meet a criterion of at least 80% interobserver agreement (type is chosen at the discretion of the supervisor) across two opportunities for the measurement method.

        i. Continuous measurement methods

            1. Count

            2. Rate

3. Duration

4. Latency

5. Inter-response time (IRT)

d. You will also need to perform at 80% or higher on the performance monitoring tool (PMT) for each measurement method.

(3) *Training*

a. Your supervisor would choose a measurement method to target.

i. This would be based on your performance at baseline.

b. **Instruction**

i. Your supervisor would give you a copy of the PMT for the targeted measurement method.

ii. You and your supervisor would review each step of the PMT together.

1. Example = Step 1: Gathered all necessary materials before beginning the session.

a. Explanation: To gather data effectively, you will need a writing tool, data sheet, and any other required materials. If you do not have these items, you will either miss instances of the target behavior or will attempt to memorize data, which can increase your errors and decrease your accuracy.

c. **Model**

i. Your supervisor would present you with a video for observation and data taking.

1. As noted earlier, this may be substituted with in vivo opportunities.

ii. Your supervisor would provide you with the same items from the baseline assessment.

1. Operational definition(s) of the behavior(s)

2. Data sheet(s) for behavior(s)

3. Measurement method to be utilized

iii. Your supervisor would prepare for data taking following the PMT provided for you during instruction.

iv. Your supervisor would take data on the video.

1. Your supervisor may stop, rewind, and replay certain parts of the video to show you specific instances of the behavior.

v. Your supervisor would demonstrate any required calculations and recording of data in specific locations (e.g., on data sheet, summary sheet, or in program binder).

d. **Rehearsal**

i. Your supervisor would provide you with the same video and materials from the model.

    ii. You would complete the preparation steps on the PMT.

    iii. You would gather data on the target behavior from the video.

    iv. Your supervisor would run interobserver agreement (IOA) calculations on your data.

  e. **Feedback**

    i. If the IOA between your supervisor's data and your data does not meet or exceed 80%, your supervisor would review the video and data taken with you.

    ii. **Your supervisor would also review your performance on the PMTs.**

    iii. **If the criteria for data and PMT performance are not met, your supervisor would have you repeat the process.**

(4) *Generalization*

  a. Your supervisor would require at least three different target behaviors (on video) using the same measurement method for the mastery criteria.

  b. Once generalization is met with video data taking, your supervisor would target the same measurement methods in field-based opportunities.

    i. After meeting the criteria for at least two different behaviors in vivo, your supervisor may state you have met the competency.

      1. Note: Supervisors have different requirements for how many behaviors will be measured before competency is determined.

WORKSHEET 9.2.1   MEASUREMENT CHART TO BE COMPLETED BY SUPERVISEE

Measure	Measurable dimension of behavior	Data collection procedure	When graphing, the y-axis should be labeled	Advantages for using the measure	Disadvantages for using the measure	The measure is appropriate for which type of behaviors or procedures (list at least five behaviors)
Frequency/ rate						
Duration per session						
Duration per occurrence						
Latency						
IRT						
Percentage of occurrence						
Trials to criterion						
Whole-interval recording						
Partial-interval recording						
Momentary time sampling						
Planned activity check						
Permanent product						

IRT, inter-response time.

Competency 2. Possible Group Supervision Activities

Case Scenario 9.2.1 is one example of how your supervisor may choose to work with you on this competency, which he or she could do during individual or group supervision activities. In addition, to work on your behavior measurement skills for Competency 2, your supervisor may require you and your peers to observe several different videos and to develop behavior measurement tools to record data. Your supervisor may ask you to calculate IOA and justify why your behavior measurement method and measurement tool are appropriate for capturing the behavior assigned. In addition, your supervisor may bring samples of hypothetical data, or real data from de-identified client cases, and ask you to graph and interpret the data. All of these activities provide you with opportunities to practice your skills in selecting appropriate behavior measurement methods, communicating why your tool or method of measurement is appropriate, and summarizing data in a manner that is easily digestible by others (e.g., graphs).

Competency 2. Specific Task Lists for the Component Skills and Additional Resources

In addition to the case scenario and suggestions for group supervision activities, we outline the tasks you need to accomplish to meet each component skill in Competency 2. Competency Task Lists 9.2.1 to 9.2.4 will help you initiate the tasks and select activities to complete with your supervisor. Again, we encourage you to hold conversations with your supervisor(s) to determine which of these tasks, or any additional tasks, are appropriate for you at each stage of your supervision experience.

COMPETENCY TASK LIST 9.2.1 CONSIDER INITIATING AND COMPLETING THE FOLLOWING TASKS FOR THE COMPONENT SKILL OF SELECTING AND TARGETING BEHAVIOR FOR CHANGE, WITH YOUR SUPERVISOR

	(Mark done or record benchmark)
I. Review BACB ethical guidelines	
A. Review and discuss with supervisor • Ethical practices in selecting and assessing potential target behaviors	
II. Develop and use worksheets to prioritize target behaviors	
A. Evaluating the social significance of potential target behaviors	
B. Prioritizing potential target behaviors	
III. Define target behaviors in observable and measurable terms	
A. Define behavior topographically (define at least 10 different behaviors) in measurable and observable terms	
1. Discuss definitions with supervisor and make necessary changes	
2. Include the final written operational definitions in this tab	
B. Define behavior functionally (define at least 10 different behaviors) in measurable and observable terms	
1. Discuss definitions with supervisor and make necessary changes	
2. Include the final written operational definitions in this tab	
C. Describe and explain behavior, including private events, in behavior-analytic (non-mentalistic) terms	

PERFORMANCE MONITORING TOOL 9.2.1   EXAMPLE PERFORMANCE CHECKLIST YOU AND YOUR SUPERVISOR CAN USE TO GAUGE YOUR PERFORMANCE IN THIS COMPONENT SKILL

Competency	Criterion	Rating	Performance Feedback
I. Review BACB ethical guidelines and discuss with supervisor			

A. Ethical practices in assessing and selecting potential target behaviors
B. Include a written summary of ethical practices in selection of target behaviors in this tab
	• Presented a written summary of ethical practices in selection of target behaviors that included:
	  A. Definition of client
	  B. Responsibility to client and others
	  C. Consultation and third-party requests for services
	  D. Client rights
		❏ Met the criterion as it is written
		❏ Did not meet the criterion as it is written
			Given on ___/___/___

II. Show competency developing and using worksheets to prioritize target behaviors			
A. Evaluating the social significance of potential target behaviors	• Correctly used a worksheet to evaluate the social significance of potential target behaviors at least on *two different occasions*	❏ Met the criterion as it is written ❏ Did not meet the criterion because the worksheet was not completed correctly	Given on ___/___/___
B. Prioritizing potential target behaviors	• Correctly used the worksheet to evaluate the social significance of potential target behaviors at least on *two different occasions*	❏ Met the criterion as it is written ❏ Did not meet the criterion because the worksheet was not completed correctly	Given on ___/___/___
III. Define behavior in observable and measurable terms			

A. Show competency defining behavior topographically (define at least five different behaviors) in measurable and observable terms	• The topographical definitions of all five target behaviors must be
	  o **Technological** (passed the stranger rule)
	  o **Observable** (passed the Dead Man's test)
	  o **Measurable** (includes a measurable dimension of the behavior)
		❏ Met the criterion (definition included all the components described in the criterion for this competency)
		❏ Did not meet the criterion (definition did not include *one or more* of the components described in the criterion for this competency)
			Given on ___/___/___

(continued)

114

PERFORMANCE MONITORING TOOL 9.2.1   *(continued)*

Competency	Criterion	Rating	Performance Feedback
	o **If necessary**, include **exclusionary factors** (e.g., a student can leave his or her seat if given permission) o **Parsimonious** (e.g., aggression, self-injury, and elopement are defined as separate behaviors and not as part of a "tantrum")		
B. Show competency defining behavior functionally (define at least five different behaviors) in measurable and observable terms	• The functional definitions of all five target behaviors must be: • **Technological** (passed the stranger rule) • **Observable** (passed the Dead Man's test) • **Measurable** (includes a measurable dimension of the behavior) • **If necessary**, include **exclusionary factors** (e.g., a student can leave his or her seat if given permission) • **Parsimonious** (e.g., aggression, self-injury, and elopement are defined as separate behaviors and not as part of a "tantrum")	❏ Met the criterion (definition included all the components described in the criterion for this competency) ❏ Did not meet the criterion (definition did not include *one or more* of the components described in the criterion for this competency)	Given on ___/___/___
C. Included revised operational definitions for each behavior reviewed with the supervisor in the supervision folder under Tab B		❏ Met the criterion as it is written ❏ Did not meet the criterion as it is written	Given on ___/___/___

COMPETENCY TASK LIST 9.2.2 CONSIDER INITIATING AND COMPLETING THE FOLLOWING TASKS FOR THE COMPONENT SKILL OF MEASURING TARGET BEHAVIORS USING VARIOUS DIRECT OBSERVATION MEASUREMENT METHODS, WITH YOUR SUPERVISOR

	(Mark done or record benchmark)
I. Review BACB ethical guidelines	
A. Review and discuss with supervisor • Ethical practices relevant to data collection and data-based decision making	
II. Select a *measurement system* to obtain representative data given the dimensions of the behavior and the logistics of observing and recording the behavior	
A. Create a basic table for the advantages and disadvantages of using continuous and discontinuous measurement procedures • Discuss the summary table with supervisor and include the final product in this tab **B. When conducting assessments or developing treatment plans, select an appropriate measurement method and design data collection forms for the measurement methods listed below** • Discuss your selection and the data collection forms with supervisor, obtain feedback, and include the final product in this tab	
➢ **Design continuous measurement procedures**	
1. Frequency/rate	
2. Duration	
3. Latency	
4. IRT	
5. Percentage of occurrence	
6. Trials to criterion	
➢ **Design discontinuous measurement procedures**	
7. Partial-interval recording	
8. Whole-interval recording	
9. Momentary time sampling	
10. Planned activity check	
11. Permanent product (e.g., number of math facts completed)	

(continued)

COMPETENCY TASK LIST 9.2.2 *(continued)*

	(Mark done or record benchmark)
III. Select a *schedule of observation* and recording periods and measure the target behavior for change	
A. When conducting assessments or monitoring progress during the intervention phase, select appropriate observation periods and collect baseline or intervention data using an appropriate measurement procedure • Discuss your selection with supervisor and obtain feedback **B. Collect data and share the results with supervisor** • Evaluate if changes need to be made to your data sheet and make necessary changes **C. Graph the results and obtain feedback from supervisor**	
➢ **Implement continuous measurement procedures**	
A-02 1. Measure frequency/rate	
A-03 2. Measure duration	
A-04 3. Measure latency	
A-05 4. Measure IRT	
A-06 5. Measure percentage of occurrence	
A-07 6. Use trials to criterion	
➢ **Implement discontinuous measurement procedures**	
A-13 7. Use partial-interval recording	
8. Use whole-interval recording	
9. Use momentary time sampling	
10. Measure behavior by permanent product	

IRT, inter-response time.

PERFORMANCE MONITORING TOOL 9.2.2.A EXAMPLE PERFORMANCE CHECKLIST YOU AND YOUR SUPERVISOR CAN USE TO GAUGE YOUR PERFORMANCE IN THIS COMPONENT SKILL

Competency	Criterion	Rating 1	Rating 2	Rating 3
III. **Use data recording forms and directly measure target behavior for change**				
Use of technology	❏ Used stopwatch with count up and down options or appropriate smartphone application with similar options	❏ Yes ❏ No	❏ Yes ❏ No	❏ Yes ❏ No
Data collection	• Collected data using every measurement method listed below with 90% IOA. Used each measurement method at least twice with 90% IOA.	**IOA 1**	**IOA 2**	**IOA 3**
A.	Frequency/rate	❏	❏	❏
A.	Duration	❏	❏	❏
A.	Latency	❏	❏	❏
A.	IRT	❏	❏	❏
A.	Momentary time sampling	❏	❏	❏
A.	Partial-interval recording	❏	❏	❏
A.	Whole-interval recording	❏	❏	❏
A.	Trials to criterion or percentage of occurrence	❏	❏	❏
A.	Planned activity check	❏	❏	❏

IOA, interobserver agreement; IRT, inter-response time.

PERFORMANCE MONITORING TOOL 9.2.2.B ANOTHER EXAMPLE PERFORMANCE CHECKLIST YOU AND YOUR SUPERVISOR CAN USE TO GAUGE YOUR PERFORMANCE FOR THE PREVIOUS COMPONENT SKILL (COOPER, HERON, & HEWARD, 2007)

Performance Monitoring Tool: Rate/Frequency Data Collection

	Date				
Step	Mark +, −, or N/A				
1. Gathered all necessary materials before beginning the session (e.g., pen, data sheet)					
2. Prepared data sheet					
a. Wrote date and initials at the top of the data sheet					
b. Recorded the target behavior(s) to be observed					
c. Recorded the start time of the observation session (e.g., hour:min a.m./p.m.)					
3. Each time the target behavior(s) occurred, marked a tally on the data sheet within 3–5 seconds of its occurrence[1]					
4. At the end of the observation session, recorded the end time (e.g., hour:min a.m./p.m.)					
5. Recorded the total number of tallies marked[1]					
6. Calculated the total number of observation minutes using the recorded start and end times					
7. Calculated the rate of the target behavior(s) (total count of the behavior(s)/total number of observation minutes)[1]					
8. Recorded the frequency of the target behavior(s) as count/minute on the data sheet					
Percent correct (number of steps with "+"/total number of steps with "+" or "−")					
Comments:					

Source: Cooper, J. O, Heron, T. E., & Heward, W. L. (2007). *Applied behavior analysis* (2nd ed.). Upper Saddle River, NJ: Pearson.

COMPETENCY TASK LIST 9.2.3 CONSIDER INITIATING AND COMPLETING THE FOLLOWING TASKS FOR THE COMPONENT SKILL OF ASSESSING QUALITY OF BEHAVIORAL MEASUREMENT, WITH YOUR SUPERVISOR

	(Mark done or record benchmark)
I. Create a basic table that summarizes threats to measurement accuracy, validity, and reliability	
A. Include a table in this tab that summarizes the variables that could threaten: • Validity of behavioral data • Reliability of behavioral data • Accuracy of behavioral data	
II. Assess and interpret interobserver agreement	
A. Determine an appropriate method to obtain (sample) interobserver data for the given data collection method • Discuss the chosen method with the supervisor and make necessary changes	
B. Create a summary table that includes • Type of IOA • Method of calculation for each type of IOA • Acceptable level of IOA • Format for reporting IOA	
C. Conduct, interpret, and report IOA • When collecting baseline or intervention data, use IOA to evaluate the accuracy and reliability of data and measurement procedures • When supervising implementation of treatment plans, use IOA to evaluate the accuracy and reliability of data collection • Calculate IOA using an appropriate method for the given data and report the IOA data • Use IOA data to make changes to measurement procedures or use Behavior Skills Training to improve data collection skills of implementers	
Use total count IOA and report the results	
Use total duration IOA and report the results	
Use mean duration per occurrence IOA and report the results	
Use interval-by-interval IOA and report the results	
Use scored and unscored interval IOA and report the results	
Use trial-by-trial IOA and report the results	

IOA, interobserver agreement.

PERFORMANCE MONITORING TOOL 9.2.3 EXAMPLE PERFORMANCE CHECKLIST YOU AND YOUR SUPERVISOR CAN USE TO GAUGE YOUR PERFORMANCE IN THIS COMPONENT SKILL

IOA method	Type of data collection method for which the IOA is appropriate	When to use this IOA method	Calculating IOA using this procedure	Example	Advantages of using the IOA	Disadvantages of using the IOA
Total count IOA						
Mean count per interval IOA						
Exact count per interval IOA						
Trial-by-trial IOA						
Total duration IOA						
Mean duration per occurrence IOA						
Mean latency per response						
Mean IRT per response						
Interval-by-interval IOA						
Scored interval IOA						
Unscored interval IOA						

IOA, interobserver agreement; IRT, inter-response time.

121

COMPETENCY TASK LIST 9.2.4   CONSIDER INITIATING AND COMPLETING THE FOLLOWING TASKS FOR THE COMPONENT SKILL OF GRAPHING AND ANALYZING DATA, WITH YOUR SUPERVISOR

	(Mark done or record benchmark)
I. Review BACB ethical guidelines	
A. Review ethical guidelines relevant to data collection, visual display, and analysis **B.** Discuss the guidelines with supervisor	
II. Design, plot, and interpret data	
A. Plot data using equal-interval graphs (A-10) o Use Excel or other graphing tools to generate	
• Bar graphs	
• Multiple baseline graphs	
• Multiple probe graphs	
• ABAB graphs	
• Alternating treatments	
• Multi-element	
• Simultaneous	
• Chaining criterion graphs	
B. Plot and interpret data using SCCs	
C. Plot data using a cumulative record (A-11)	
D. Interpret visually displayed data using baseline logic (A-10 and A-11)	
o Draw level and trend lines	
o Evaluate changes in level, trend, and variability	
o Measure effect size using	
• Points of nonoverlap	
• Dual-criterion method	
E. Print and place all graphs in this tab	

SCCs, Standard Celeration Charts.

**PERFORMANCE MONITORING TOOL 9.2.4   EXAMPLE
PERFORMANCE CHECKLIST YOU AND YOUR SUPERVISOR
CAN USE TO GAUGE YOUR PERFORMANCE IN THIS
COMPONENT SKILL**

	Yes	No
1. The graph has a title that describes the data it depicts		
2. The graph represents the data correctly (e.g., bar graph for categorical or nominal data, line graph for continuous data such as sessions or days)		
3. The y-axis is the same range across participants		
4. The y-axis is labeled correctly (e.g., percentage of correct responses)		
5. The x-axis is labeled correctly (e.g., sessions)		
6. The x-axis tics appear aligned with the data points		
7. There are condition labels (e.g., baseline, DRA, withdrawal) that represent the condition (or independent variables)		
8. There are condition phase lines between conditions (for each independent variable): solid lines between conditions with clear IV change and dashed lines between condition that share components		
9. The data path is not connected across the conditions		
10. The grid lines on the graphs have been removed		
11. The graph for each subject aligns with the ones below it (sessions line up)		
12. x-Axis ticks appear aligned with the data points		
13. The graph contains a legend if there are multiple dependent variables or data paths		

DRA, differential reinforcement of alternative behavior; IV, independent variable.

Additional Resources to Consider

Baer, D. M. (1977). Reviewer's comment: Just because it's reliable doesn't mean that you can use it. *Journal of Applied Behavior Analysis, 10,* 117–119.

Baer, D. M., Wolf, M. M., & Risley, T. R. (1968). Some current dimensions of applied behavior analysis. *Journal of Applied Behavior Analysis, 1,* 91–97.

Bailey, J., & Burch, M. (2016). *Ethics for behavior analysis* (3rd ed.). New York, NY: Routledge.

Cooper, J. O., Heron, T. E., & Heward, W. L. (2007). *Applied behavior analysis* (2nd ed.). Upper Saddle River, NJ: Pearson.

Cummings, A. R., & Carr, J. E. (2009). Evaluating progress in behavioral programs for children with autism spectrum disorders via continuous and discontinuous measurement. *Journal of Applied Behavior Analysis, 42,* 57–71. doi:10.1901/jaba.2009.42-57

Deochand, N., Costello, M. S., & Fuqua, R. W. (2015), Phase-change lines, scale breaks, and trend lines using Excel 2013. *Journal of Applied Behavior Analysis, 48,* 478–493. doi:10.1002/jaba.198

Fiske, K., & Delmolino, L. (2012). Use of discontinuous methods of data collection in behavioral intervention: Guidelines for practitioners. *Behavior Analysis in Practice, 5*(2), 77–81. doi:10.1007/BF033

Gast, D. L. (2010). *Single subject research methodology in behavioral sciences.* New York, NY: Routledge.

Johnson, J. M., & Pennypacker, H. S. (2008). *Strategies and tactics in behavioral research* (3rd ed.). New York, NY: Routledge

Kazdin, A. E. (2011). *Single-case research designs: Methods for clinical and applied settings* (2nd ed.). New York, NY: Oxford University Press.

LeBlanc, L. A., Raetz, P. B., & Sellers, T. P. (2016). A proposed model for selecting measurement procedures for the assessment and treatment of problem behavior. *Behavior Analysis in Practice, 9,* 77–83. doi:10.1007/s40617

Lerman, D. C., Dittlinger, L. H., Fentress, G., & Lanagan, T. A. (2011). Comparison of methods for collecting data on performance during discrete trial teaching. *Behavior Analysis in Practice, 4,* 53–62. doi:10.1007/BF03391775.

Mayer, R. G., Sulzer-Azaroff, B., & Wallace, M. (2013). *Behavior analysis for lasting change* (3rd ed.). Cornwall-on-Hudson, NY: Sloan Publishing.

O'Neil, R. E., Horner, R. H., Albin, R. W., Sprague, J. R., Sorey, K., & Newton, J. S. (1997). *Functional assessment and program development for problem behavior: A practical handbook.* Pacific Grove, CA: Brooks/Cole Publishers.

Umbreit, J., Ferro, J., Liaupsin, C. J., & Lane, K. L. (2006). *Functional behavioral assessment and function-based intervention: An effective, practical approach.* Englewood Cliffs, NJ: Prentice Hall.

Wolf, M. M. (1978). Social validity: The case for subjective measurement or how applied behavior analysis is finding its heart. *Journal of Applied Behavior Analysis, 11,* 203–214.

COMPETENCY 3. CONDUCT BEHAVIOR ASSESSMENTS (e.g., FUNCTIONAL BEHAVIOR ASSESSMENT, PREFERENCE ASSESSMENT, REINFORCER ASSESSMENT)

The third competency is focused on conducting behavior assessments. Behavior analysts conduct several types of behavior assessments when clients are referred for behavioral services (i.e., baseline assessment) so that they can determine the clients' needs. Initially, behavior analysts conduct assessments to understand what skills their clients have in their repertoire, their clients' preferences, the function of any problem behaviors the client emits, and the contextual factors (e.g., familial situation, previous treatment plans) that affect the referral problem(s) and treatment planning. Conducting assessments that are useful for your intervention planning and progress monitoring requires that you learn the purpose of each type of assessment, how to carry out the procedures for each, as well as how to interpret the results. In addition, when conducting an assessment, you will often learn new things about the client and contextual factors to consider during your assessment. Sometimes you may experience road blocks you will need to troubleshoot to remove. As a competent behavior analyst, you will need to be able to identify the correct assessment to utilize as well as to make the necessary adjustments to obtain the information you need for your intervention planning. You should also be able to justify why you selected a particular assessment, to explain the assessment procedures to a third party, and to explain how the results you obtain will help you make solid, evidence-based decisions for the intervention (i.e., why did you spend time on the assessment?).

For this competency, we have identified two component skills: (a) functional behavior assessment and (b) preference/reinforcer assessment. Diagram 9.3.1 provides some benchmarks to help you gauge your skill development in this competency.

DIAGRAM 9.3.1   Competency benchmarks for conducting behavior assessments

<u>**Elementary Skills**</u>

■ **Functional Behavior Assessment**
- Can explain the purpose and benefits of conducting functional behavior assessments
- Can explain the steps of functional behavior assessment process
- Can explain the differences between indirect and direct assessments
- Can list indirect assessment tools
- Can list the differences between descriptive behavior assessment and functional analysis
- Can list different types of descriptive data collection methods (e.g., ABC continuous recording, ABC narrative recording) and strengths and weakness of each
- Can list different types of functional analysis methods and strengths and weaknesses of each method
- Can accurately describe conditions of typical functional analysis

■ **Preference/Reinforcer Assessment**
- Can explain the purpose of conducting preference assessment
- Can explain the purpose of conducting reinforcer assessment
- Can list different types of preference assessments

<u>**Intermediate Skills**</u>

■ **Functional Behavior Assessment**
- Can conduct indirect assessment using review of records, interviews, and rating scale (e.g., FAST)
- Can accurately collect baseline data using the most appropriate measurement methods
- Can accurately collect data using various descriptive assessment methods (e.g., continuous ABC recording)
- Can accurately calculate conditional probabilities from descriptive assessment data
- Can accurately conduct functional analysis conditions and collect data
- Can graph and accurately interpret descriptive assessment and functional analysis data

■ **Preference/Reinforcer Assessment**
- Can conduct various preference assessments (e.g., free operant, paired choice or MSWO)
- Can conduct reinforcer assessment
- Can graph and accurately interpret preference and reinforcer assessment results

(continued)

DIAGRAM 9.3.1 *(continued)*

<u>Advanced Skills</u>

■ **Functional Behavior Assessment**
- Can obtain informed consent to conduct behavior assessment
- Can select appropriate schedule of observation and recording periods and most appropriate measurement method to collect baseline data
- Can select appropriate type of functional analyses by considering severity of target behaviors, available resources, and setting
- Can generate hypothesized functions of target behavior(s) based on indirect and descriptive assessment results
- Can design functional analysis conditions that ensure experimental control
- Can write comprehensive functional behavior assessment reports and treatment recommendations based on assessment results
- Can clearly explain the assessment results to caregivers/teachers
- Can use behavior skills training to teach others how to conduct functional analysis conditions and descriptive assessments

■ **Preference/Reinforcer Assessment**
- Can select preference and reinforcer assessments based on client's skills, available resources, and setting
- Can incorporate preference and reinforcer assessment results into functional behavior assessment reports and treatment plans
- Can use behavior skills training to teach others how to conduct various types of preference assessments

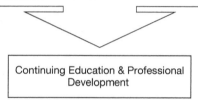

Continuing Education & Professional Development

Competency 3. Example Case Scenario 9.3.1. Teaching Component Skill: Indirect Assessment

(1) *Scenario*

    a. You are completing the first assessment visit for a new client. The client's name is Sudiah Ramas and she is a 3-year-old girl with a diagnosis of autism spectrum disorder. The supervisor has asked you to complete the indirect assessment with the family next Monday at 10:00 a.m. at the family's home.

        1. You will be using the Vineland Adaptive Behavior Skills, third edition, and the Functional Assessment Screening Tool (FAST) as part of your indirect assessment.

        2. Your fieldwork also requires the following forms to be completed during the initial assessment:

        a. Consent for Assessment

        b. Privacy Practices

        c. Financial Responsibility Form

(2) *Baseline Assessment of Your Skills*

      i. List all of the steps you need to complete prior to your assessment visit.

      ii. Role-play the initial assessment visit with your supervisor (who would play the role of Sudiah's mother or father).

      iii. Your supervisor will evaluate your performance using the Performance Monitoring Checklist (PMC) for indirect assessment visits.

  b. If you reach the criterion for competency (at least 90% of the required steps in correct order as listed on the PMC), you will move to the role-play scenario.

      i. If you do not reach 80% of the required steps listed on the PMC, you will move to training.

(3) *Training*

  a. **Step 1**

    i. Instruction:

      1. Your supervisor would give you a copy of the PMC for the indirect assessment to follow along as he or she models the interview.

      2. You and your supervisor would review each step of the PMC.

        a. Example = Step 1: Confirm approximate travel time to assessment site using Google Maps. Add a minimum of 15 minutes to the travel time for commute.

          i. Explanation: The reason that you will add an additional 15 minutes is to ensure that you arrive to the assessment on time.

    ii. Model:

      1. You will act the role of the parent using the script.

      2. You will take data on your supervisor's performance using the PMC provided.

      3. Your supervisor will make intentional errors on at least three portions of the PMC. You are responsible for noting those errors.

        a. If you note all the errors correctly, you will move to the competency check.

        b. If you do not note all the errors correctly, you will repeat the exercise with your supervisor after discussing which portions of the role-played interview were correct and which portions were incorrect.

    iii. Competency check:

      1. Write out all the steps of preparation for and completion of indirect assessment.

b. **Step 2**

    i. *Role-play*

        1. Your supervisor will play the role of Sudiah's parent and you will complete all the steps of the preparation for and completion of the indirect assessment.

            a. For the Vineland, you will complete one section (e.g., Communication: Receptive Communication).

            b. For the FAST, you will assess aggression as the target behavior.

        2. Your supervisor will act as the parent based on his or her past experiences with parents during indirect assessments.

            a. You are responsible for completing the indirect assessment given the supervisor's responses.

        3. Your supervisor will provide feedback on two areas:

            a. Performance on PMC items

            b. Other areas that the supervisor feels you did well or could improve upon (e.g., tone, pacing between items or note taking and asking questions, clarity of the questions you asked)

        4. If you complete the indirect assessment at 80% or greater fidelity, you will move to the direct assessment competency.

            a. If you complete it at less than 80% fidelity, you will complete the role-play again.

            b. This will continue until you meet the competency criteria.

(4) *Generalization*

    a. Completion of indirect assessment steps with a parent in the field.

        i. Your supervisor will use the same PMC as the one used for your training.

        ii. The parent may be given a feedback form to evaluate your performance based on his or her perspective.

PERFORMANCE MONITORING CHECKLIST 9.3.1 PMC FOR INDIRECT ASSESSMENT

Indirect Assessment PMC			
Date			
Preparation			
(1) Three business cards to give caregiver(s)			
(2) Copy of Vineland-II			
(3) Copy of all required paperwork (e.g., consent to assess, financial responsibility, privacy practices)			
(4) Confirmed address and approximate drive time			
(5) Memorized client and caregiver(s) names			
Arrival			
(1) Arrived at least 10 minutes before scheduled appointment			
(2) Confirmed all required items on person			
(3) Arrived in professional dress			
Introduction			
(1) Introduced self with eye contact			
(2) Included name, company, and reminder of appointment in introduction			
(3) Asked if caregiver is ready for interviewee			
(4) Asked caregiver where interview would take place			
(5) Went to the area indicated by caregiver			
Required paperwork			
For consent to assess, financial responsibility, and privacy practices			
(1) Described each specific form to caregiver			
(2) Explained reason for each form to be signed and how to proceed if form is not signed			
(3) Asked if caregiver had questions about the form			
(4) Accurately answered any questions delivered by caregiver			
(5) Obtained caregiver signature on form OR noted reason parent did not sign document			
(6) Scanned and emailed copy of documents to caregiver(s)			
Interview form (IISCA, FAI, or other)			
(1) Informed parent of the purpose of the interview form			
(2) Presented 80% or more of questions as open-ended questions			

(continued)

PERFORMANCE MONITORING CHECKLIST 9.3.1 *(continued)*

Indirect Assessment PMC			
(3) Read all questions clearly			
(4) Recorded caregiver's responses to questions			
(5) Answered any questions asked by caregiver			
Vineland-II			
(1) Informed parent of the purpose of the interview form and rules to be followed (e.g., floor and ceiling)			
(2) Presented response sheet (scale to be used to answer all questions) in front of caregiver			
(3) Read all questions clearly			
(4) When required, prompted caregiver to use response sheet (minimum 80% of provided opportunities)			
(5) Recorded caregiver's responses to questions			
(6) Answered any questions asked by caregiver			
(7) Transitioned between various scales of Vineland (minimum 80% of provided opportunities)			
Interviewing skills (measured throughout interview forms)			
(1) Asked caregiver if a break was needed at least once during interview			
(2) Gave eye contact when posing questions and during caregiver's responses			
(3) Posed questions and clarifications objectively (not leading questions) for 80% or more of presented questions/clarifications			
(4) Maintained a professional tone and demeanor throughout the interview forms			
(5) Completed the interview in an appropriate time frame (maximum = 2.5 hours)			
Completing interview			
(1) Thanked caregiver for completing the interview			
(2) Asked caregiver if there are any additional questions			
(3) Informed caregiver about the next steps of the assessment process			
(4) Confirmed next assessment visit date/time			
(5) Provided caregiver with copies of business cards and number to call to be reached			
Total Yes/41			

WORKSHEET 9.3.1   BASIC SCRIPT FOR ROLE-PLAYING INTERVIEW WITH SUPERVISEE

Content guide

(1) Part of PMC targeted

    a. Specific task/verbal behavior of assessor: *Example of what might be said*

        i. Potential responses to assessor's statements

            1. Follow-up to response (assessor)

                a. Follow-up to assessor (last portion of role-play for this section)

(2) Introduction

    a. Assessor greets caregiver(s): *Good morning, my name is Darren Jeffers. I am a behavior analyst from ABC and we spoke about having our first assessment appointment today at 9:00 a.m. Is this still a good time for the interview?*

        i. Affirmative (*Yes, this is a good time for the interview.*)

            1. Assessor to move to b.

        ii. Negative (*Sorry, something has come up and I cannot do the interview at this time.*)

            1. Assessor to set up a new appointment: *I am sorry this time does not work. If it would be okay, I would like to call you later today and set up a day and time that might work better.*

                a. Affirmative (*Okay, I will wait for your call.*).

                b. Negative (*I am not sure I will have any time available.*)

                c. Propose a time (*Would you be able to come back at 10 a.m?.*)

    b. Assessor asks caregiver where the interview will take place: *Mrs. Gonzales, where would you like to conduct the interview today?*

        i. Convenient location (e.g., dining room, kitchen table, place with space to take notes)

            1. Assessor to proceed to location and set up for step 3.

        ii. Inconvenient location (e.g., sitting on floor, in the kitchen while a parent prepares a meal, in the living room with TV on and a parent watching)

            1. Assessor to ask if more appropriate space is available: *I apologize but I was hoping to set up my computer so I can take notes. Is there a location where we can talk and I can take notes? If not, I am happy to conduct the interview wherever it is convenient.* Move to step 3.

                a. Affirmative (*Yes, we have a spot where that will be possible.*)

                b. Negative (*No, this is the best place for me to do the interview.*)

                    i. Assessor to move to the correct location.

(continued)

WORKSHEET 9.3.1 (*continued*)

(3) Required paperwork

a. Introduction to consent for assessment: *This first document details what the assessment will entail. If you sign the document, you are consenting for me to run the assessment. You can revoke your consent at any time and can revoke it for specific portions of the assessment or all parts. If you choose not to sign the document, we will end the assessment process and discuss the next steps. Do you have any questions before you sign this form?*

    i. Affirmative (*I will sign the document.*)

        1. Assessor thanks the caregiver and moves to step b. *Thank you very much for signing this document. Next...*

    ii. Negative (*I will not sign the document.*)

        1. Assessor confirms decision, asks for questions, if any, and informs the caregiver) of the next step. *Thank you for telling me your decision. Do you have any questions that I can answer before we confirm your decision regarding this? Okay, then the next steps will be ...*

        a. Confirmation of no consent

        b. Question regarding form *(Can you please explain ____ portion of this form?)*

    iii. Question (*Can you please explain ____ portion of this form?*)

        1. Assessor accurately answers question based on form: *Thank you for your question. That portion of the form refers to.... Did I answer your question?*

        a. Affirmative (*Yes you did answer that question for me. I am comfortable to sign this document.*) Move to step b.

        b. Negative (*Actually you did not answer my question.*)

            i. Assessor attempts to answer question more clearly.

    c. Question (*Can you please answer ____ for me?*)

b. Financial responsibility form: *This form details the cost of the assessment for you based on your insurance. By signing this document, you are confirming that you are willing to be responsible for the cost listed on this form. If you are unable to pay that cost and choose not to sign, we will end the assessment at this time and I will walk you through the next steps to take.*

    i. Affirmative (*I will sign the document.*)

        1. Assessor thanks and moves to step b. *Thank you very much for signing this document. Next...*

    ii. Negative (*I will not sign the document.*)

        1. Assessor confirms decision, asks for questions, if any, and informs the caregiver of the next step. *Thank you for telling me your decision. Do you have any questions that I can answer before we confirm your decision regarding this? Okay, then the next steps will be ...*

        a. Confirmation of no consent

        b. Question regarding form (*Can you please explain ____ portion of this form?*)

(continued)

WORKSHEET 9.3.1   (continued)

iii. Question (*Can you please explain _____ portion of this form?*)

   1. Assessor accurately answers question based on the form: *Thank you for your question. That portion of the form refers to…. Did I answer your question?*

      a. Affirmative (*Yes you did answer that question for me. I am comfortable to sign this document.*) Move to step b.

      b. Negative (*Actually you did not answer my question.*)

         i. Assessor attempts to answer question more clearly.

      c. Question (*Can you please answer _____ for me?*)

Competency 3. Possible Group Supervision Activities

Case Scenario 9.3.1 is one example of how your supervisor may choose to target skills in this competency area. In a group setting, your supervisor may require you and your peers to role-play specific portions of the target assessment together. This role play may include breaking you into smaller groups based on your baseline performance, assigning group members to specific roles (e.g., parent, assessor, other observer), and having your performance measured using PMCs. An example group supervision meeting would be as follows: One group member serves as the assessor, a second individual serves as the parent, and a third serves as the data collector. The individual in the role of the assessor would complete the assigned portion of the assessment as the second individual follows a script on how to respond. All group members would then switch roles to ensure that practice opportunities occur for each group member. Additionally, your supervisor may provide you with hypothetical assessment data and require you to present the findings from an assessment to the group. Your performance may be evaluated in the areas of presentation skills, evaluation of provided information, and communication of information to various third-party individuals (e.g., funding source, parent, and other professional).

Competency 3. Specific Task Lists for the Component Skills and Additional Resources

In addition to the case scenario and suggestions for group supervision activities, we outline the tasks you need to accomplish to meet each component skill in Competency 3. Competency Task Lists 9.3.1 to 9.3.4 are intended to help you initiate tasks and select activities to complete with your supervisor. Again, we encourage you to hold conversations with your supervisor(s) to determine which of these tasks, or any additional tasks, are appropriate for you at each stage of your supervision experience. Feedback:

COMPETENCY TASK LIST 9.3.1   CONSIDER INITIATING AND COMPLETING THE FOLLOWING TASKS FOR THE COMPONENT SKILL OF COMPLETING A FUNCTIONAL BEHAVIOR ASSESSMENT, WITH YOUR SUPERVISOR

	(Mark done or record benchmark)
I. Review BACB ethical guidelines 1.0, 2.0, and 3.0 and discuss with supervisor	
A. Ethical practices in conducting behavior assessments **B.** Discuss with supervisor the ethical practices and the importance of practicing within one's limits of professional competence and obtaining consultation, supervision, training, or making referrals as necessary	
II. Conduct a preliminary assessment to identify the referral problem	
A. Obtain informed consent for assessment	
B. Identification of the problem	

1. Conduct indirect assessment
 • Review records and available data
 • Conduct interviews using semi-structured format (e.g., FAI)
 • Use rating scales
  i. FAST
  ii. MAS
  iii. SIT
 • Consider biological/medical variables that may be affecting the client
 • Include completed indirect assessment forms and notes on your interview under this tab	

2. Observe the client in the natural environment • Identify variables that could have an evocative effect on target behaviors	
C. Develop a hypothesis statement based on the preliminary assessment of the client	

• For each target behavior, identify potential
  i. Biological/medical variables that may affect the client
  ii. Immediate antecedents
  iii. Consequences	

D. Define target behaviors in observable and measurable terms	
• Operationally define target behaviors in measurable and observable terms before conducting direct assessment • Discuss the definitions with the supervisor and make necessary changes	

(continued)

COMPETENCY TASK LIST 9.3.1   *(continued)*

	(Mark done or record benchmark)
III. Use direct observation to collect baseline data	
A. Select observation periods to obtain baseline data given the dimensions of the behavior and the logistics of observing and recording the data • Use scatterplot data to select observation periods, **or** • Use information obtained from interviews to select observation periods	
B. Select a measurement system to obtain baseline data given the dimensions of the behavior and the logistics of observing and recording	

• Create a basic table incorporating:
  o Fundamental measures (e.g., count, duration, temporal locus)
  o Procedures for measuring behavior (e.g., event recording, time sampling)
  o Examples of behaviors you may measure using each method and procedure of data collection
• For each measurement system, develop data recording sheets to be used for data collection	

C. Directly observe the target behavior(s)	
• Use the data recording sheet to obtain baseline data given the dimensions of the behavior	

o Obtain baseline data
  o Discuss baseline data with supervisor
  o Conduct IOA
  o Evaluate whether changes need to be made to your data collection method or recording sheets	

D. Select and use a data display that effectively communicates relevant quantitative relations	

• Use Excel to generate graphs to display results of baseline data
• Graphs must include
  o Correctly labeled y- and x-axes
  o Title
  o Correct data points and markers
  o Figure captions
• Analyze and interpret observed data	

IV. Identify variables that influence the occurrence of problem behavior	
A. Create a basic table that includes uses and limitations of • ABC recording and functional analysis (FA) • Response-dependent ABC recording and response-independent (scheduled observation) ABC recording	

(continued)

COMPETENCY TASK LIST 9.3.1 *(continued)*

	(Mark done or record benchmark)
<ul><li>Discuss with supervisor what information can be obtained from ABC recording</li><li>Discuss with supervisor the many limitations of ABC recording and why behavior analysts cannot draw accurate conclusions regarding function when using descriptive assessments</li><li>If ABC recording is used<ul><li>Define environmental variables in observable and measurable terms (e.g., define antecedents and consequences)</li><li>Evaluate temporal relations between observed variables</li></ul></li></ul>	
B. Design and conduct functional analysis	
<ul><li>Create a table that includes<ul><li>Various types of FA procedures</li><li>Examples of target behaviors assessed using each type of FA procedure</li><li>Limitations of each type of FA procedure</li></ul></li></ul>	
<ul><li>Choose an appropriate FA procedure for the given target behavior<ul><li>Discuss with supervisor the risks associated with the assessment</li><li>Discuss how to reduce the risks</li><li>Propose the FA procedure that is most appropriate for the given target behavior and that minimizes the risk to the client</li></ul></li></ul>	
<ul><li>Obtain informed consent to conduct FA from caregiver or client</li></ul>	
<ul><li>Conduct FA under direct supervision of supervisor<ul><li>Graph and analyze the FA results</li><li>Evaluate temporal relations between observed variables</li></ul></li></ul>	
V. Write functional behavior assessment (FBA) report	
<ul><li>The FBA should include the following components:</li></ul>	
A. Reason for referral B. Background information C. Behavior-analytic description of reported target behaviors and environmental variables that could influence the target behaviors D. Hypothesis statement for each target behavior E. Baseline data F. FA results G. Summary	

(continued)

COMPETENCY TASK LIST 9.3.1   (*continued*)

	(Mark done or record benchmark)
H. Recommendations o Make recommendations regarding behaviors that must be established, maintained, increased, or decreased i. State intervention goals in observable and measurable terms o Identify potential interventions based on assessment results and the best available scientific evidence • Include the completed FBAs in this tab (de-identify client information first)	

FAI, Functional Assessment Inventory; FAST, Functional Assessment Screening Tool; MAS, Motivation Assessment Scale; SIT, Self-Injury Trauma Scale.

PERFORMANCE MONITORING CHECKLIST 9.3.2   EXAMPLE PERFORMANCE CHECKLIST YOU AND YOUR SUPERVISOR CAN USE TO GAUGE YOUR PERFORMANCE IN THIS COMPONENT SKILL

Task Analysis	Y/N/NA			Feedback
	S1	S2	S3	
1. Assessor checked whether the data collector was ready				
2. Assessor provided the client with moderately preferred items				
3. Assessor had the client attend to the items				
4. Assessor said, "I am going to do some work; you can play with these"				
5. Assessor turned away from the client and pretended to be busy				
6. In 100% of opportunities, contingent on hand biting, assessor provided social attention in the form of a verbal reprimand (e.g., "Don't do that." "Stop it.") and light physical contact				
7. Used a natural tone when providing verbal attention				
8. In 100% of opportunities, after delivering the attention, the assessor turned away from the client and pretended to be busy				
9. In 100% of opportunities, any other behavior (inappropriate or appropriate) was ignored by the assessor				
10. Condition was completed within set time interval				

WORKSHEET 9.3.2   EXAMPLE INFORMED CONSENT DOCUMENT

Informed Assent

This informed assent form explains all terms and conditions for the services that will be provided by _____ under the supervision of _____.

I, _____, understand that my parents /guardian have/has given permission (said it's okay) for me to get direct services (help with work completion, planning, organization) from _____.

I understand that I have the following rights:

- I understand that any personal information I share with _____ will be kept confidential **unless I break the law and/or there's a direct danger to myself or others.**
- I have the right to get information regarding my treatments, services, or tests, including risks and benefits of the treatments, services, or tests.
- I have the right to get enough information to make the best decision about accepting or refusing the treatments, services, or tests.
- I have the right to have _____ give me a written and/or oral explanation of any and all treatments, services, or tests in a way that I can fully understand and that includes the following:
  - o Test results
  - o Nature of the treatments, services, and/or tests/procedures
  - o Dosage or frequency of services
  - o Expected end of services
  - o Any expected benefits
  - o Known side effects and risks
  - o Whether other services are available
  - o Information on what can happen if treatments, services, and/or tests are not used

Services will be on_____(day(s) of the week & time frame).

If _____ have to cancel a session they will call my parents /guardian and let them know that they will be cancelling the session for the day at least 30 minutes before the session starts.

_____ will also let my parents know when they plan on rescheduling the session.

If I or my parents have to cancel the session, my parents will let _____ know at least 30 minutes before the session starts for that day. I promise to let my parents know if I have to cancel a session so that they can let the _____ know as soon as possible.

Contact Information
If you have any questions, comments, or concerns please feel to contact the case supervisors

Dr. Peter Adzhyan, L.E.P., BCBA-D
petros.adzhyan.87@csun.edu
(818) 677-7724
Sierra Tower 306
California State University, Northridge

Dr. Ellie Kazemi, BCBA-D
ellie.kazemi@csun.edu
(818) 677- 7224
Sierra Tower 306
California State University, Northridge

Student Interns' Contact Information
XXXXXXXXXX
Graduate Student, MS-ABA
XXXXXXXXXX@my.csun.edu
(XXX) XXXX
California State University, Northridge

XXXXXXXXXX
Graduate Student, MS-ABA
XXXXXXX.790@my.csun.edu
(XXX) XXXXXX
California State University, Northridge

I am taking part in these services because I want to and because I understand the risks and benefits.

Signature _____ Date _____
Student Intern Signature _____ Student Intern Signature _____

COMPETENCY TASK LIST 9.3.2 CONSIDER INITIATING AND COMPLETING THE FOLLOWING TASKS FOR THE COMPONENT SKILL OF CONDUCTING PREFERENCE ASSESSMENTS, WITH YOUR SUPERVISOR

	(Mark done or record benchmark)
I. Design and conduct preference assessments to identify putative reinforcers (A-14)	

A. Create a basic table that includes uses and limitations of:
 o Indirect preference assessment
 o Direct observation (approach based)
 o Systematic assessment of preferred stimuli
   o Multiple stimulus presentations without replacement (MSWO)
   o Multiple stimulus presentations with replacement (MSW)
   o Paired stimulus presentation (PS)	

B. Design and conduct preference assessment i. Taking the resources in the setting, type of stimuli being examined, and client's level of functioning into consideration, design a preference assessment for the client ii. Discuss the designed preference assessment with supervisor	
C. Conduct MSWO, PS, and approach-based preference assessments under direct supervision of supervisor	
D. Develop a performance monitoring checklist to evaluate the fidelity of preference assessments and have the supervisor use the form to rate and give feedback on conducting preference assessments (see Tab 24)	
E. Include the completed checklist with feedback in this tab and Tab 24	
II. Write summary of preference assessment results	
➢ Summarize the preference assessment results using the appropriate visual display ➢ Present the summary of the preference assessment results to the supervisor and make necessary changes	
➢ Share the results with parents or teachers	

PERFORMANCE MONITORING CHECKLIST 9.3.3   EXAMPLE PERFORMANCE CHECKLIST YOU AND YOUR SUPERVISOR CAN USE TO GAUGE YOUR PERFORMANCE IN THIS COMPONENT SKILL

- **Performance monitoring check list for multiple stimulus preference assessment (MSWO)**

Scoring key:

- 1 = step completed correctly
- 0 = step completed incorrectly
- NA = No opportunity to observe

Task Analysis	1	2	3	4	5	6	7	8	9	10	% Correct
Seven items selected for the assessment											
The table was clear of all stimuli before presenting the items											
All seven items were presented simultaneously in an arc											
After the child selected an item, the assessor removed all the items											
Recorded the selection of the item											
The assessor let the child play with the selected item for 10 seconds before presenting the next pair											
The remaining items were presented again and the items at the corners were switched (item to the assessor's left was moved to the assessor's right and the item on the assessor's right was moved to the assessor's left)											
If the child reached for more than one item, the assessor blocked access to the items											
If the child reached for both items, after clocking, the assessor waited 5 seconds and presented the same items											
If child did not select an item, the assessor removed the items after 5 seconds and presented the entire array again by switching the corners											
All steps completed correctly 1 = all steps in the trial completed correctly 0 = any of the steps in the trial missed											

_____
_____
_____
_____

Goals for the next session:

1. _____
2. _____
3. _____

COMPETENCY TASK LIST 9.3.3   CONSIDER INITIATING AND COMPLETING THE FOLLOWING TASKS FOR THE COMPONENT SKILL OF CONDUCTING REINFORCER ASSESSMENTS, WITH YOUR SUPERVISOR

	(Mark done or record benchmark)
I. Design and conduct reinforcer assessments to identify putative reinforcers	
A. Design a reinforcer assessment 　i.　Conduct a literature search and develop a procedure for reinforcer assessment 　ii.　Discuss with supervisor the procedure and make necessary changes 　iii.　Include the procedure in this tab	
B. Conduct a reinforcer assessment 　i.　Conduct the approved reinforcer assessment under direct supervision of supervisor	
C. Develop a performance monitoring checklist to evaluate the fidelity of reinforcer assessments and have the supervisor use the form to rate and give feedback on conducting the assessment (see Tab 24)	
D. Include the completed checklist with feedback in this tab and Tab 24	
II. Write a summary of reinforcer assessment results	
• Summarize the assessment results using the appropriate visual display • Present the summary of the reinforcer assessment results to the supervisor and make necessary changes	
• Share the results with parents or teachers	

PERFORMANCE MONITORING CHECKLIST 9.3.4   EXAMPLE PERFORMANCE CHECKLIST YOU AND YOUR SUPERVISOR CAN USE TO GAUGE YOUR PERFORMANCE IN THIS COMPONENT SKILL

Simple reinforcer assessment

Task Analysis	Y/N/NA			Feedback
	S1	S2	S3	
1. Assessor chose a behavior that is in the learner's repertoire and occurs in a free operant arrangement				
2. Assessor operationally defined the behavior being used to conduct reinforcer assessment				
3. Assessor conducted at least three baseline observation sessions to determine current rate of occurrence for behavior				
4. Assessor did not deliver items/activities or other specific consequences contingent on behavior occurring				
5. Assessor chose item/activity to serve as reinforcer				
6. Assessor set time frame for assessment of specific reinforcer being evaluated				
7. Assessor delivered item/activity contingent on occurrence of target behavior in 100% of observed opportunities				
8. Assessor conducted at least three reinforcer observation sessions to determine if any behavior change was observed				
9. Assessor completed a reversal to the baseline conditions				
10. Assessor accurately determined if the item/activity evaluated functioned as a reinforcer				

COMPETENCY TASK LIST 9.3.4   CONSIDER INITIATING AND COMPLETING THE FOLLOWING TASKS FOR THE COMPONENT SKILL OF CONDUCTING A PARAMETRIC ANALYSIS, WITH YOUR SUPERVISOR

	(Mark done or record benchmark)
I. Design and conduct parametric analysis	

A. Design parametric analysis
  i. Conduct a literature search and develop a procedure for parametric analysis for:
   • Assessing the effects of various schedules of reinforcement on target behaviors
   • Assessing the effects of various magnitudes of reinforcement on target behaviors
   • Assessing the effects of various tasks (for escape maintained behaviors) on target behaviors
  ii. Discuss with supervisor the proposed design and make necessary changes
   • Include the procedures in this tab	

B. Conduct a parametric analysis
  i. Conduct the parametric assessment under the direct supervision of supervisor
  ii. Develop a performance monitoring checklist to evaluate the fidelity of the parametric assessment and have the supervisor use the form to rate and give feedback on conducting the assessment
   • Include the completed checklist with feedback in this tab	

II. Write a summary of assessment results	
i. Summarize the parametric assessment results using the appropriate visual display ii. Present the summary of the assessment results to the supervisor and make necessary changes iii. Use the assessment results in treatment planning	
iv. Share the results with parents or teachers	

PERFORMANCE MONITORING CHECKLIST 9.3.5   EXAMPLE PERFORMANCE CHECKLIST YOU AND YOUR SUPERVISOR CAN USE TO GAUGE YOUR PERFORMANCE IN THIS COMPONENT SKILL

Performance monitoring checklist for parametric analysis
Scoring key: 1 = step completed correctly; 0 = step completed incorrectly; NA = no opportunity to observe

Task Analysis

Pre-assessment preparation	1	2	3	4	5	6	7	8	9	10	Comments
1. All required materials for data collection were ready											
2. The definition of the target problem behavior was observable and measurable											
3. All required materials for introduction of IV were ready											
4. The criteria for terminating the IV contingent on occurrence and nonoccurrence of the problem behavior were clear and measurable											
5. The presentation of the sequence for the levels of IV was correctly listed on the data sheet (e.g., starting with 1 trial, then 2, ...)											
Conducting parametric analysis											
6. Made sure the client was ready before presenting the first level of IV (e.g., made sure the client was attending to the assessor before the instruction correlated with the trial was provided; or made sure that the client was engaged with the preferred activity before starting the timer for access to the activity)											
7. Presented the levels of IV from lowest to highest magnitude											
8. Contingent on occurrence of the problem behavior, stopped the assessment and recorded correct data											

(continued)

PERFORMANCE MONITORING CHECKLIST 9.3.5   (*continued*)

9. Contingent on nonoccurrence of the problem behavior, continued to increase levels of IV when criteria for change were met												
10. Replicated the results to establish the functional relationship between levels of IV and the problem behavior by showing verification and replication												
11. Graphed the assessment results												
Total %												

Feedback:

Goals for the next session:

Supervisor Signature: _____ Date: _____

Therapist Signature: _____ Date: _____

Additional Resources to Consider

Bloom, S. E., Iwata, B. A., Fritz, J. N., Roscoe, E. M., & Carreau, A. B. (2011). Classroom application of a trial-based functional analysis. *Journal of Applied Behavior Analysis, 44,* 19–31. doi:10.1901/jaba.2011.44-19

Carr, J. E., Nicolson, A. C., & Higbee, T. S. (2000). Evaluation of a brief multiple-stimulus preference assessment in a naturalistic context. *Journal of Applied Behavior Analysis, 33,* 353–357. doi:10.1901/jaba.2000.33-353

DeLeon, I. G., & Iwata, B. A. (1996). Evaluation of a multiple-stimulus presentation format for assessing reinforcer preferences. *Journal of Applied Behavior Analysis, 29,* 519–533. doi:10.1901/jaba.1996.29-519

Fahmie, T. A., Iwata, B. A., Harper, J. M., & Querim, A. C. (2013). Evaluation of the divided attention condition during functional analyses. *Journal of Applied Behavior Analysis, 46,* 71–78. doi:10.1002/jaba.20

Fisher, W., Piazza, C. C., Bowman, L. G., Hagopian, L. P., Owens, J. C., & Slevin, I. (1992). A comparison of two approaches for identifying reinforcers for persons with severe and profound disabilities. *Journal of Applied Behavior Analysis, 25,* 491–498. doi:10.1901/jaba.1992.25-491

Fritz, J. N., Iwata, B. A., Hammond, J. L., & Bloom, S. E. (2013). Experimental analysis of precursors to severe problem behavior. *Journal of Applied Behavior Analysis, 46,* 101–129. doi:10.1002/jaba.27

Hagopian, L. P., Long, E. S., & Rush, K. S. (2004). Preference assessment procedures for individuals with developmental disabilities. *Behavior Modification, 28*, 668–677. doi:10.1177/0145445503259836

Hagopian, L. P., Rooker, G. W., Jessel, J., & DeLeon, I. G. (2013). Initial functional analysis outcomes and modifications in pursuit of differentiation: A summary of 176 inpatient cases. *Journal of Applied Behavior Analysis, 46*, 88–100. doi:10.1002/jaba.25

Hammond, J. L., Iwata, B. A., Rooker, G. W., Fritz, J. N., & Bloom, S. E. (2013). Effects of fixed versus random condition sequencing during multielement functional analyses. *Journal of Applied Behavior Analysis, 46*, 22–30. doi:10.1002/jaba.7

Hanley, G. P. (2012). Functional assessment of problem behavior: Dispelling myths, overcoming implementation obstacles, and developing new lore. *Behavior Analyst in Practice, 5*, 54–72. doi:10.1007/BF03391818

Hanley, G. P., Iwata, B. A., McCord, B. E. (2003). Functional analysis of problem behavior: A review. *Journal of Applied Behavior Analysis, 36*, 147–185. doi:10.1901/jaba.2003.36-147

Iwata, B. A., Dorsey, M. F., Slifer, K. J., Bauman, K. E., & Richman, G. S. (1994). Toward a functional analysis of self-injury. *Journal of Applied Behavior Analysis, 27*, 197–209. doi:10.1901/jaba.1994.27-197

Iwata, B. A., & Dozier, C. L. (2008). Clinical application of functional analysis methodology. *Behavior Analysis in Practice, 1*, 3–9. doi:10.1007/BF033

Jessel, J., Hanley, G. P., & Ghaemmaghami, M. (2016), Interview-informed synthesized contingency analyses: Thirty replications and reanalysis. *Journal of Applied Behavior Analysis, 49*, 576–595. doi:10.1002/jaba.316

Neidert, P. L., Iwata, B. A., Dempsey, C. M., & Thomason-Sassi, J. L. (2013). Latency of response during the functional analysis of elopement. *Journal of Applied Behavior Analysis, 46*, 312–316. doi:10.1002/jaba.11

O'Neil, R. E., Horner, R. H., Albin, R. W., Sprague, J. R., Sorey, K., & Newton, J. S. (1997). *Functional assessment and program development for problem behavior: A practical handbook.* Pacific Grove, CA: Brooks/Cole Publishers.

Querim, A. C., Iwata, B. A., Roscoe, E. M., Schlichenmeyer, K. J., Ortega, J. V., & Hurl, K. E. (2013). Functional analysis screening for problem behavior maintained by automatic reinforcement. *Journal of Applied Behavior Analysis, 46*, 47–60. doi:10.1002/jaba.26

Repp, A. C., & Horner, R. (1998). *Functional analysis of problem behavior: From effective assessment to effective support.* Belmont, CA: Wadsworth Publishing.

Thompson, R. H., & Iwata, B. A. (2007). A comparison of outcomes from descriptive and functional analyses of problem behavior. *Journal of Applied Behavior Analysis, 40*, 333–338. doi:10.1901/jaba.2007.56-06

Touchette, P. E., MacDonald, R. F., & Langer, S. N. (1985). A scatter plot for identifying stimulus control of problem behavior. *Journal of Applied Behavior Analysis, 18*, 343–351. doi:10.1901/jaba.1985.18-343

COMPETENCY 4. EVALUATE AND DEVELOP EVIDENCE-BASED INTERVENTION PLANS

As a competent behavior analyst, it is your ethical duty to recommend treatment strategies that are evidence based. Evidence-based practice means relying on the best scientific evidence, and your clinical experience, to make decisions for your clients. Although evidence-based practice is the standard in many applied professions (e.g., medicine, clinical psychology, physical therapy), researchers continuously find large gaps in applied fields between science and practice. The gap exists in part because practitioners and scientists have different skill sets, which makes it difficult for practitioners to digest the research outcomes that scientists publish. Behavior analysts are no different. Often, teachers in graduate programs assign peer-reviewed journal articles in their coursework in an attempt to train emerging practitioners to read, digest, and apply research. However, science is progressive and new discoveries are made every year that impact evidence-based practice. Therefore, as a competent behavior analyst, you must be an educated consumer of research and continue to stay on top of the literature long after your graduate training concludes. You have to read research articles and determine if the research evidence for a particular behavior-analytic strategy warrants its use with your client(s).

In addition to making evidence-based decisions, a core belief of every behavior analyst is that behavior occurs as a function of environmental variables. Therefore, it is imperative that, as a competent behavior analyst, your treatment protocols are also based on the results of your comprehensive assessments. You must be adept at conducting thorough assessments of function to determine the variables that evoke, maintain, or increase problem behaviors. You will also need to know how to obtain information on motivating operations, competing contingencies, stimuli that function as reinforcers, reinforcing consequences for target behavior, and antecedent stimuli that may have evocative or abatement effects on the problem behavior or its alternative(s). Therefore, for this competency, the two component skills you must gain are (a) obtain, summarize, and evaluate research articles as part of recommendations and development of intervention plans and (b) recommend intervention strategies based on the assessment results and the best available scientific evidence. In Diagram 9.4.1, we provide some benchmarks to help you gauge your skill development in this competency.

DIAGRAM 9.4.1 COMPETENCY BENCHMARKS FOR DEVELOPING EVIDENCE-BASED INTERVENTION PLANS BASED ON ASSESSMENT RESULTS AND BASELINE DATA.

Elementary Skills

- Can discuss the seven dimensions of applied behavior analysis (ABA) and give examples of each that show application of the seven dimensions to treatment evaluation
- Can name journals that regularly publish behavior analytic studies
- Can explain the difference between randomized clinical trials and single-subject studies
- Can state the criteria set by American Psychological Association for considering an intervention to be evidence based (for group and single-subject designs)
- Can explain the difference between evidence-based, emerging, and non-evidence-based, treatments

Intermediate Skills

- Can search behavior-analytic journals for peer-reviewed articles using specific keywords related to hypothetical scenarios (e.g., staff training)
- Can accurately evaluate if retrieved articles meet the seven dimensions of ABA
- Can accurately summarize relevant information from retrieved articles
- Can recommend evidence-based treatments by taking into consideration the client's needs, available resources, assessment results, and the best available scientific evidence
- Can develop technological behavior reduction and skill acquisition treatment plans for hypothetical scenarios, by incorporating treatment information from behavior-analytic studies

Advanced Skills

- Can search behavior-analytic journals for peer-reviewed articles that meet the seven dimension of ABA using specific keywords related to the needs of specific clients (e.g., SIB maintained by escape from task, or deficits in echoics)
- Can recommend evidence-based treatments for initial assessment or for progress reports by taking into consideration the client's needs, available resources, assessment results, and the best available scientific evidence
- Can develop technological behavior reduction and skill acquisition treatment plans to address the client's needs, by incorporating treatment information from behavior-analytic studies

Continuing Education & Professional Development

Competency 4. Example Case Scenario for Teaching Component Skill: Developing Evidence-Based Interventions

(1) *Prerequisites*

   a. Read and be able to discuss the following resources:

   i. Chambless, D., Sanderson, W., Shoham, V., Johnson, S., Pope, K., Crits-Christoph, P., . . . McCurry, S. (1996). An update on empirically validated therapies. *The Clinical Psychologist, 49,* 5–18.

   ii. Chambless, D. L., & Hollon, S. D. (1998). Defining empirically supported therapies. *Journal of Consulting and Clinical Psychology, 66*(1), 7–18. doi:10.1037/0022-006X.66.1.7

   iii. Nathan, P. E., & Gorman, J. M. (Eds.). (1998). *A guide to treatments that work*. New York, NY: Oxford University Press.

   b. Discriminate between the following types of information:

   i. Anecdotal

   ii. Consumer report

   iii. Case study

   iv. Correlational research

   v. Quasi-experimental research

   vi. Experimental research

   vii. Meta-analyses

(2) *Baseline assessment of your skills*

   a. Your supervisor would provide you with a list of treatment options for an area that affects the population with whom you work.

   b. You would be responsible for analyzing and explaining the strength of the evidence using the criteria discussed in both Chambless et al. (1998) and Nathan and Gorman (1998).

   i. **Example of task:**

   1. Use the criteria discussed in Chambless et al. (1998) and Nathan and Gorman (1998) to order the following interventions for attention-deficit/hyperactivity disorder (AD/HD) in the order of best to least established interventions.

   a. Biomedical interventions (e.g., specialized diets)

   b. Neurofeedback

   c. Behavioral interventions

   d. Stimulant medications (e.g., Adderall)

   e. Sensory integration therapy

   2. You can use any article database or other appropriate resource to complete this task.

   c. Your supervisor would evaluate you on the following areas:

      i. Identification of category for each intervention type

      ii. Type of empirical articles found and evaluated

      iii. Written evaluation of each intervention type and the evidence provided

         1. Citations of research would be included here as well.

      iv. Verbal communication of quality of each intervention based on your categorization.

      v. If you meet the criteria set by your supervisor, you would move to generalization aspect of training.

         1. If you do not meet the criteria set by your supervisor, you would move to training.

(3) *Training*

   a. **Instruction and modeling**

      i. Prior to you attempting this task, your supervisor will model for you the process of finding evidence-based interventions.

      ii. Your supervisor would complete this model for a non-ABA or intervention for a specific diagnosis (e.g., effective sunburn interventions).

      iii. This model may include:

         1. How to search available resources (e.g., university library, Google Scholar)

         2. How to evaluate research articles:

            a. Source of research

            b. Journal of publication

            c. Determining research design

            d. Evaluating social/statistical significance provided in studies

            e. Looking for replications of studies and evaluating differences from originals.

            f. Evaluating effectiveness

            g. Using criteria from articles mentioned earlier to determine level of the evidence's strength

         3. Compare findings to groups researching evidence for interventions for the specific effect

   b. **Rehearsal**

      i. Your supervisor would ask you to complete the same process for another intervention from the public sphere.

         1. Examples:

            a. Weight loss methods

            b. Increasing energy

      ii. Your supervisor would have you complete a presentation on the evidence or nonevidence for the intervention chosen.

     1. Your supervisor would provide you with an assignment prompt and rubric similar to Evaluating an Intervention to Determine If It Is Evidence Based.

(4) *Generalization*

  a. Your supervisor would have you create an evaluation of a specific ABA assessment or procedure:

    i. Your performance would be evaluated based on the Evidence Description Presentation PMC.

    ii. If you meet the criteria, you will move to the competencies of writing behavior programs and skill acquisition programs.

WORKSHEET 9.4.1   DETERMINING EVIDENCE BASE FOR A NON–BEHAVIOR-ANALYTIC INTERVENTION

Select a common intervention, medication, or supplement (e.g., Emergency-C; Collagen, Airborne) and conduct a brief research. Keep your search as well as your search question simple. Answer the following questions:

  1. What is the intervention, medication, or supplement? (1 point)

  2. What are the claimed gains of the intervention? (1 point)

  3. Who are the main consumers of the product or intervention? (1 point)

Is there any scientific evidence that the intervention is effective? Support your claim by providing information regarding the evidence below.

  4. Did you find peer-reviewed empirical research that evaluated the intervention?

    A. If yes, provide the citations in the American Psychological Association (APA) format and answer the following questions. (2 points)

      a. Was the intervention the independent variable in the study(ies)? (1 point)

      b. Was the dependent variable (DV; what was supposed to improve) the claim made about the product? (1 point)

      c. Use APA standards to demonstrate if the claims are evidence based.

        i. Used randomized clinical trials, control groups, and other design factors? (2 points)

        ii. Had two independent research teams support these claims? (2 points)

        iii. If a single-subject design, had more than nine participants across studies? (2 points)

        iv. The studies used

          1. a treatment manual? (1 point)

          2. reliable and valid outcome measures? (1 point)

          3. appropriate analyses? (1 point)

        v. Was the study behavioral (DV was measurable and observable; 2 points)?

    B. If no, clearly explain which methods of search and keywords you used (2 points). Suggest another intervention for evaluation until you find one that has some empirical evidence.

PERFORMANCE MONITORING CHECKLIST 9.4.1 PMC FOR EVIDENCE DESCRIPTION PRESENTATON

Criteria		Met?
General formatting, grammar, and APA style		
1	The following headings were included and adhered to APA Style Manual: Introduction, Method, Results, Discussion, References	Y/N/NA
2	The following subheadings were included under the Method section and adhered to the APA Style Manual: Participants and Setting, Dependent Variable (or Response Measurement), Interobserver Agreement, Design, Procedure	Y/N/NA
3	The following subheadings appeared and adhered to the APA Style Manual as subheadings under Procedure: Baseline and Intervention	Y/N/NA
4	Font size was 32 points (or minimum of 28 points) and easy to see	Y/N/NA
5	Font type was professional and easy to read (e.g., Arial)	Y/N/NA
6	Font color was either white against black (or dark background) or black against a light color (white) for an easy contrast between font and background colors	Y/N/NA
7	Background color and images did not detract from the content of the slides	Y/N/NA
8	In-text citations adhered to APA style	Y/N/NA
9	Content on each slide was well digested such that few words appeared on each slide	Y/N/NA
10	Slides were spelling error free (i.e., no more than one misspelling)	Y/N/NA
11	Citations and quotations were accurate and correctly referenced	Y/N/NA
12	Author refrained from using subjective (e.g., "he understands") or mentalistic ("his anxiety") words and refrained from using circular thinking ("because he knows")	Y/N/NA
	Total	()/12
	% age	
Sections of the presentation		
Introduction		
	The title was unique but accurately described the project	Y/N/NA
	Introduction began with a general statement related to the project (e.g., the problem behavior and its social significance or how ABA is related to the intervention)	Y/N/NA
	– Included a summary of a relevant research study (what was the objective of the study, who were the participants, what did the researchers do, what were their findings)	Y N NA

(continued)

PERFORMANCE MONITORING CHECKLIST 9.4.1   *(continued)*

Criteria	Met?
-Connected how the research study mentioned was related to the project	Y/N/NA
-Ended with a correct statement of the purpose or goal of the project (essentially, a statement of the research question)	Y/N/NA
Method	
Participant and Setting had information about the participants, their age, their gender, and information relevant to project (e.g., breed of the dog, if it had previous formal training, and if it was adopted)	Y/N/NA
-Included information about the setting in which the intervention was conducted	Y/N/NA
-Included enough information so that a reader could decide to whom the intervention is applicable and in what setting	Y/N/NA
The Dependent Variable (or Response Measurement) section referred to the target behavior and provided an observable and measurable *definition* of the behavior that was measured	Y/N/NA
-Included information on how the behavior was measured	Y/N/NA
-If a response sheet (e.g., math sheet) was used, the author explained exactly what the material looked like, so that another person could replicate the materials to develop the same measures for collecting data on the target behavior	Y/N/NA
The Interobserver Agreement (IOA) included the percentage of sessions that were observed	Y/N/NA
-Included the mean agreement for IOA	Y/N/NA
-Included how the second observer was trained	Y/N/NA
-Included how the second observer collected data	Y/N/NA
The Design included the name of the design that was used	Y/N/NA
The Baseline subsection under **Procedure** provided information, in detail, regarding exactly what the participant(s) experienced at baseline	Y/N/NA
The Intervention subsection provided information, in detail, regarding what the participant(s) experienced in the intervention phase	Y/N/NA
-Included information about criteria if different criteria were used	Y/N/NA
-Included exact information about the task analysis (e.g., how many steps) if a task analysis was used	Y/N/NA
-Included information about reinforcers if they were used	Y/N/NA
-If reinforcers were used, included which type of preference assessment was used (if applicable) and the results	Y/N/NA

(continued)

PERFORMANCE MONITORING CHECKLIST 9.4.1 (*continued*)

Criteria	Met?
-If a mastery criterion was used such that the next step was not taught unless the participants' performance met a certain criterion, the criterion was explained (if applicable)	Y/N/NA
-If the author used a particular type of teaching (e.g., forward chaining, total task chaining, discrete trials, or differential reinforcement), the procedure was named correctly	Y/N/NA
Results	
Provided a summary statement about how participant(s) did at baseline (e.g., at baseline, Joe completed seven problems, on average, on his own during 2 minutes)	Y/N/NA
Provided a summary statement about how participant(s) did in the intervention (e.g., during the intervention, Joe completed 22 problems, on average, on his own during the 2-minute session)	Y/N/NA
Provided a summary statement of outcomes (e.g., the intervention was effective because there was a significant change in the level of responding and the trend was increasing)	Y/N/NA
The graph matched the data measurement mentioned in the Dependent Variable (or Response Measurement) section	Y/N/NA
The graph matched the design mentioned	Y/N/NA
The graph was correct (e.g., y- and x-axes are labeled, data paths are not connected between conditions)	Y/N/NA
When explaining the graph, oriented audience to the x-axis, then the y-axis, and explained the legend or data on the plane	Y/N/NA
Discussion	
Provided a statement about the conclusions that can be drawn (e.g., based on these findings, it seems differential reinforcement was effective in increasing Joe's math completion)	Y/N/NA
Provided a general statement about IOA (if it was acceptable, and if not, what needs to change in the future)	Y/N/NA
Explained the limitations of the project (e.g., "One limitation in this study was that there was not enough time to collect data on a separate behavior to replicate the effects of the treatment and determine if the intervention was effective")	Y/N/NA
Explained what the author will do differently in the future (e.g., future researchers should consider collecting data on two behaviors simultaneously and several weeks earlier)	Y/N/NA
References	
Used correct APA style	Y/N/NA

(*continued*)

PERFORMANCE MONITORING CHECKLIST 9.4.1   *(continued)*

Criteria	Met?
Total	()/()
Percentage	
Overall Grade	
General Formatting Percentage	
Subsection Percentage	
Mean Percentage	

Competency 4. Possible Group Supervision Activities

In addition to the information we presented in Case Scenario 9.4.1, your supervisor may choose to target this competency in a group setting. One way this may be done would be to provide background information, baseline data, and other relevant information regarding a hypothetical client. Your supervisor may ask each member of the group to find a research article to target the primary area(s) of concern for the client, and then have all group members conduct an evaluation of the level of empirical support for the intervention proposed in the article and its appropriateness for the hypothetical client.

In addition, your supervisor may require group members to form small teams to debate the validity of specific intervention procedures commonly utilized with specific populations. Two teams would take part in this debate, one on the affirmative side and the other on the contrary side of the argument. Some examples of interventions to debate would be sensory diets to reduce stereotypy, utilization of neurofeedback to treat attention deficit hyperactivity disorder, implementation of prison programs to reduce rates of recidivism, or other topics relevant to the population(s) with whom group members work. This activity may include finding and digesting the research evidence for both sides, organizing the argument in a nonoffensive manner, and engaging in verbal dialogue with individuals who may not share the same perspective regarding the topic.

Competency 4. Specific Task Lists for the Component Skills and Additional Resources

In addition to the case scenario and suggestions for group supervision activities, we outline the tasks you need to accomplish to meet each component skill in Competency 4. Competency Task Lists 9.4.1 and 9.4.2 are intended to help you initiate the tasks and select activities to complete with your supervisor. Again, we encourage you to hold conversations with your supervisor(s) to determine which of these tasks, or any additional tasks, are appropriate for you at each stage of your supervision experience.

COMPETENCY TASK LIST 9.4.1   CONSIDER INITIATING AND COMPLETING THE FOLLOWING TASKS FOR THE COMPONENT SKILL OF OBTAINING, SUMMARIZING, AND EVALUATING RESEARCH ARTICLES AS PART OF RECOMMENDATIONS AND DEVELOPMENT OF INTERVENTION PLANS, WITH YOUR SUPERVISOR

	(Mark done or record benchmark)
I. Review and interpret articles from the behavior-analytic literature	
A. Obtain and summarize research articles 　I.　Search behavior-analytic journals for peer-reviewed articles that address: 　i.　Problem behaviors with similar functions as those identified in treatment plans that you are implementing 　　　• Or 　ii.　Problem behaviors with similar functions that you are developing a treatment plan for 　iii.　Skill acquisition for specific skill acquisition programs that you are implementing 　　　• Or 　iv.　Skill acquisition for specific skills that you are developing for skill acquisition programs	
B. Summarize the articles and include the summary for each article in this tab 　I.　Summary should include: 　i.　Reference to the article in APA style 　ii.　Subjects 　iii.　Target behaviors with operational definitions 　iv.　Type of FBA conducted and results 　v.　Procedure used for the intervention 　vi.　Results of the intervention 　vii.　Strengths and limitations of the articles 　viii.　How are you planning to use the information obtained from the article for your case?	

FBA, functional behavior assessment.

157

PERFORMANCE MONITORING CHECKLIST 9.4.2 EXAMPLE PERFORMANCE CHECKLIST YOU AND YOUR SUPERVISOR CAN USE TO GAUGE YOUR PERFORMANCE IN THIS COMPONENT SKILL

Criteria	Met?
1 Reference to the article is in APA style	Y/N/NA
2 Description of participants presented accurately	Y/N/NA
3 All target behaviors accompanied by their respective operational definitions	Y/N/NA
4 Description of all assessment procedures presented accurately	Y/N/NA
5 Procedure used in the article described technologically	Y/N/NA
6 Intervention results described accurately	Y/N/NA
7 Strengths of articles discussed	Y/N/NA
8 Limitations of article discussed	Y/N/NA
9 Described potential uses of the article with regard to specific client/ participant	Y/N/NA
10 Written material contained three or fewer spelling or grammatical errors	Y/N/NA

COMPETENCY TASK LIST 9.4.2   CONSIDER INITIATING AND COMPLETING THE FOLLOWING TASKS FOR THE COMPONENT SKILL OF RECOMMENDING INTERVENTION STRATEGIES BASED ON THE ASSESSMENT RESULTS AND THE BEST AVAILABLE SCIENTIFIC EVIDENCE, WITH YOUR SUPERVISOR

	(Mark done or record benchmark)
I. Recommend intervention strategies based on FBA results	
A. Taking the client's needs, best practices, available resources, FBA results, and the best available scientific evidence into consideration, recommend conceptually systematic and effective strategies for intervention	
B. The recommendations should include, but not be limited to: i. Antecedent interventions to address identified MOs and/or SDs and decrease problem behavior (provide reference) ii. Consequence-based interventions to increase socially acceptable adaptive behaviors and decrease maladaptive behaviors (provide reference) iii. Appropriate initial reinforcement schedule and criteria for thinning iv. Shaping of replacement behaviors if not in the client's repertoire (e.g., FCT; provide reference) v. How to address the problem behavior if it occurs during intervention (provide reference) vi. Training of support staff and/or parents (provide reference) vii. Monitoring fidelity of implementation (provide reference) viii. Data collection, monitoring, and data-based decision making	
II. Recommend intervention strategies based on skills assessment results (VB-MAPP results)	
A. Taking the client's needs, best practices, available resources, skills assessment results, and the best available scientific evidence into consideration, recommend conceptually systematic and effective strategies for skill acquisition interventions	
B. The recommendations should include, but not be limited to: i. Goals for each skill deficit ii. Appropriate teaching methods for each skill (DTT, NET) iii. Appropriate chaining method iv. Appropriate method of programming for generality v. Monitoring fidelity of implementation vi. Data collection, monitoring, and data-based decision making	

DTT, discrete trial training; MOs, motivating operations; NET, natural environment teaching; SDs, discriminative stimuli.

PERFORMANCE MONITORING CHECKLIST 9.4.3   EXAMPLE PERFORMANCE CHECKLIST YOU AND YOUR SUPERVISOR CAN USE TO GAUGE YOUR PERFORMANCE IN THIS COMPONENT SKILL

Functional Behavior Assessment and Recommendations Rubric

Criteria for Components of the FBA

- **Identifying information**

- **Reason for referral**
  a. Clearly stated the source of referral (teacher, parent, regional center)
  b. Stated the reason the child/adolescent was referred, including a general description of the problem (target) behaviors (e.g., elopement or tantrum).
  c. If the target behaviors have been present in the past, included information on worsening or improvement in target behavior to justify the need for assessment

- **The purpose of the FBA**
  a. Gather baseline (e.g., frequency, duration) data on target behavior(s)
  b. Identify setting-related events that could support occurrence of the problem behavior(s)
  c. Identify antecedents that evoke the target behavior(s)
  d. Identify the function(s) of the target behavior(s)
  e. Recommend intervention strategies that address necessary environmental changes, function-based interventions, and teaching strategies that will increase occurrence of socially acceptable behaviors and decrease occurrence of the problem behaviors

Reason for referral sentence structure

BACKGROUND INFORMATION

- **Includes information about the methods used to obtain background information**
- **If records are available**
  - Record review as well as interviews with parents and/or teacher(s) must be included as methods in this section

Format of family history

Content of family history
  a. Family members with whom the child/adolescent lives
  b. Primary caretakers and their availability for parent training
  c. History of household changes, including changes in family members
  d. Recent moves
  e. Home language
  f. Regional center involvement
     - Home-based behavior services
  g. Department of Child and Family Services (DCFS) involvement
     - Placement in foster home

(continued)

PERFORMANCE MONITORING CHECKLIST 9.4.3 *(continued)*

Format of medical history

Medical history (in a paragraph format)
a. Any health, vision, and hearing issues that might impact learning and current behaviors
b Relevant medication information
c. History of hospitalizations and recent injuries

Format of educational history

Educational history (in a paragraph format)
a. History of schools attended
b. Date of initial IEP and eligibility (if applicable)
c. Instructional setting(s) and past and current services
d. History of specific behavior difficulties (e.g., difficulties that are documented in school records)
   - Frequency, duration, and intensity of each behavior
   - Include all problem behaviors documented in school records with appropriate references
     o Example: According to IEP dated November 14, 2011, John exhibited aggressive behaviors toward peers and adults.
   - Discipline history
     o Office discipline referrals (ODRs)
     o Suspensions or expulsions
   - Include a graph, if there are available data, to visually show the occurrence of problem behaviors over time
e. Brief discussion of current achievement history to document impact of behavior on access to academic curriculum
   a. Report card information (if available)
   b. Current work samples and classroom test performance (if available)

Intervention history

Summary of indirect assessments

- **Includes information about the methods used to obtain indirect assessment information**
- **If records are available**
  - Record review as well as interviews with parents and/or teacher(s) must be included as Methods in this section
  - Use of a structured interview and/or rating scales (e.g., FAI, FAST, MAS, QABF) or unstructured interview (provide a sample of questions)
  - Relevant dates of interviews included

- **The table for identification of the problem behaviors must include:**
  a. Behavior (general description is okay)
  b. Occurrence (could have a range)
  c. Duration
  d. Severity

(continued)

PERFORMANCE MONITORING CHECKLIST 9.4.3 *(continued)*

- **Possible response class hierarchy** is described if the indirect assessment results show that the parents or the teachers observe sequences of behaviors ranging from less severe to more severe

- **Appropriate behaviors**
  a. **Appropriate behaviors in the child's repertoire (including any basic verbal operant, adaptive, and social skills) are clearly described**

- **Immediate antecedents**
- **The table for identifying possible antecedents must include:**
  a. Behavior (from indirect assessment)
  b. Immediate antecedents (from indirect assessment)

- **Possible maintaining consequences**
- **The table for identifying possible consequences must include:**
  a. Behavior (from indirect assessment)
  b. Consequences (from indirect assessment)

- **Setting-related events affecting problem behavior**
  a. The setting-related events are described using language that is not technical
  b. If specific setting-related events are identified, the report should address the following for each setting-related event:
     I. List the setting-related events identified and possible factors that could have an evocative effect on the behavior
     II. Identify the possible relationship between the setting event and the target behavior (e.g., poor sleep: On days when John gets less than 8 hours of sleep, the frequency and duration of tantrums have been reported to increase)
        I. Setting events are possible correlates. Without an experimental test, authors should refrain from making causal statements.

- **Summary of indirect assessments and hypothesized predictor(s) (setting-related events and immediate antecedents) and potential function(s) of problem behavior(s) table must include for each target behavior:**
  a. Setting-related events related to each target behavior
  b. Immediate antecedents that could evoke the target behavior
  c. Possible function(s) (from indirect assessments)

DIRECT ASSESSMENT

- **The table describing direct observation session must include:**
  a. The observer
  b. The dates and times of each observation session

- **Operational definition of target behaviors**
  a. Definition is objective, is clear, and discriminates between what is and what is not an instance of the target behavior
  b. Definitions are observable and measurable; they are situation specific and individualized
     I. Target behaviors are defined topographically or functionally

(continued)

PERFORMANCE MONITORING CHECKLIST 9.4.3   *(continued)*

- **Baseline data for target behaviors**
  a. Average level is reported
  b. References to graphs are included
  c. Graphs are present and axes are correctly labeled (based on data collection method)
  d. Data are correctly plotted

DESCRIPTIVE ASSESSMENT (DA)

- **Description of DA method (e.g., ABC data, event recording) is technological**

- **Results**
  a. Data are summarized using an appropriate measure (e.g., conditional probabilities for ABC data)
  b. Graphs of results are included and correctly labeled

- **Summary**
  a. Summary statements are relevant to the indirect assessment and the data collected in the DA
  b. Hypotheses about function are tentative

FUNCTIONAL ANALYSIS (FA)

The procedures for FA are technological
  a. You can act out the procedure without having any questions about how to do it
  b. Procedure includes a reference to an article that was used as a reference for the assessment

---

If parametric analysis is used, the procedure is technological
  a. You can act out the procedure without having any questions about how to do it
  b. The materials used during the analysis are clearly described
  c. Procedure includes a reference to an article that was used as a reference for the assessment

---

For severe problem behaviors (e.g., self-injury, elopement, aggression), the FA procedure describes how the child's safety was addressed. Also, the assessor indicates that consent was obtained and by whom.

Results of functional analysis (see task analysis for sample)
  - **For each target behavior:**
    a. Reference to the graph is made
    b. Function is stated and matches the results shown on the graph
    c. Antecedent evoking the TB is stated (antecedent manipulated during the FA)

FA graph
  a. All axes are correctly labeled
  b. Data are correctly plotted
  c. All graphing requirements (see Cooper, Heron, & Heward, 2007) are met (e.g., black data points, conditions are labeled)

(continued)

PERFORMANCE MONITORING CHECKLIST 9.4.3   *(continued)*

SUMMARY OF FUNCTIONAL BEHAVIOR ASSESSMENT

Summary has three separate paragraphs

First paragraph includes the following:
- a. Referral question
- b. School of attendance, grade, and class
- c. Eligibility for special education and current services
- d. Current academic performance
- e. Previous and current interventions and their effectiveness
- f. Medical history

Second paragraph includes the following:
- a. Reported setting events match the setting events included in the report
- b. Reported baseline data match the baseline data included in the report

Third paragraph includes the following:
- **For each behavior**
   - **a.** Antecedents that have most control over the behavior
   - **b.** Consequence that maintains the behavior

RECOMMENDATION

- Recommended antecedent interventions are evidence based

- Recommendations for antecedent interventions do not need to be technological but have to meet the following criteria:
   - a. For each setting event, there is an antecedent intervention that addresses the setting event
   - b. For each problem behavior, there is a recommended antecedent intervention
   - c. All antecedent interventions include specific details (do not have to be technological) that will help in development of the intervention plans
      - i. Procedure for initial implementation
      - ii. Use of prompts (if needed)
      - iii. How to fade in and out the antecedent stimulus (criteria for fading)

- Recommended consequence interventions are evidence based

- Consequence-based interventions do not need to be technological but have to meet the following criteria:
   - a. For each problem behavior, there is a recommend function based on consequence-based intervention
   - b. The least intrusive intervention is recommended
   - c. If recommending punishment strategies (time out or response cost):
      - i. There is a statement as to why the assessor recommends a more restrictive intervention (e.g., research evidence that the intervention is most effective with the presenting problem or evidence that evidence-based, less-restrictive interventions were used but were ineffective)
      - ii. Punishment procedures are combined with reinforcement procedures (i.e., research-based interventions that combine punishment strategies with reinforcement procedures)

(continued)

PERFORMANCE MONITORING CHECKLIST 9.4.3 *(continued)*

---

   d. All consequence-based interventions must include specific details that will help in development of the intervention plans
     i. The initial schedule of reinforcement (based on the baseline data)
     ii. Specific items or actions to be used as possible reinforcers (from preference assessment)
     iii. Use of prompts
     iv. When to thin the schedule of reinforcement

Data collections and analysis
   a. How often data should be collected
   b. Data collection forms (include a sample in the Appendix)
   c. Person responsible for data entry and analysis
   d. Clear criterion for review of effectiveness of the plan is set

---

FAI, Functional Assessment Inventory; FAST, Functional Assessment Screening Tool; MAS, Motivation Assessment Scale; QABF, Questions About Behavior Function.

Additional Resources to Consider

- Association for Science in Autism Treatment (ASAT) evaluates research studies and provides summary reports that are digestible by families and practitioners. Go to www.asatonline.org > Treatment > Autism Treatments: Descriptions and Research Summaries > Summaries of Scientific Research on Interventions on Autism

- The National Autism Center developed the Scientific Merit Rating Scale (SMRS) in its National Standards Report (2009, 2015) as well as the Strength of Evidence Classification System, with a four-point format (Established, Emerging, Unestablished, and Ineffective/Harmful) for interpretation of outcomes. Access the report at www.nationalautismcenter.org/national-standards-project/phase-2

Bibliography

Bailey, J., & Burch, M. (2002). *Research methods in applied behavior analysis.* Thousand Oaks, CA: Sage.

Behavior Analyst Certification Board. (2010). Guidelines for responsible conduct for behavior analysts. Retrieved from http://www.bacb. com/index.php?page=57

Carr, J. E., & Briggs, A. M. (2010). Strategies for making regular contact with the scholarly literature. *Behavior Analysis in Practice, 3,* 13–18. doi:10.1007/BF033

Cochrane Library. (n.d.). Cochrane reviews. Retrieved from https://www.cochranelibrary.com/cdsr/reviews

Cooper, J. O., Heron, T. E., & Heward, W. L. (2007). *Applied behavior analysis* (2nd ed.). Upper Saddle River, NJ: Pearson.

Dubuque, E. M. (2011). Automating academic literature searches with RSS feeds and Google reader. *Behavior Analysis in Practice, 4,* 63–69. doi:10.1007/BF033

Gillis, J. M., & Carr, J. E. (2014). Keeping current with the applied behavior-analytic literature in developmental disabilities: Noteworthy articles for the practicing behavior analyst. *Behavior Analysis in Practice, 7*, 10–14. doi:10.1007/s4061

Normand, M. P. (2008). Science, skepticism, and applied behavior analysis. *Behavior Analysis in Practice, 1*(2), 42–49. doi:10.1007/BF03391727

Parsons, M. B., & Reid, D. H. (2011). Reading groups: A practical means of enhancing professional knowledge among human service practitioners. *Behavior Analysis in Practice, 4*, 53–60. doi:10.1007/BF033

Slocum, T. A., Detrich, R., Wilczynski, S. M., Spencer, T. D., Lewis, T., & Wolfe, K. (2014). The evidence-based practice of applied behavior analysis. *The Behavior Analyst, 37*, 41–56. doi:10.1007/s40614-014-0005-2

Smith, T. (2013). What is evidence-based behavior analysis? *The Behavior Analyst, 36*, 7–33. doi:10.1007/BF03392290

Van Houten, R., Axelrod, S., Bailey, J. S., Favell, J. E., Foxx, R. M., Iwata, B. A., & Lovaas, O. I. (1988). The right to effective behavioral treatment. *Journal of Applied Behavior Analysis, 21*, 381–384. doi:10.1901/jaba.1988.21-381

COMPETENCY 5. DESIGN AND IMPLEMENT SKILL ACQUISITION PROCEDURES BASED ON INITIAL ASSESSMENT

Behavior analysts are experts in learning; the principles and concepts of behavior analysis are firmly rooted in theories of learning. Therefore, as a competent behavior analyst, you must know how to conduct and interpret skill assessments. Furthermore, you need to know how to design and carry out skill acquisition programs based on the assessments to teach clients new skills (e.g., communication, play, socialization) that are then generalized across contexts and maintained over time by natural contingencies. Teaching your clients new skills is very rewarding because the more skills your clients gain in their repertoire, the more they can be free and make personal choices in their lives.

Depending on the context and the population with whom you work, you may find yourself working with individuals with very few basic skills (e.g., children with severe autism and intellectual disability). For example, you may work on gaining eye contact during instruction, tracking objects with eyes, and orienting one's body toward a speaker. You may also teach imitating a model, following through with basic requests from a speaker, and communicating basic needs and wants. Alternatively, you may teach various adaptive living skills (e.g., toileting, grooming, commuting) depending on your client(s)' baseline levels of skills to aid them achieve independence for the first time, or in some cases to regain skills after trauma.

Furthermore, you may teach more complex behaviors to your clients. For example, you may teach various play skills to children to increase their learning opportunities in the natural environment and their likelihood of making and maintaining friends. You may teach conversational and social skills to adolescents or adults to increase their social partners and decrease their self-report of loneliness. Or, you may teach complex independent living skills to adults, such as crossing the street, catching the bus, or meeting an employer's expectations at work. Outside of the area of developmental disabilities, you may be tasked with instructing a group of college students in a university course or training individuals in a business setting to implement new safety procedures correctly. Regardless of the specific type of acquisition program, you likely will engage in all of the following behaviors as a competent behavior analyst. You will explain the purpose of your assessment and your goals for intervention to caregivers and other stakeholders to obtain consent for the assessment, conduct an initial assessment of the skills in your client's repertoire, prioritize the skills you want to teach, target teaching pivotal or high-priority skills, select a teaching method that is suitable for the individual and the skill, program for generalization and maintenance of the skill, and consider the milestones that must be achieved throughout the intervention. You will monitor your skill acquisition goals by reviewing your client's data and making adjustments in the intervention based on the data path trend, level, and variability. You will also observe your direct staff to assure they are following the teaching procedures with sufficient procedural integrity.

To reach competency in this area, you must work on the following component skills: (a) explain the differences between norm- and criteria-referenced assessments and what information you gain from each type of assessment; (b) conduct formal assessments using the Verbal Behavior Milestones Assessment and Placement

DIAGRAM 9.5.1   Competency benchmarks for designing and implementing skill acquisition procedures based on initial assessment.

<u>**Elementary Skills**</u>

■ **Skill Acquisition Assessment**
- Can explain the purpose and benefits of conducting skill acquisition assessments
- Can explain the difference between between norm- and criterion-referenced skill acquisition tests (e.g., Vineland-3 versus VB-MAPP)
- Can label and explain the ranges of standardized test scores (e.g., average = standard scores of 95 to 105 and scaled scores of 9 to 11)
- Can name criterion-and norm-referenced skill acquisition tests (e.g., VB-MAPP and Vineland-3)

■ **Design and Implement Skill Acquisition Procedures**
- Can explain the importance of early intervention
- Can define and give examples of verbal operants, imitation, and social and adaptive skills
- Can define and give examples of stimulus control, generality, and maintenance
- Can list various methods of programing for generality at the onset of intervention (e.g., multiple exemplars, program common stimuli)
- Can define behavior cusps and explain the importance of teaching behavior cusps
- Can list evidence-based behavior-analytic procedures that can be used to teach new skills (e.g., discrete trial teaching, shaping)

<u>**Intermediate Skills**</u>

■ **Skill Acquisition Assessment**
- Can accurately conduct skills assessments using criterion-referenced tests (e.g., VB-MAPP, AFLS)
- Can accurately conduct skills assessments using norm-referenced tests (e.g.,Vineland-3)
- Can score and interpret criterion- and norm-referenced skill assessment results

■ **Design and Implement Skill Acquisition Procedures**
- Can teach attending, verbal and listener behaviors, imitation, discrimination, and academic skills using discrete-trial or naturalistic teaching arrangements
- Can accurately implement different generality methods to ensure generality of targeted skills
- Can probe for generality and maintenance of the skills taught
- Can teach play, social, and adaptive skills using shaping and chaining
- Can accurately implement least to most and most to least prompting methods and prompt fading to ensure independent responding
- Can use precision teaching to build fluency of the acquired skills
- Can use direct instruction to teach academic skills

(continued)

168

DIAGRAM 9.5.1 *(continued)*

<u>Advanced Skills</u>

■ **Skill Acquisition Assessment**
   - Can obtain informed consent to conduct skills assessment
   - Can select and administer the appropriate skills assessment test(s) by taking into consideration client's behaviors, interview, and observation results
   - Can write comprehensive skills assessment reports and recommend treatment goals and intervention procedures based on assessment results
   - Can clearly explain the assessment results, recommended goals, and intervention procedures to caregivers/teachers
   - Can use norm- and criterion-referenced tests

■ **Design and Implement Skill Acquisition Procedures**
   - Can write skill complete acquisition goals (e.g., goal incudes specific context, observable behavior, and clear and measurable criterion)
   - Can use the skills assessment results and develop skill acquisition treatment plans with goals that address the client's needs
   - Can use different methods of programming for generality at the onset of the interventions to support generality of the taught skills
   - Can select appropriate and efficient evidence-based skill acquisition teaching method(s) based on skill assessment results (client's current repertoires), resources, risks, and the best available scientific evidence
   - Can develop and supervise implementation of prompt fading plans to ensure independent responding
   - Can select equivalence-based instruction that will optimize goal achievement (e.g., client can be taught "car" first, and then the same target probed for emergence of symmetry for listener skills [receptive identification]; client is asked to point to "car")
   - Can select appropriate reinforcement schedules to ensure acquisition, generality, and maintenance of the skills
   - Can use BST to teach others how to implement discrete-trial teaching or naturalistic teaching arrangements, shaping, chaining, prompting, and prompt fading procedures

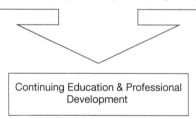

Continuing Education & Professional Development

Program (VB-MAPP) or Assessment of Basic Language and Learning Skills, Revised (ABLLS-R); (c) implement skills acquisition programs to teach verbal behavior, imitation, and discrimination using direct instruction (e.g., discrete trial training [DTT]), precision teaching, and/or natural environment/incidental teaching; (d) develop skills acquisition programs to teach verbal behavior, imitation, and discrimination using direct instruction (e.g., DTT), precision teaching, and/or natural environment/ incidental teaching; (e) implement daily living skills programs based on formal assessment results; (f) develop daily living skills programs based on formal assessment results; (g) implement social and play skills programs based on formal assessment results; and (h) develop social and play skills programs. Diagram 9.5.1 offers some benchmarks to help you gauge your skill development in this competency.

Competency 5. Example Case Scenario for Teaching Component Skill: Using Discrete Trial Training in Skill Acquisition Programming

(1) *Scenario*

    a. You are assigned a new participant for whom the program focuses on skill acquisition programming. Your supervisor has chosen to utilize discrete trial training (DTT) as the teaching methodology for a listener responding stimulus selection (LRSS) and matching to sample (MTS) program.

        i. You are tasked with implementing these programs in the home with the participant.

(2) *Baseline assessment of your skills*

    a. Choose one of the following target lists:

        i. LRSS: three-dimensional objects, field of five objects:

            1. Car (toy)

            2. Cup

            3. Crayon

            4. Cat (toy)

            5. Corn (play food)

        ii. LRSS: two-dimensional objects, field of four objects:

            1. Dog

            2. Bus

            3. Toothbrush

            4. Fork

        iii. MTS: Matching identical three-dimensional objects, field of three objects:

            1. Ball

            2. Block

            3. Doll

        iv. MTS: matching identical two-dimensional objects, field of five objects:

            1. Table

            2. Spoon

            3. Tree

            4. Pencil

            5. Apple

    b. For each set of targets, your supervisor would provide you with the prompts to use.

    c. Your supervisor would play the role of the participant while you implement the chosen program.

    i. Your supervisor would NOT engage in problem behavior in this role-play.

      1. The goal is to assess your implementation of DTT programming, not managing problem behaviors.

   ii. Your supervisor would engage in the following response types:

      1. *Correct response* = participant behavior matches the discriminative stimulus for the program (SD).

        a. Example

          i. SD = "Touch the car"

          ii. Response = participant touches the car

      2. *Incorrect response* = participant behavior does not match the SD delivered.

        a. Example:

          i. SD = "Match" + picture of pen.

          ii. Response = participant places picture of pen anywhere *except* on the picture of the pen in the field of pictures.

            1. Also, participant engages in any response unrelated to the SD delivered.

      3. *No response* = participant does not engage in any response for a period of 5 seconds.

        a. Example:

          i. SD = "Touch the flower."

          ii. Response = participant engages in no response to SD.

            1. Excluded are responses such as breathing and body repositioning.

d. You would be responsible for:

    i. Assembling all required materials

    ii. Setting up the required data sheet

    iii. Delivering the SD

    iv. Determining the response type (correct, incorrect, no response)

    v. Delivering the correct consequence

    vi. Delivering the appropriate prompt

    vii. Data taking

e. You would run a minimum of 10 trials with your supervisor in the role of the participant:

    i. Your supervisor would assess your fidelity of implementation using a performance monitoring checklist (PMC) for DTT.

    ii. If you perform at least 80% of the trials (8/10) at 100% fidelity (all steps done correctly on trial), you will move to the generalization step.

      1. If you fail to meet the listed criteria, you will move to the training step.

(3) *Behavior skills training (BST)*

    a. If you fail to meet the criteria, your supervisor would train you on the procedure using BST.

    b. *Step 1: Instruction*

        i. Your supervisor would provide you with written instructions for the program targets/type chosen in baseline.

        ii. Your supervisor would explain the instructions to you.

        iii. This explanation will likely include:

            1. Materials required

            2. Prompt hierarchy to use

            3. Data collection procedures

            4. General programming procedures

            5. Error correction method

            6. Rationale for program and error correction method chosen

        iv. Your supervisor would also likely provide you with a copy of the PMC being used in evaluating your fidelity.

    c. *Step 2: Modeling*

        i. Your supervisor would model (demonstrate) the program for you.

        ii. The model would cover how an implementer should respond to:

            1. Correct response to SD

            2. Incorrect response to SD

            3. No response to SD

                 a. Your supervisor may categorize no response as a type of incorrect response.

        iii. All steps noted in the instructions will be covered in the model.

    d. *Step 3: Rehearsal*

        i. Your supervisor would serve as the participant as you practice implementing the program.

        ii. Your supervisor would play the role of the participant while you implement the chosen program.

            1. Your supervisor would *NOT* engage in problem behavior in this role-play.

            2. Your supervisor would engage in the following response types:

                 a. Correct response to SD

                 b. Incorrect response to SD

                 c. No response to SD

e. *Step 4: Feedback*

   i. Your supervisor would use the PMC to deliver feedback on your performance.

   ii. Your supervisor would focus on both items done correctly (things to keep) and those done incorrectly (things to improve on).

      1. Your supervisor may deliver the feedback during a trial **or**

      2. Your supervisor may deliver feedback following the completion of a trial

f. *Step 5: Repeat steps 3 and 4*

   i. Your supervisor would continue with rehearsal and feedback until you reach 100% fidelity on three consecutive trials.

(4) *Generalization 1*

a. Once you have met the mastery criteria (100% fidelity on three consecutive trials), your supervisor would have you run 10 trials for a target list/program different from that done in baseline.

b. If you meet the criteria for at least 80% of the trials (8/10) at 100% fidelity (all steps done correctly on trial), you will move to generalization 2.

   i. If you do not meet the criteria, your supervisor would move to the rehearsal/feedback step for this program.

   ii. Once the criteria for feedback rehearsal are met, a new target list would be implemented.

      1. This step would be repeated until the criteria are met.

(5) *Generalization 2*

a. Once you have met the mastery criteria (100% fidelity on 80% of generalization trials), your supervisor would have you run 10 trials with an actual participant.

   i. If you meet the criteria at least for 80% of the trials (8/10) at 100% fidelity (all steps done correctly on trial), you would move to periodic check-ins (to be determined by your supervisor).

   ii. If you fail to meet the criteria, your supervisor would provide feedback in vivo with the participant until it is met in a single 10-trial block.

PERFORMANCE MONITORING CHECKLIST 9.5.1   PMC FOR EVIDENCE DESCRIPTION PRESENTATION

Discrete Trial Training: Simultaneous Method		

Observer:_____   Implementer: _____   Date: _____

Instructions:
1. All items will be scored as either "1" or "0."
2. For trial scoring, any component scored as "0" will result in the entire trial scored as zero.
3. For items 7, 8, and 9, mark "0" for subcomponents that were incorrectly implemented. Marked items will count as zeros toward the overall trial score.

Before Teaching Trials		Score
1	*Gathered necessary materials (e.g., data sheet, pen, stimuli)[1]*	
2	*Selected effective reinforcers (e.g., unsatiated stimuli, ranked high on a preference[1]*	
3	*Identified the essential components of a written skill acquisition plan (e.g., target responses and prompting method)[1&3]*	
4	*Identified method of stimuli presentation (i.e., simultaneous, sequential)[4]*	

During Teaching Trials		Trials				
		1	2	3	4	5
5	*Secured child's attention (e.g., child makes eye contact with therapist or stimili for 1 seconds)[1]*					
6	*Presented correct instruction (in accordance with the written plan)[1]*					
7	Instruction was[2&4] **Concise** (i.e., delivered without distractors and with minimal words)[4]	__ Concise	__Concise	__Concise	__Concise	__Concise
	Neutral (i.e., delieverd with minimal voice modulation)[2]	__Neutral	__Neutral	__Neutral	__Neutral	__Neutral
8	Absent of inadvertent cues[4]: **Eye gaze:** Therapist looked at the client, rather than the stimuli when delivering	__Eye gaze	__Eye gaze	__Eye gaze	__Eye gaze	__Eye gaze
	Physical movements: Therapist minimized change in body posture and positioning following instruction (excluding prompted trials)	__Phys. Mov.	__Phys. Mov.	__Phys. Mov.	__Phys. Mov.	__Phys. Mov.

(continued)

PERFORMANCE MONITORING CHECKLIST 9.5.1 (*continued*)

9	(If applicable) Stimuli were[4]: **Presented equidistant apart Rotated systematically across trials**	__Equidistant __Rotated	__Equidistant __Rotated	__Equidistant __Rotated	__Equidistant __Rotated	__Equidistant __Rotated
	Correct prompt delivered[4] *(Skip if no prompt was used)*					
10	**Prompt Level**[4]: Repeat verbal instruction, partial verbal, full verbal, textual, visual, gestural, model, positional cue, partial physical, full physical, etc.	_____	_____	_____	_____	_____
	If **correct** response					
11	*Reinforcer was delivered*[1]	1	1			
12	*Reinforcer was delivered immediately (within 2 seconds)*[1]	1	1			
13	*Appropriate potency/amount/size of reinforcer*[4]	1	1			
	If **incorrect** response					
14	*Blocked respose and removed materials*[1]	1	1			
	General Criteria					
15	*Begun next trial within 3–5 seconds*[1]	1	1			
16	*Collected data*[1]	1	1			
	Totals	0/1	1/1	/1	/1	/1
	Percent correct (Total trials scored as 1/Total trials)	/5 = _____ x 100 = _____ %				

Note.
1. Components on DTTEF (Fazzio et al., 2007).
2. Components found on PMTs outside of DTTEF.
3. BACB Registered Behavior Technician Task List.
4. Components absent from DTT training literature.

Competency 5. Possible Group Supervision Activities

The aforementioned case scenario may be utilized as part of a group supervision meeting to target the skills for this competency. Your supervisor may assign to your group graphical representations of client data along with the procedures and have you utilize the information therein to determine the next steps for a specific client. Another possible group activity would be the creation of performance monitoring checklists (PMCs) for a skill acquisition procedure, training another group member on that procedure, and then taking fidelity data. In this scenario, each group member may be assigned a different skill acquisition area (i.e., daily living skills, social skills, verbal skills, listener skills, academic skills) and procedure to train the group on during the meeting. Finally, your supervisor may assign you to review and edit a skill acquisition procedure. This process would target the identification of specific errors and could then be expanded to the review of group written procedures for skill acquisition.

Competency 5. Specific Task Lists for the Component Skills and Additional Resources

In addition to the case scenario and suggestions for group supervision activities, we outline the tasks you need to accomplish to meet each component skill in Competency 5. Competency Task Lists 9.5.1 to 9.5.7 are intended to help you initiate the tasks and select activities to complete with your supervisor. Again, we encourage you to hold conversations with your supervisor(s) to determine which of these tasks, or any additional tasks, are appropriate for you at each stage of your supervision experience.

COMPETENCY TASK LIST 9.5.1   CONSIDER INITIATING AND COMPLETING THE FOLLOWING TASKS FOR THE COMPONENT SKILL OF CONDUCTING FORMAL ASSESSMENT USING VB-MAPP OR ABLLS-R, WITH YOUR SUPERVISOR

	(Mark done or record benchmark)
I. Review BACB ethical guidelines 1.0, 2.0, and 3.0 and discuss with supervisor	
A. Ethical practices in conducting behavior assessments	
B. Discuss with supervisor the ethical practices and the importance of practicing within one's limits of professional competence, and obtaining consultation, supervision, or training, or making referrals as necessary	
II. Conduct formal assessment	
A. Obtain informed consent for assessment	
B. Administer the entire VB-MAPP or ABLLS-R	
C. Develop a performance monitoring form to evaluate the administration of VB-MAPP or ABLLS-R and have the supervisor use the form to give you feedback on administration of VB-MAPP or ABLLS-R i. Include the feedback in this tab	
D. Score and graph completed VB-MAPP or ABLLS-R	
E. Discuss the results with the supervisor	
III. Write assessment report	
A. The skills assessment report should include the following components: • Reason for referral (see scoring rubric) • Background information • Results for each area assessed • Summary • Recommendations	
B. Include the final product in this tab	

COMPETENCY TASK LIST 9.5.2   CONSIDER INITIATING AND COMPLETING THE FOLLOWING TASKS FOR THE COMPONENT SKILL OF IMPLEMENTING SKILLS ACQUISITION PROGRAMS TO TEACH VERBAL BEHAVIOR, IMITATION, AND DISCRIMINATION USING DIRECT INSTRUCTION (E.G., DTT), PRECISION TEACHING, AND/OR NATURAL ENVIRONMENT/INCIDENTAL TEACHING, WITH YOUR SUPERVISOR

	(Mark done or record benchmark)
I. Review BACB ethical guidelines	
A. Before beginning to work with your first client (as an implementer) and before developing your first treatment plan, review the ethical guidelines for your work with the client **For example, if you are implementing or developing behavior change plans that are not part of a research program, you would review:** i. 1.0 Responsible Conduct of a Behavior Analyst ii. 2.0 The Behavior Analyst's Responsibility to Clients iii. 3.0 Assessing Behavior iv. 4.0 The Behavior Analyst and the Individual Behavior Change Program v. 6.0 The Behavior Analyst and the Workplace vi. 8.0 The Behavior Analyst's Responsibility to Colleagues	
II. Implement skill acquisition programs to teach verbal behavior	
A. Implement the listed skill acquisition programs and obtain at least 90% implementation fidelity on at least two consecutive performance monitoring checklists for each program • Include the completed performance checklists for each program in this tab	
• Use the dimensions of applied behavior analysis (Baer, Wolf, & Risley, 1968) to evaluate whether the interventions you are asked to implement are behavior analytic in nature	

Skill acquisition program   **Teaching method**
                                               • Discrete Trial Training (DTT)
                                             • Natural Environment Teaching/ Incidental Teaching (NET/IT)
                                             • Precision Teaching (PT) Other: _____ (___)	

(continued)

COMPETENCY TASK LIST 9.5.2 *(continued)*

Echoic training		
Mand training with various topographies (at least two)		
Speech		
Pictures		
ASL		
Augmentative devices		
Tact training		
Actions		
Objects		
Color and shapes		
Using prepositions		
Using adjectives		
Using adverbs		
Using complete sentences		
Other		
Other		
Other		
Intraverbal training		
What questions		
When questions		
Where questions		
Who questions		
Answering questions after reading a story		
Other		
Other		
Other		
Listener training		
Attending to speaker		
Following one-component actions		

(continued)

COMPETENCY TASK LIST 9.5.2 *(continued)*

Following two-component actions		
Selecting a stimulus in an array		
Selecting stimuli based on function, feature, and class		
Following instructions involving prepositions		
Discriminating between different adjectives		
Following two- to three-step directions		
Other		
Other		
III. Implement skill acquisition programs to teach imitation and equivalence		
Motor imitation training		
Gross motor actions (e.g., jumping)		
Fine motor actions (e.g., wiggle fingers)		
Functional skills (e.g., using spoon)		
Other		
Other		
Other		
Stimulus equivalence and discrimination training		
Matching to sample		
Sorting		
Completing patterns and sequences		
Other		
Other		
Other		

(continued)

COMPETENCY TASK LIST 9.5.2 *(continued)*

IV. Use behavior change elements in skill acquisition programs

Use pairing procedures to establish new conditioned reinforcers

---

Use appropriate schedules of reinforcement

Initial implementation phase

Thinning

Maintenance

Use of prompts and prompt fading

Use errorless learning and prompt fading

Use of differential reinforcement

COMPETENCY TASK LIST 9.5.3   CONSIDER INITIATING AND COMPLETING THE FOLLOWING TASKS FOR THE COMPONENT SKILL OF DESIGNING SKILLS ACQUISITION PROGRAMS TO TEACH VERBAL BEHAVIOR, IMITATION, AND DISCRIMINATION USING DIRECT INSTRUCTION (E.G., DTT), PRECISION TEACHING, AND/OR NATURAL ENVIRONMENT/INCIDENTAL TEACHING, WITH YOUR SUPERVISOR

	(Mark done or record benchmark)
I. Review BACB ethical guidelines	
A. Before beginning to work with your first client (as an implementer) and before developing your first treatment plan, review the following ethical guidelines and discuss with supervisor 　i. 1.0 Responsible Conduct of a Behavior Analyst 　ii. 2.0 The Behavior Analyst's Responsibility to Clients 　iii. 4.0 The Behavior Analyst and the Individual Behavior Change Program 　iv. 6.0 The Behavior Analyst and the Workplace 　v. 8.0 The Behavior Analyst's Responsibility to Colleagues 　vi. 9.0 The Behavior Analyst's Ethical Responsibility to Society 　vii. 10.0 The Behavior Analyst and Research	
II. Develop skill acquisition programs to teach verbal behavior	
A. Select intervention strategies based on assessment results and the best available scientific evidence 　i. Consult with supervisor and offer rational and supporting articles for selected intervention strategies	
B. Discuss with supervisor and take into account: 　i. Client's preferences and current repertoires 　ii. Environmental and resource constraints 　iii. Social validity of the intervention **C.** Develop technological and conceptually systematic skill acquisition programs for the following skills: 　i. State goals in observable and measurable terms 　ii. Program for stimulus and response generalization and maintenance of the skills **D.** Have the supervisor use written program performance checklists to evaluate whether the written programs are behavior analytic in nature and give feedback 　i. Make needed changes and place the final product and the feedback in this tab	

(continued)

COMPETENCY TASK LIST 9.5.3 *(continued)*

	(Mark done or record benchmark)
E. Use Behavior Skills Training to train the staff on how to implement the plans i. Develop and use performance monitoring checklists to monitor procedural integrity during implementation of treatment plans	
F. Evaluate the effectiveness of interventions through ongoing data collection and analysis and make data-based decisions	

BACB task list number   **Skill acquisition Programs (see items in implementing section for full description)**   **Teaching method**
  • Discrete Trial Training (DTT)
  • Natural Environment Teaching/Incidental Teaching (NET/IT)
  • Precision Teaching (PT)
  • Other:_____
  (___)	

COMPETENCY TASK LIST 9.5.4 CONSIDER INITIATING AND COMPLETING THE FOLLOWING TASKS FOR THE COMPONENT SKILL OF IMPLEMENTING DAILY LIVING SKILLS PROGRAMS BASED ON FORMAL ASSESSMENT RESULTS, WITH YOUR SUPERVISOR

	(Mark done or record benchmark)
I. Review BACB ethical guidelines	
A. Before beginning to work with your first client (as an implementer) and before developing your first treatment plan, review the following ethical guidelines and discuss with supervisor i. Responsible Conduct of a Behavior Analyst ii. The Behavior Analyst's Responsibility to Clients iii. The Behavior Analyst and the Individual Behavior Change Program iv. The Behavior Analyst and the Workplace v. The Behavior Analyst's Responsibility to Colleagues vi. The Behavior Analyst's Ethical Responsibility to Society vii. The Behavior Analyst and Research	
II. Implement skill acquisition programs to teach daily living skills	
A. Implement the listed skill acquisition programs and obtain at least 90% implementation fidelity on at least two consecutive performance monitoring checklists for each program • Include the completed performance checklists for each program in this tab	
B. Use the dimensions of applied behavior analysis (Baer et al., 1968) to evaluate whether interventions you are asked to implement are behavior analytic in nature	
Daily living skills Acquisition program **Chaining method** • Forward • Backward • Total task	
Dressing	
Clothing selection appropriate for weather	
Putting on and removing shirts, pants, socks	
Putting on and removing jackets	
Putting on and removing shoes	
Other	
Other	
Other	
Toileting	

(continued)

COMPETENCY TASK LIST 9.5.4 (continued)

	(Mark done or record benchmark)
Personal hygiene	
Brushing teeth	
Washing hands and face	
Showering	
Combing hair	
Eating and drinking	
Using utensils	
Drinking from a cup	
Meal preparation	
Use of kitchen appliances	
Other	
Other	
Other	
Household chores	
Cleaning	
Making bed	
Setting and cleaning table	
Washing dishes	
Feeding animals	
Other	
Other	
Other	
Laundry	
Washing and drying clothes	
Folding and putting away washed clothing	
Other	
Other	
Safety awareness	
Abduction-prevention	
Crossing streets	
Safety/danger signs and signals	

(continued)

COMPETENCY TASK LIST 9.5.4   *(continued)*

	(Mark done or record benchmark)
First aid skills	
Using public transportation	
Money management	
Employment skills	
III. Use behavior change elements in skill acquisition programs	
Use pairing procedures to establish new conditioned reinforcers	
Use appropriate schedules of reinforcement	
Initial implementation phase	
Thinning	
Maintenance	
Use prompts and prompt fading	
Use errorless learning and prompt fading	
Use of differential reinforcements	

COMPETENCY TASK LIST 9.5.5   CONSIDER INITIATING AND COMPLETING THE FOLLOWING TASKS FOR THE COMPONENT SKILL OF DESIGNING DAILY LIVING SKILLS PROGRAMS BASED ON FORMAL ASSESSMENT RESULTS, WITH YOUR SUPERVISOR

	(Mark done or record benchmark)
I. Review BACB ethical guidelines	

A. Before beginning to work with your first client (as an implementer) and before developing your first treatment plan, review the following ethical guidelines and discuss with supervisor
  i. Responsible Conduct of a Behavior Analyst
  ii. The Behavior Analyst's Responsibility to Clients
  iii. The Behavior Analyst and the Individual Behavior Change Program
  iv. The Behavior Analyst and the Workplace
  v. The Behavior Analyst's Responsibility to Colleagues
  vi. The Behavior Analyst's Ethical Responsibility to Society
  vii. The Behavior Analyst and Research	

(continued)

COMPETENCY TASK LIST 9.5.5 (*continued*)

	(Mark done or record benchmark)
II. Develop skill acquisition programs to teach daily living skills	
A. For each daily living skill listed here develop a task analysis i. Establish a baseline using the task analysis ii. Graph the baseline data using appropriate graphs iii. Discuss with supervisor the assessment results and the graphs iv. Place task analysis with baseline data in this tab	
B. Select intervention strategies based on task analysis results and the best available scientific evidence i. Consult with supervisor and offer rational and supporting articles for your selections	
C. Discuss with supervisor and take into account: i. Client's preferences and current repertoires ii. Environmental and resource constraints iii. Social validity of the intervention **D.** Develop technological and conceptually systematic daily living skill acquisition programs for the skills listed here i. State goals in observable and measurable terms ii. Program for stimulus and response generalization and maintenance of the skills **E.** Have the supervisor use written program performance checklists to evaluate whether the written programs are behavior analytic in nature and give feedback i. Make needed changes and place the final product and the feedback in this tab	
F. Use behavior skills training to train the staff on how to implement the plans i. Develop and use performance monitoring checklists to monitor procedural integrity during implementation of treatment plans	
G. Evaluate the effectiveness of interventions through ongoing data collection and analysis and make data-based decisions	
BACB task list number **Daily living skills Acquisition programs (see items in implementing section for full description)** **Chaining method** • Forward • Backward • Total task	

COMPETENCY TASK LIST 9.5.6   CONSIDER INITIATING AND COMPLETING THE FOLLOWING TASKS FOR THE COMPONENT SKILL OF IMPLEMENTING SOCIAL AND PLAY SKILLS PROGRAMS BASED ON FORMAL ASSESSMENT RESULTS, WITH YOUR SUPERVISOR

	(Mark done or record benchmark)
I. Review BACB ethical guidelines	
A. Before beginning to work with your first client (as an implementer) and before developing your first treatment plan, review the following ethical guidelines and discuss with supervisor i. Responsible Conduct of a Behavior Analyst ii. The Behavior Analyst's Responsibility to Clients iii. The Behavior Analyst and the Individual Behavior Change Program iv. The Behavior Analyst and the Workplace v. The Behavior Analyst's Responsibility to Colleagues vi. The Behavior Analyst's Ethical Responsibility to Society vii. The Behavior Analyst and Research	
II. Implement skill acquisition programs to teach social and play skills	
A. Implement the listed skill acquisition programs and obtain at least 90% implementation fidelity on at least two consecutive performance monitoring checklists for each program i. Include the completed performance checklists for each program in this tab	
B. Use the dimensions of applied behavior analysis (Baer et al., 1968) to evaluate whether interventions you are asked to implement are behavior-analytic in nature	
Social and play skills Acquisition program	**Chaining method** • Forward • Backward • Total task	
Independent play skills	
Functional play	
Creative play	
Independent indoor play	
Independent outdoor play	

(continued)

COMPETENCY TASK LIST 9.5.6   (continued)

	(Mark done or record benchmark)
Other	
Other	
Other	
Social play	
Sharing toys	
Turn taking	
Initiating and sustaining indoor and outdoor play activities with peers	
Joining in an ongoing indoor or outdoor play activity	
Pretend play with peers	
Team sports and sportsmanship	
Other	
Other	
Other	
Other	
Social interactions	
Initiating and maintaining eye contact	
Greetings	
Beginning and ending intraverbal exchanges	
Intraverbal behavior with others on non-reinforcing topics	
Giving and accepting compliments	
Discriminating and tacting feelings of others	
Offering and receiving help	
Negotiations	
Perspective taking	
Joint attention	
Other	
Other	

(continued)

COMPETENCY TASK LIST 9.5.6   *(continued)*

	(Mark done or record benchmark)
Other	

III. Program behavior change elements in skill acquisition programs

Program pairing procedures to establish new conditioned reinforcers	
Program appropriate schedules of reinforcement	
Initial implementation phase	
Thinning	
Maintenance	
Program use of prompts and prompt fading	
Program errorless learning and prompt fading	
Program use of differential reinforcements	

COMPETENCY TASK LIST 9.5.7   CONSIDER INITIATING AND COMPLETING THE FOLLOWING TASKS FOR THE COMPONENT SKILL OF DESIGNING SOCIAL AND PLAY SKILLS PROGRAMS BASED ON FORMAL ASSESSMENT RESULTS, WITH YOUR SUPERVISOR

	(Mark done or record benchmark)

I. Review BACB ethical guidelines

A. Before beginning to work with your first client (as an implementer) and before developing your first treatment plan, review the following ethical guidelines and discuss with supervisor
  i.   Responsible Conduct of a Behavior Analyst
  ii. The Behavior Analyst's Responsibility to Clients
  iii. The Behavior Analyst and the Individual Behavior Change Program
  iv. The Behavior Analyst and the Workplace
  v.   The Behavior Analyst's Responsibility to Colleagues
  vi. The Behavior Analyst's Ethical Responsibility to Society
  vii. The Behavior Analyst and Research	

(continued)

COMPETENCY TASK LIST 9.5.7   (*continued*)

	(Mark done or record benchmark)
II. Develop skill acquisition programs to teach daily living skills	
A. For each social and play skill listed here, develop a task analysis i. Establish a baseline using the task analysis ii. Graph the baseline data using appropriate graphs iii. Discuss with supervisor the assessment results and the graphs iv. Place task analysis with baseline data in this tab	
B. Select intervention strategies based on task analysis results and the best available scientific evidence i. Consult with supervisor and offer rational and supporting articles for your selections	
C. Discuss with supervisor and take into account: i. Client's preferences and current repertoires ii. Environmental and resource constraints iii. Social validity of the intervention **D.** Develop technological and conceptually systematic daily living skill acquisition programs for skills listed here i. State goals in observable and measurable terms ii. Program for stimulus and response generalization and maintenance of the skills **E.** Have the supervisor use written program performance checklists to evaluate whether the written programs are behavior-analytic in nature and give feedback i. Make needed changes and place the final product and the feedback in this tab	
F. Use behavior skills training to train the staff on how to implement the plans i. Develop and use performance monitoring checklists to monitor procedural integrity during implementation of treatment plans	
G. Evaluate the effectiveness of interventions through ongoing data collection and analysis and make data-based decisions	

BACB   **Social and play skills**
  task   **Acquisition program (see items**
  list   **in implementing section for full**
  number **description)**   **Chaining method**
                    • Forward
                    • Backward
                    • Total task	

Additional Resources to Consider

Ala'i-Rosales, S., & Zeug, N. (2010). Three important things to consider when starting intervention for a child diagnosed with autism. *Behavior Analysis in Practice, 3,* 54–55. doi:10.1007/BF03391766

Albert, K. M., Carbone, V. J., Murray, D. D., Hagerty, M., & Sweeney-Kerwin, E. J. (2012). Increasing the mand repertoire of children with autism through the use of an interrupted chain procedure. *Behavior Analysis in Practice, 5*(2), 65–76. doi:10.1007/BF033

Baer, D. M., Wolf, M. M., & Risley, T. R. (1968). Some current dimensions of applied behavior analysis. *Journal of Applied Behavior Analysis, 1,* 91–97.

Barnes, C. S., Mellor, J. R., & Rehfeldt, R. A. (2014). Implementing the verbal behavior milestones assessment and placement program (VB-MAPP): Teaching assessment techniques. *The Analysis of Verbal Behavior, 30,* 36–47. doi:10.1007/s40616-013-0004-5

Bosch, S., & Fuqua, R.W. (2001). Behavioral cusps: A model for selecting target behaviors. *Journal of Applied Behavior Analysis, 34,* 123–125. doi:10.1901/jaba.2001.34-123

Carroll, R. A., Kodak, T., & Fisher, W. W. (2013). An evaluation of programmed treatment-integrity failures during discrete-trial instruction. *Journal of Applied Behavior Analysis, 46,* 379–394. doi:10.1002/jaba.49

Dixon, M. R., Belisle, J., Stanley, C., Rowsey, K., Daar, J. H., & Szekely, S. (2015). Toward a behavior analysis of complex language for children with autism: Evaluating the relationship between PEAK and the VB-MAPP. *Journal of Developmental and Physical Disabilities, 27,* 223–233. doi:10.1007/s1088

Esch, J. W., Esch, B. E., & Love, J. R. (2009). Increasing vocal variability in children with autism using a lag schedule of reinforcement. *The Analysis of Verbal behavior, 25,* 73–78. doi:10.1007/BF033

Geiger, K. B., Carr, J. E., LeBlanc, L. A., Hanney, N. M., Polick, A. S., & Heinicke, M. R. (2012). Teaching receptive discriminations to children with autism: A comparison of traditional and embedded discrete trial teaching. *Behavior Analysis in Practice, 5,* 49–59. doi:10.1007/BF033

Grow, L., & LeBlanc, L. (2013). Teaching receptive language skills: Recommendations for instructors. *Behavior Analysis in Practice, 6,* 56–75. doi:10.1007/BF03391791

Grow, L. L., Carr, J. E., Kodak, T., Jostad, C. M., & Kisamore, A. N. (2011). A comparison of methods for teaching auditory visual conditional discriminations to children diagnosed with autism spectrum disorders. *Journal of Applied Behavior Analysis, 44,* 475–498. doi:10.1901/jaba.2011.44-475

Hall, G., & Sundberg, M. L. (1987). Teaching mands by manipulating conditioned establishing operations. *Analysis of Verbal Behavior, 5,* 41–53. doi:10.1007/BF033

Hanley G. P., Heal, N. A., Ingvarsson, E. T., & Tiger, J. H. (2007). Evaluation of a classwide teaching program for developing preschool life skills. *Journal of Applied Behavior Analysis, 40,* 277–300. doi:10.1901/jaba.2007.57-06

Hood, S. A., Luczynski, K. C., & Mitteer, D. R. (2017), Toward meaningful outcomes in teaching conversation and greeting skills with individuals with autism spectrum disorder. *Journal of Applied Behavior Analysis, 50,* 459–486. doi:10.1002/jaba.388

Libby, M. E., Weiss, J. S., & Ahearn, W. H. (2008). A comparison of most-to-least and least-to-most prompting on the acquisition of solitary play skills. *Behavior Analysis in Practice, 1,* 37–43. doi:10.1007/BF033

Lovaas, O. I. (2003). *Teaching individuals with developmental delays: Basic intervention techniques.* Austin, TX: Pro-Ed.

McGee, G. G., Almeida, M. C., Sulzer-Azaroff, B., & Feldman, R. S. (1992). Promoting reciprocal interactions via peer incidental teaching. *Journal of Applied Behavior Analysis, 25,* 117–126. doi:10.1901/jaba.1992.25-117

Petursdottir, A. I., & Carr, J. E. (2011). A review of recommendations for sequencing receptive and expressive language instruction. *Journal of Applied Behavior Analysis, 44,* 859–876. doi:10.1901/jaba.2011.44-859

Rosales, R., & Rehfeldt, R. (2007). Contriving transitive conditioned establishing operations to establish derived manding skills in adults with severe developmental disabilities. *Journal of Applied Behavior Analysis, 40,* 105–121. doi:10.1901/jaba.2007.117-05

Rosales-Ruiz, J., & Baer, D. M. (1997). Behavioral cusps: A developmental and pragmatic concept for behavior analysis. *Journal of Applied Behavior Analysis, 30,* 533–544. doi:10.1901/jaba.1997.30-533

Smith, T., Mruzek, D. W., Wheat, L. A., & Hughes, C. (2006). Error correction in discrimination training for children with Autism. *Behavioral Interventions, 21,* 245–263. doi:10.1002/bin.223

Sundberg, M. L. (2008). *Verbal behavior milestones assessment and placement program.* Concord, CA: AVB.

Sundberg, M. L., & Michael, J. (2001). The benefits of Skinner's analysis of verbal behavior for children with autism. *Behavior Modification, 25,* 698–724. doi:10.1177/0145445501255003

Sundberg, M. L., & Partington, J. W. (1998). *Teaching language to children with autism or other developmental disabilities.* Pleasant Hill, CA: Behavior Analysts, Inc.

Taylor, B. A., & Fisher, J. (2010). Three important things to consider when starting intervention for a child diagnosed with autism. *Behavior Analysis in Practice, 3,* 52–53. doi:10.1007/BF03391765

Vets, T. L., & Green, G. (2010). Three important things to consider when starting intervention for a child diagnosed with autism. *Behavior Analysis in Practice, 3,* 56–57. doi:10.1007/BF03391767

Weiss, M. J., & Zane, T. (2010). Three important things to consider when starting intervention for a child diagnosed with autism. *Behavior Analysis in Practice, 3,* 58–60. doi:10.1007/BF03391767

White, P. J., O'Reilly, M., Streusand, W., Levine, A., Sigafoos, J., Lancioni, G., . . . Aguilar, J. (2011). Best practices for teaching joint attention: A systematic review of the intervention literature. *Research in Autism Spectrum Disorders, 5,* 1283–1295. doi:10.1016/j.rasd.2011.02.003

COMPETENCY 6. DESIGN AND IMPLEMENT BEHAVIOR REDUCTION PROCEDURES

Although behavior analysts work with all types of individuals, with people of all ages across the life span, and with various behaviors, your skills in reducing problem behavior makes you, and the profession of behavior analysis, most visible and at the forefront of human care services. Reducing problem behaviors, such as self-injury and aggression, is socially significant because such behaviors can lead to long-term physical damage for the individual and even death! Aggression and self-injurious behaviors harm more than the individual engaging in them; such problem behaviors are often highly damaging for family members and the community at large.

Furthermore, other problem behaviors, such as stereotypy, make it more likely that the individual engaging in them will access punishers (e.g., reprimands, stares, restraint) in his or her natural environment. Stereotypy also impedes the individual's learning curve, such that engaging in stereotypy often interrupts learning. When individuals engage in stereotypy, they are less likely to attend to other reinforcers. Therefore, individuals who engage in high rates of stereotypy often have a narrow menu of reinforcers and rarely engage with social partners. For some of these reasons, stereotypy has perplexed all practitioners in human care services (e.g., medicine, marriage and family therapy, clinical psychology) for many years. Lastly, problem behavior emitted in a group setting can interrupt others and can have ripple effects sometimes such that the whole group engages in problem behaviors. Therefore, school systems have begun to look to behavior analysts for school-wide behavior plans and classroom behavior management techniques.

Despite the intensity and topography of the problem behavior, behavioral strategies have been effective in mitigating them. Furthermore, behavior analysts never attribute the cause of the problem behavior to the individuals' diagnosis, choices, or family members. As a behavior analyst, your fundamental belief that behavior is a function of its circumstances makes you uniquely qualified to reduce your client(s) problem behaviors without personal judgment and by changing the circumstances surrounding behavior. Just as with skill acquisition, with problem behavior you must begin by conducting a comprehensive functional behavior assessment to identify the environmental sources that maintain or increase the problem behavior, or the function of the problem behavior. Once you have determined the function, you will need to develop a function- and evidence-based behavioral intervention to reduce the problem behavior. You will also need to give much consideration to the natural environment surrounding the problem behavior to assure that your intervention effects last. For this competency, we identify four component skills you must learn: (a) antecedent-based interventions, (b) consequent-based interventions, (c) group contingencies, and (d) self-management strategies. Diagram 9.6.1 provides some benchmarks to help you gauge your skill development in this competency.

DIAGRAM 9.6.1 Competency benchmarks for designing and implementing behavior reduction procedures based on initial assessment.

Elementary Skills

- Can define and give examples of reinforcement, punishment, and extinction
- Can define and give examples of response class
- Can define matching law
- Can define and give examples of differential reinforcement
- Can define and give examples of discriminative stimulus and motivating operations
- Can discriminate between discriminative stimulus and motivating operations
- Can define and give examples of simple and compound schedules of reinforcement (including time based)
- Can define and give examples of rule-governed behaviors
- Can give examples of unwanted effects of using punishment and extinction

Intermediate Skills

- Can implement procedures accurately to strengthen behavior (e.g., DRI, DRA, DNRA/I, FCT) with and without extinction
- Can implement procedures accurately to weaken behavior (e.g., NCR, high-probability requests, time out, response cost, overcorrection)
- Can implement token exchange systems accurately
- Can implement behavior contracts and group contingencies accurately
- Can probe for generality and maintenance of socially appropriate behaviors

Advanced Skills

- Can write behavior reduction and alternative behavior goals (e.g., goal includes specific context, observable behavior, and clear and measurable criterion)
- Can select appropriate and efficient evidence-based procedures based on assessment results, the best available evidence, and the available resources and risks
- Can develop technological treatment plans that incorporate antecedent and consequent-based procedures to address problem and socially acceptable alternative behaviors
- Can select appropriate schedules of reinforcement/punishment to ensure of strengthening the alternative behaviors and of weakening the problem behaviors
- Can select appropriate schedules of reinforcement to support generality and maintenance of the alternative behaviors
- Can explain the treatment plans to caregivers/teachers using nontechnical language
- Can use BST to teach others how to implement procedures to strengthen and weaken behaviors

Continuing Education & Professional
Development

Competency 6. Example Case Scenario for Teaching Component Skill: Writing Behavior Reduction Plans

(1) *Scenario*

    a. You have been assigned to write a behavior reduction procedure for a participant. This participant engages in attention-maintained self-injurious behavior. The topography of this self-injurious behavior is striking his forehead with the heel of his hand. As part of your assignment, your supervisor requests that you do the following:

        i. Gather baseline data on the target behavior

        ii. Research evidence-based interventions

        iii. Write an intervention to reduce the occurrence of the target behavior to be implemented by the clinical team

(2) *Baseline assessment of your skills*

    a. Your supervisor would provide you with a hypothetical client scenario (similar to that listed in 1) and you would write a behavior reduction plan.

    b. Your supervisor would provide feedback using a performance monitoring tool (PMT) for evaluating behavior reduction plans.

        i. If you reach the mastery criteria (meet a minimum of 80% of steps on the PMT), you would move to the generalization component.

        ii. If you do not reach the mastery criteria, you would proceed to the training process.

(3) *Behavior Skills Training (BST)*

    a. Your supervisor would provide you with a copy of the PMT used in your evaluation.

    b. Your supervisor would give you a behavior reduction plan (written by another individual) seeded with specific errors.

        i. You would provide feedback on the provided behavior reduction plan using the PMT.

        ii. Your supervisor would review your feedback on this task and deliver feedback on any errors that you missed.

    c. Once you have reached the mastery criteria with this task (criteria to be determined by your supervisor), your supervisor would model the process of writing a behavior intervention.

    d. Your supervisor would provide you with additional case scenarios for you to write behavior interventions.

        i. You would be evaluated using the same PMT and criteria as done at the baseline assessment of your skills.

        ii. You will move to the generalization phase after meeting 80% of the PMT on two behavior reduction plans.

(4) *Generalization*

   a. Your supervisor would provide you with a client opportunity to write a behavior plan.

   b. This means that you would be responsible for the behavior plan from assessment through decision making about the procedure's effectiveness.

PERFORMANCE MONITORING TOOL 9.6.1   PMT FOR BEHAVIOR REDUCTION PLAN

Behavior Reduction Plan PMT			
Date			
(1) All background information is correct (score yes if 100% correct)			
(a) Participant name			
(b) Participant identification number (if applicable)			
(c) Date intervention introduced			
(d) Name of supervising BCBA			
(2) Behavior reduction goal is present and appropriate			
(a) Written in observable terms			
(b) Written in measurable terms			
(c) Contains a date to be met (e.g., in 6 months, by January 2019)			
(d) Contains participant name			
(e) Contains criteria for goal being met			
(3) Procedure for taking baseline measurement of problem behavior or summary of baseline data is presented			
(4) Function of the behavior is noted in plan			
(5) References for the plan are presented			
(6) References are presented in APA format			
(7) Data collection method is presented in plan			
(8) Data collection matches both baseline measure and goal measure			
(9) Behavior plan matches function presented in assessment information			
(10) Specific behaviors are operationally defined correctly			
(a) Technological (passes stranger rule)			
(b) Observable (passes Dead Man's test)			
(c) Measurable (includes a measurable dimension of behavior)			

(continued)

PERFORMANCE MONITORING TOOL 9.6.1   *(continued)*

Behavior Reduction Plan PMT			
(d) Parsimonious (behaviors are separated as appropriate)			
(e) Objective (no mentalistic language used)			
(11) Behavior reduction procedures are conceptually systematic			
(12) Behavior reduction procedures are written in clear and concise language			
(13) Procedures describe typical antecedent events associated with the problem behaviors targeted			
(14) Procedures describe how to proceed in the event problem behaviors occur			
(15) Plan contains criteria for fading plan			
(16) Plan contains description of fading plan			
(17) If applicable, plan contains safety procedures for participant and interventionist			
(18) Plan contains reinforcement procedure			
(19) Plan contains parent training component			
(20) Plan contains all required steps to implement the procedure			
Total Yes/			

APA, American Psychological Association; BCBA, Board Certified Behavior Analyst; PMT, performance monitoring tool.

Competency 6. Possible Group Supervision Activities

The group activities for behavior reduction procedures will bear a strong resemblance to those presented in the skill acquisition competency due to the similarity of process from start to finish. The case scenario presented earlier may be utilized as part of a group supervision meeting to target the skills for this competency. Your supervisor may also assign your group graphical representations of client data along with the current procedures and have you utilize the information therein to determine the next steps for a specific client and his or her intervention. Another possible group activity would be the creation of performance monitoring checklists (PMCs) for a specific behavior reduction procedure for a problem behavior, training another group member on that procedure, and then gathering fidelity data. In this scenario, each group member may be assigned a single problem behavior (e.g., vocal stereotypy, self-injury, elopement) and be required to determine the intervention to utilize for that behavior. In some cases, the intervention choices will vary across individuals, necessitating an in-depth discussion of why that intervention was chosen in this particular instance. Lastly, your supervisor may assign you to review and edit a behavior reduction procedure. This process would target the identification of specific errors and could then be expanded to the review of group written procedures for behavior reduction.

Competency 6. Specific Task Lists for the Component Skills and Additional Resources

In addition to the case scenario and suggestions for group supervision activities, we outline the tasks you need to accomplish to meet each component skill in Competency 6. Competency Task Lists 9.6.1 to 9.6.8 are intended to help you initiate tasks and select activities to complete with your supervisor. Again, we encourage you to hold conversations with your supervisor(s) to determine which of these tasks, or any additional tasks, are appropriate for you at each stage of your supervision experience.

COMPETENCY TASK LIST 9.6.1 CONSIDER INITIATING AND COMPLETING THE FOLLOWING TASKS FOR THE COMPONENT SKILL OF IMPLEMENT ANTECEDENT-BASED INTERVENTIONS

	(Mark done or record benchmark)
I. Review BACB ethical guidelines	

A. Before beginning to work with your first client (as an implementer) and before developing your first treatment plan, review the following ethical guidelines and discuss with supervisor
    i.   1.0 Responsible Conduct of a Behavior Analyst
    ii. 2.0 The Behavior Analyst's Responsibility to Clients
    iii. 4.0 The Behavior Analyst and the Individual Behavior Change Program
    iv. 6.0 The Behavior Analyst and the Workplace
    v.   8.0 The Behavior Analyst's Responsibility to Colleagues
    vi. 9.0 The Behavior Analyst's Ethical Responsibility to Society
    vii. 10.0 The Behavior Analyst and Research	

II. Implement antecedent-based interventions	

A. Implement the listed interventions and obtain at least 90% implementation fidelity on at least two consecutive performance monitoring checklists for each program
    B. Include the completed performance checklists for each program in this tab
    C. Use the dimensions of applied behavior analysis (Baer, Wolf, & Risley, 1968) to evaluate whether the interventions you are asked to implement are behavior analytic in nature	

(continued)

COMPETENCY TASK LIST 9.6.1 *(continued)*

	(Mark done or record benchmark)
Intervention	
Identify and make changes to the physical environment (e.g., manipulate discriminative stimuli)	
Use noncontingent reinforcement for behaviors maintained by:	
Attention	
Escape	
Access to tangibles	
Automatic reinforcement	
Use stimulus fading-in (e.g., food blending or for task refusal)	
Use choice making	
Use high-probability request sequences	
Use task-interspersal (e.g., academic work completion)	
Other	
Other	
III. Use behavior change elements during implementation	
Use appropriate parameters and schedules of reinforcement	
Use fixed and variable time schedules	
Initial implementation phase	
Thinning the schedules	
Use prompts and prompt fading	
Use extinction	
Use the matching law and recognize factors influencing choice	

COMPETENCY TASK LIST 9.6.2   CONSIDER INITIATING AND COMPLETING THE FOLLOWING TASKS FOR THE COMPONENT SKILL OF DEVELOPING ANTECEDENT-BASED INTERVENTIONS, WITH YOUR SUPERVISOR

	(Mark done or record benchmark)
I. Review BACB ethical guidelines	
A. Review the following ethical guidelines and discuss with supervisor i. 1.0 Responsible Conduct of a Behavior Analyst ii. 2.0 The Behavior Analyst's Responsibility to Clients iii. 4.0 The Behavior Analyst and the Individual Behavior Change Program iv. 6.0 The Behavior Analyst and the Workplace v. 8.0 The Behavior Analyst's Responsibility to Colleagues vi. 9.0 The Behavior Analyst's Ethical Responsibility to Society vii. 10.0 The Behavior Analyst and Research	
II. Develop antecedent-based interventions	

A. Select potential antecedent-based intervention or combination of interventions (e.g., noncontingent reinforcement with stimulus fading in) based on assessment results and the best available scientific evidence
i.   Consult with supervisor and offer a rationale and supporting articles for your choice
ii. Discuss the limits of each procedure with supervisor and address the limits in the plan
iii. Discuss with supervisor and take into account:
   i.   Client's preferences and current repertoires
   ii. Environmental and resource constraints
   iii. Social validity of the intervention	

B. Propose an appropriate single-subject design that will allow evaluation of the effectiveness of the behavioral programs	
C. Develop technological and conceptually systematic treatment plan(s) for the given problem behavior(s) (developing plans for all areas listed here is strongly recommended) i. State intervention goals in observable and measurable terms ii. Program for stimulus and response generalization and maintenance iii. Combine antecedent-based procedures with reinforcement and extinction procedures	

(continued)

COMPETENCY TASK LIST 9.6.2   *(continued)*

	(Mark done or record benchmark)
iv. Design and include a data collection form to obtain representative data given the dimensions of the behavior and the logistics of observing and recording **D.** Have the supervisor use a written program performance checklist to evaluate whether the written treatment plans are behavior-analytic in nature and give feedback i. Make needed changes and place the final product and the feedback in this tab	
E. Use behavior skills training to train the staff on how to implement the plans i. Develop and use performance monitoring checklists to monitor procedural integrity during implementation of treatment plans	
F. Evaluate the effectiveness of interventions through ongoing data collection and analysis and make data-based decisions	
Antecedent Interventions	
Identify and make changes to the physical environment (e.g., manipulate discriminative stimuli).	
Use noncontingent reinforcement for behaviors maintained by:	
Attention	
Escape	
Access to tangibles	
Automatic reinforcement	
Use stimulus fading-in (e.g., food blending or for task refusal)	
Use choice making	
Use high-probability request sequences	
Use task-interspersal (e.g., academic work completion)	
Other	
Other	
Other	

(continued)

COMPETENCY TASK LIST 9.6.2 *(continued)*

	(Mark done or record benchmark)
III. Use behavior change elements during implementation	
Use appropriate parameters and schedules of reinforcement	
Use fixed and variable time schedules	
Initial implementation phase	
Thinning the schedules	
Use prompts and prompt fading	
Use extinction	
Use the matching law and recognize factors influencing choice	

PERFORMANCE MONITORING TOOL 9.6.2 EXAMPLE PERFORMANCE CHECKLIST YOU AND YOUR SUPERVISOR CAN USE TO GAUGE YOUR PERFORMANCE IN THIS COMPONENT SKILL

Is the Intervention Proposed Behavior-Analytic?			
Date			
1. Is it applied? (targeting behavior(s) of social significance)			
2. Is it behavioral?			
3. Is it analytic?			
4. Is it technological?			
5. Is it conceptually systematic?			
6. Is it effective?			
7. Is it generalizable?			

COMPETENCY TASK LIST 9.6.3   CONSIDER INITIATING AND COMPLETING THE FOLLOWING TASKS FOR THE COMPONENT SKILL OF IMPLEMENTING CONSEQUENCE-BASED INTERVENTIONS, WITH YOUR SUPERVISOR

	(Mark done or record benchmark)
I. Review BACB ethical guidelines	

A. Before beginning to work with your first client (as an implementer) and before developing your first treatment plan, review the following ethical guidelines and discuss with supervisor
   i. 1.0 Responsible Conduct of a Behavior Analyst
   ii. 2.0 The Behavior Analyst's Responsibility to Clients
   iii. 4.0 The Behavior Analyst and the Individual Behavior Change Program
   iv. 6.0 The Behavior Analyst and the Workplace
   v. 8.0 The Behavior Analyst's Responsibility to Colleagues
   vi. 9.0 The Behavior Analyst's Ethical Responsibility to Society
   vii. 10.0 The Behavior Analyst and Research	

II. Implement consequence-based interventions	
A. Implement the listed interventions and obtain at least 90% implementation fidelity on at least two consecutive performance monitoring checklists for each program **B.** Include the completed performance checklists for each program in this tab **C.** Use the dimensions of applied behavior analysis (Baer et al., 1968) to evaluate whether interventions you are asked to implement are behavior-analytic in nature	
Intervention	
Implement treatment plans using positive and negative reinforcement	
Differential reinforcement of alternative/incompatible behavior	
Functional communication training	
Differential negative reinforcement of alternative/incompatible behavior (DNRA/DNRI)	
Differential reinforcement of other behavior (DRO)	
Differential reinforcement of high rates of behavior (DRH; e.g., reading fluency)	
Differential reinforcement of low rates of behavior (DRL)	

(continued)

COMPETENCY TASK LIST 9.6.3 *(continued)*

	(Mark done or record benchmark)
Full-session DRL	
Interval DRL	
Spaced-responding DRL	
Implement treatment plans using the Premack principle	
Implement treatment plans using a token economy	
Implement treatment plans using extinction	
Implement treatment plans using positive and negative punishment	
Identify and use punishers	
Time out	
Response cost	
Reprimands	
Response blocking	
Overcorrection	
Implement treatment plans using combinations of reinforcement, punishment, and extinction	
Other	
Other	
Other	
Other	
III. Use behavior change elements during implementation of treatment plans	
Appropriate parameters and schedules of reinforcement:	
Fixed and variable time schedules	
Initial implementation phase	
Thinning the schedules	
Use pairing procedures to establish new conditioned reinforcers	
Use appropriate parameters and schedules of punishment	
Use prompts and prompt fading	

COMPETENCY TASK LIST 9.6.4   CONSIDER INITIATING AND COMPLETING THE FOLLOWING TASKS FOR THE COMPONENT SKILL OF DESIGNING CONSEQUENCE-BASED INTERVENTIONS, WITH YOUR SUPERVISOR

	(Mark done or record benchmark)
I. Review BACB ethical guidelines	

A. Before beginning to work with your first client (as an implementer) and before developing your first treatment plan, review the following ethical guidelines and discuss with supervisor
  i.   1.0 Responsible Conduct of a Behavior Analyst
  ii. 2.0 The Behavior Analyst's Responsibility to Clients
  iii. 4.0 The Behavior Analyst and the Individual Behavior Change Program
  iv. 6.0 The Behavior Analyst and the Workplace
  v.   8.0 The Behavior Analyst's Responsibility to Colleagues
  vi. 9.0 The Behavior Analyst's Ethical Responsibility to Society
  vii. 10.0 The Behavior Analyst and Research	

II. Develop and implement consequence-based interventions	

A. Select a potential consequence-based intervention or combination of interventions (e.g., DRO with token economy and response cost) based on assessment results and the best available scientific evidence
  o Consult with supervisor and offer rationale and supporting articles for your choice
  o Discuss the limits of each procedure with supervisor and address the limits in the plan
  o Discuss with supervisor and take into account:
     i.   Client's preferences and current repertoires
     ii. Environmental and resource constraints
     iii. Social validity of the intervention	

B. Before developing treatment plans, discuss with supervisor and plan for possible unwanted effects of:
  o Reinforcement
  o Punishment
  o Extinction
  o Plan for behavioral contrast effects
C. Develop technological and conceptually systematic treatment plans for given problem behavior(s) (developing plans for all areas listed here is strongly recommended)
  o State intervention goals in observable and measurable terms
  o When a behavior is to be decreased, select an acceptable alternative behavior to be established or increased
  o Program for stimulus and response generalization and maintenance	

(continued)

COMPETENCY TASK LIST 9.6.4 *(continued)*

	(Mark done or record benchmark)

o If reinforcement and extinction procedures are not effective, consider least restrictive punishment procedure(s)
    o Design and include a data collection form to obtain representative data given the dimensions of the behavior and the logistics of observing and recording
D. Have the supervisor use a written program performance checklist to evaluate whether the written treatment plans are behavior-analytic in nature and give feedback
    o Make needed changes and place the final product and the feedback in this tab	

E. Use behavior skills training to train the staff on how to implement the plans o Develop and use performance monitoring checklists to monitor procedural integrity during implementation of treatment plans	
F. Evaluate the effectiveness of interventions through ongoing data collection and analysis and make data-based decisions	
Consequence-Based Intervention	
Develop treatment plans using positive and negative reinforcement	
Develop treatment plans using the Premack principle	
Develop treatment plans using a token economy	
Develop treatment plans using extinction	
Develop treatment plans using positive and negative punishment	
Develop treatment plans using combinations of reinforcement, punishment and extinction	
Other	
III. Incorporate behavior change elements into the treatment plans	
Appropriate parameters and schedules of reinforcement	
Fixed and variable time schedules	
Initial implementation phase	
Thinning the schedules	
Use pairing procedures to establish new conditioned reinforcers	
Use appropriate parameters and schedules of punishment	
Prompts and prompt fading	
Consider matching law and recognize factors influencing choice	

COMPETENCY TASK LIST 9.6.5   CONSIDER INITIATING AND COMPLETING THE FOLLOWING TASKS FOR THE COMPONENT SKILL OF IMPLEMENTING GROUP CONTINGENCIES, WITH YOUR SUPERVISOR

	(Mark done or record benchmark)
I. Review BACB ethical guidelines	
A. Before beginning to work with your first client (as an implementer) and before developing your first treatment plan, review the following ethical guidelines and discuss with supervisor i. 1.0 Responsible Conduct of a Behavior Analyst ii. 2.0 The Behavior Analyst's Responsibility to Clients iii. 4.0 The Behavior Analyst and the Individual Behavior Change Program iv. 6.0 The Behavior Analyst and the Workplace v. 8.0 The Behavior Analyst's Responsibility to Colleagues vi. 9.0 The Behavior Analyst's Ethical Responsibility to Society vii. 10.0 The Behavior Analyst and Research	
II. Implement group contingencies	
A. Implement the listed group contingencies and obtain at least 90% implementation fidelity on at least two consecutive performance monitoring checklists for each program **B.** Include the completed performance checklists for each program in this tab **C.** Use the dimensions of applied behavior analysis (Baer et al., 1968) to evaluate whether interventions you are asked to implement are behavior-analytic in nature	
Group Contingency	
Use independent group contingencies	
Use interdependent group contingencies	
Use dependent group contingencies	
Other	
III. Use behavior change elements during implementation of treatment plans	
Use positive and negative reinforcement	
Appropriate parameters and schedules of reinforcement	
Fixed and variable time schedules	
Initial implementation phase	
Thinning the schedules	

(continued)

COMPETENCY TASK LIST 9.6.5 *(continued)*

	(Mark done or record benchmark)
Use prompts and prompt fading	
Use pairing procedures to establish new conditioned reinforcers	
Use appropriate parameters and schedules of punishment	
Use extinction	
IV. Data collection and display	
• During implementation of interventions, collect appropriate data and generate graphs • Discuss the visually displayed data with supervisor • Make necessary changes and include the final graph for each skill in this tab	
Collect data on:	
Rate/frequency	
Duration	
Latency	
IRT	
Plot and interpret data using equal-interval graphs	
Use withdrawal/reversal designs	
Use changing criterion designs	
Use multiple baseline designs	

IRT, inter-response time.

COMPETENCY TASK LIST 9.6.6   CONSIDER INITIATING AND COMPLETING THE FOLLOWING TASKS FOR THE COMPONENT SKILL OF DESIGNING GROUP CONTINGENCIES, WITH YOUR SUPERVISOR

	(Mark done or record benchmark)
I. Review BACB ethical guidelines	

A. Before beginning to work with your first client (as an implementer) and before developing your first treatment plan, review the following ethical guidelines and discuss with supervisor
   i. 1.0 Responsible Conduct of a Behavior Analyst
   ii. 2.0 The Behavior Analyst's Responsibility to Clients
   iii. 4.0 The Behavior Analyst and the Individual Behavior Change Program
   iv. 6.0 The Behavior Analyst and the Workplace
   v. 8.0 The Behavior Analyst's Responsibility to Colleagues
   vi. 9.0 The Behavior Analyst's Ethical Responsibility to Society
   vii. 10.0 The Behavior Analyst and Research	

II. Develop group contingencies	

A. Select potential group contingency intervention(s) based on assessment results and the best available scientific evidence
   a. Consult with supervisor and offer a rationale and supporting articles for your choice
   b. Discuss the limits of each procedure with supervisor and address the limits in the plan
   c. Discuss with supervisor and take into account:
      i. Client's preferences and current repertoires
      ii. Environmental and resource constraints
      iii. Social validity of the intervention	

B. Before developing treatment plans, discuss with supervisor and plan for possible unwanted effects of:
   a. Reinforcement
   b. Punishment
   c. Extinction
   d. Plan for behavioral contrast effects
C. Develop technological and conceptually systematic treatment plans for given problem behavior(s) (developing plans for all areas listed here is strongly recommended)
   a. State intervention goals in observable and measurable terms
   b. Program for stimulus and response generalization and maintenance	

(continued)

COMPETENCY TASK LIST 9.6.6 *(continued)*

	(Mark done or record benchmark)
D. If reinforcement and extinction procedures are not effective, consider least restrictive punishment procedure(s)	
E. Have the supervisor use a written program performance checklist to evaluate whether the written treatment plans are behavior-analytic in nature and give feedback a. Make needed changes and place the final product and the feedback in this tab	
F. Use behavior skills training to train the staff on how to implement the plans a. Develop and use performance monitoring checklists to monitor procedural integrity during implementation of treatment plans	
G. Evaluate the effectiveness of interventions through ongoing data collection and analysis and make data-based decisions	
Group Contingency	
Develop plans using independent group contingencies	
Develop plans using interdependent group contingencies	
Develop plans using dependent group contingencies	
Other	
Other	
Other	
III. Use behavior change elements during implementation of treatment plans	
Use positive and negative reinforcement	
Appropriate parameters and schedules of reinforcement	
Fixed and variable time schedules	
Initial implementation phase	
Thinning the schedules	
Use prompts and prompt fading	
Use pairing procedures to establish new conditioned reinforcers	
Use appropriate parameters and schedules of punishment	
Use extinction	

COMPETENCY TASK LIST 9.6.7 CONSIDER INITIATING AND COMPLETING THE FOLLOWING TASKS FOR THE COMPONENT SKILL OF IMPLEMENTING SELF-MANAGEMENT STRATEGIES AND CONTINGENCY CONTRACTS, WITH YOUR SUPERVISOR

	(Mark done or record benchmark)
I. Review BACB ethical guidelines	

A. Before beginning to work with your first client (as an implementer) and before developing your first treatment plan, review the following ethical guidelines and discuss with supervisor
  i. 1.0 Responsible Conduct of a Behavior Analyst
  ii. 2.0 The Behavior Analyst's Responsibility to Clients
  iii. 4.0 The Behavior Analyst and the Individual Behavior Change Program
  iv. 6.0 The Behavior Analyst and the Workplace
  v. 8.0 The Behavior Analyst's Responsibility to Colleagues
  vi. 9.0 The Behavior Analyst's Ethical Responsibility to Society
  vii. 10.0 The Behavior Analyst and Research	

II. Implement self-management procedures and contingency contracts	
A. Implement the listed interventions and obtain at least 90% implementation fidelity on at least two consecutive performance monitoring checklists for each program **B.** Probe for generalization and maintenance **C.** Include the completed performance checklists for each program in this tab Use the dimensions of applied behavior analysis (Baer et al., 1968) to evaluate whether the interventions you are asked to implement are behavior-analytic in nature	
Intervention	
Implement self-management plans addressing the following behaviors:	
Task completion	
Reducing problem behaviors	
Following schedules (e.g., time management)	
Weight management and diet	
Exercise	
Repetitive (not self-injurious) behaviors maintained by automatic reinforcement	

(continued)

COMPETENCY TASK LIST 9.6.7 *(continued)*

	(Mark done or record benchmark)
Medication management (e.g., insulin administration)	
Other	
Other	
Other	
Other	
Implement and monitor contingency contracts	
Implement treatment plans using combination of self-management strategies and contingency contracts	
Other	
Other	
III. Use behavior change elements during implementation	
Appropriate parameters and schedules of reinforcement	
Fixed and variable time schedules	
Initial implementation phase	
Thinning the schedules	
Token economies and other conditioned reinforcement systems	
Pairing procedures to establish new conditioned reinforcers	
Use of appropriate parameters and schedules of punishment	
Prompts and prompt fading	
Use of antecedent manipulation, such as motivating operations and discriminative stimuli	
Use of instructions and rules	
Consider matching law and recognize factors influencing choice	

COMPETENCY TASK LIST 9.6.8 CONSIDER INITIATING AND COMPLETING THE FOLLOWING TASKS FOR THE COMPONENT SKILL OF DESIGNING SELF-MANAGEMENT STRATEGIES AND CONTINGENCY CONTRACTS, WITH YOUR SUPERVISOR

	(Mark done or record benchmark)
I. Review BACB ethical guidelines	
A. Before beginning to work with your first client (as an implementer) and before developing your first treatment plan, review the following ethical guidelines and discuss with supervisor i. 1.0 Responsible Conduct of a Behavior Analyst ii. 2.0 The Behavior Analyst's Responsibility to Clients iii. 4.0 The Behavior Analyst and the Individual Behavior Change Program iv. 6.0 The Behavior Analyst and the Workplace v. 8.0 The Behavior Analyst's Responsibility to Colleagues vi. 9.0 The Behavior Analyst's Ethical Responsibility to Society vii. 10.0 The Behavior Analyst and Research	
II. Develop consequence-based interventions	
A. Select a potential self-management intervention or combination of self-management intervention with a behavior contract based on assessment results and the best available scientific evidence a. Consult with supervisor and offer a rationale and supporting articles for your choice b. Discuss the limits of each procedure with supervisor and address the limits in the plan c. Discuss with supervisor and take into account: i. Client's preferences and current repertoires ii. Environmental and resource constraints iii. Social validity of the intervention	
B. Before developing treatment plans, discuss with supervisor and plan for possible unwanted effects of: a. Reinforcement b. Punishment c. Extinction d. Plan for behavioral contrast effects **C.** Develop technological and conceptually systematic treatment plans for given problem behavior(s) (developing plans for all areas listed here is strongly recommended) i. State intervention goals in observable and measurable terms ii. When a behavior is to be decreased, select an acceptable alternative behavior to be established or increased iii. Program for stimulus and response generalization and maintenance iv. Use instructions and rules	

(continued)

COMPETENCY TASK LIST 9.6.8 *(continued)*

	(Mark done or record benchmark)
v. If antecedent, reinforcement, and extinction procedures are not effective, consider least restrictive punishment procedure(s) vi. Design and include a data collection form to obtain representative data given the dimensions of the behavior and the logistics of observing and recording **D.** Have the supervisor use written program performance checklists to evaluate whether the written treatment plans are behavior-analytic in nature and give feedback i. Make needed changes and place the final product and the feedback in this tab	
E. Use behavior skills training to train the staff on how to implement the plans i. Develop and use performance monitoring checklists to monitor procedural integrity during implementation of treatment plans	
F. Evaluate the effectiveness of interventions through ongoing data collection and analysis and make data-based decisions	
Intervention	
Develop self-management plans addressing the following behaviors:	
Task completion	
Reducing problem behaviors	
Following schedules (e.g., time management)	
Weight management and diet	
Exercise	
Repetitive (not self-injurious) behaviors maintained by automatic reinforcement	
Medication management (e.g., insulin administration)	
Other	
Other	
Other	
Other	
Develop and monitor contingency contracts	
Develop treatment plans using combination of self-management strategies and contingency contracts	

(continued)

215

COMPETENCY TASK LIST 9.6.8   (continued)

	(Mark done or record benchmark)
Other	
Other	
III. Incorporate behavior change elements into the treatment plans	
Appropriate parameters and schedules of reinforcement	
Fixed and variable time schedules	
Initial implementation phase	
Thinning the schedules	
Token economies and other conditioned reinforcement systems	
Pairing procedures to establish new conditioned reinforcers	
Use of appropriate parameters and schedules of punishment	
Prompts and prompt fading	
Use of antecedent manipulation, such as motivating operations and discriminative stimuli	
Use of instructions and rules	
Consider matching law and recognize factors influencing choice	

Additional Resources to Consider

Ahrens, E. N., Lerman, D. C., Kodak, T., Worsdell, A. S., & Keegan, C. (2011). Further evaluation of response interruption and redirection as treatment for stereotypy. *Journal of Applied Behavior Analysis, 44,* 95–108. doi:10.1901/jaba.2011.44-95

Athens, E. S., & Vollmer, T. R. (2010). An investigation of differential reinforcement of alternative behavior without extinction. *Journal of Applied Behavior Analysis, 43,* 569–589. doi:10.1901/jaba.2010.43-569

Austin, J. E., & Tiger, J. H. (2015). Providing alternative reinforcers to facilitate tolerance to delayed reinforcement following functional communication training. *Journal of Applied Behavior Analysis, 48,* 663–668. doi:10.1002/jaba.215

Austin, J. L., & Bevan, D. (2011). Using differential reinforcement of low rates to reduce children's requests for teacher attention. *Journal of Applied Behavior Analysis, 44,* 451–461. doi:10.1901/jaba.2011.44-451

Bachmeyer, M. H. (2009). Treatment of selective and inadequate food intake in children: A review and practical guide. *Behavior Analysis in Practice, 2,* 43–50. doi:10.1007/BF033

Bancroft S. L., & Bourret, J. C. (2008). Generating variable and random schedules of reinforcement using Microsoft Excel macros. *Journal of Applied Behavior Analysis, 41,* 227–235. doi:10.1901/jaba.2008.41-227

Becraft, J. L., Borrero, J. C., Davis, B. J., Mendres-Smith, A. E., & Castillo, M. I. (2018). The role of signals in two variations of differential-reinforcement-of-low-rate procedures. *Journal of Applied Behavior Analysis, 51,* 3–24. doi:10.1002/jaba.431

Bloom, S. E., & Lambert, J. M. (2015). Implications for practice: Resurgence and differential reinforcement of alternative responding. *Journal of Applied Behavior Analysis, 48,* 781–784. doi:10.1002/jaba.266

Call, N. A., Pabico, R. S., Findley, A. J., & Valentino, A. L. (2011). Differential reinforcement with and without blocking as treatment for elopement. *Journal of Applied Behavior Analysis, 44,* 903–907. doi:10.1901/jaba.2011.44-903

Carr, E. G., & Durand, V. M. (1985). Reducing behavior problems through functional communication training. *Journal of Applied Behavior Analysis, 18,* 111–126. doi:10.1901/jaba.1985.18-111

Davis, T. N., Machalicek, W., Scalzo, R., Kobylecky, A., Campbell, V., Pinkelman, S., & Sigafoos, J. (2015). A review and treatment selection model for individuals with developmental disabilities who engage in inappropriate sexual behavior. *Behavior Analysis in Practice,* 1–14. doi:10.1007/s40617-015-0062-3

Ducharme, J. M., & Worling, D. E. (1994). Behavioral momentum and stimulus fading in the acquisition and maintenance of child compliance in the home. *Journal of Applied Behavior Analysis, 27,* 639–647. doi:10.1901/jaba.1994.27-639

Fisher, W. W., Greer, B. D., Fuhrman, A. M., & Querim, A. C. (2015). Using multiple schedules during functional communication training to promote rapid transfer of treatment effects. *Journal of Applied Behavior Analysis, 48,* 713–733. doi:10.1002/jaba.254

Geiger, K. B., Carr, J. E., & LeBlanc, L. A (2010). Function-based treatments for escape-maintained problem behavior: A treatment-selection model for practicing behavior analysts. *Behavior Analysis in Practice, 3,* 22–32. doi:10.1007/BF033

Grow, L. L., Carr, J. E., & LeBlanc, L. A. (2009). Treatments for attention-maintained problem behavior: Empirical support and clinical recommendations. *Journal of Evidence-Based Practices for Schools, 10,* 70–92.

Hagopian, L. P., Boelter, E. W., & Jarmolowicz, D. P. (2011). Reinforcement schedule thinning following functional communication training: Review and recommendations. *Behavior Analysis in Practice, 4,* 4–16. doi:10.1007/BF033

Hanley, G. P. (2010). Toward effective and preferred programming: A case for the objective measurement of social validity with recipients of behavior-change programs. *Behavior Analysis in Practice, 3,* 13–21. doi:10.1007/BF033

Hanley, G. P., Jin, C. S., Vanselow, N. R., & Hanratty, L. A. (2014). Producing meaningful improvements in problem behavior of children with autism via synthesized analyses and treatments. *Journal of Applied Behavior Analysis, 47,* 16–36. doi:10.1002/jaba.106

Hanley, G. P., Piazza, C. C., & Fisher, W. W. (1997). Noncontingent presentation of attention and alternative stimuli in the treatment of attention-maintained destructive behavior. *Journal of Applied Behavior Analysis, 30,* 229–237. doi:10.1901/jaba.1997.30-229

Harper, J. M., Iwata, B. A., & Camp, E. M. (2013). Assessment and treatment of social avoidance. *Journal of Applied Behavior Analysis, 46,* 147–160. doi:10.1002/jaba.18

Jessel, J., & Ingvarsson, E. T. (2016). Recent advances in applied research on DRO procedures. *Journal of Applied Behavior Analysis, 49,* 991–995. doi:10.1002/jaba.323

Lipschultz, J., & Wilder, D. A. (2017). Recent research on the high-probability instructional sequence: A brief review. *Journal of Applied Behavior Analysis, 50,* 424–428. doi:10.1002/jaba.378

Luiselli, J. K. (Ed.). (2006). *Antecedent assessment and intervention: Supporting children and adults with developmental disabilities in community settings.* Baltimore, MD: Paul H. Brookes.

Luiselli, J. K. (2015). Behavioral treatment of rumination: Research and clinical applications. *Journal of Applied Behavior Analysis, 48,* 707–711. doi:10.1002/jaba.221

Luiselli, J. K., & Cameron, M. J. (Eds.). (1998). *Antecedent control: Innovative approaches to behavioral support.* Baltimore, MD: Paul H. Brookes.

Marcus, B. A., & Vollmer, T. R. (1996). Combining noncontingent reinforcement and differential reinforcement schedules as treatment for aberrant behavior. *Journal of Applied Behavior Analysis, 29,* 43–51. doi:10.1901/jaba.1996.29-43

McCord, B. E., Iwata, B. A., Galensky, T. L., Ellingson, S. A., & Thomson, R. J. (2001). Functional analysis and treatment of problem behavior evoked by noise. *Journal of Applied Behavior Analysis, 34,* 447–462. doi:10.1901/jaba.2001.34-447

Michael, J. L. (1982). Distinguishing between discriminative and motivational functions of stimuli. *Journal of the Experimental Analysis of Behavior, 37,* 149–155. doi:10.1901/jeab.1982.37-149

Piazza, C. C., Patel, M. R., Gulotta, C. S., Sevin, B. M., & Layer, S. A. (2003). On the relative contributions of positive reinforcement and escape extinction in the treatment of food refusal. *Journal of Applied Behavior Analysis, 36,* 309–324. doi:10.1901/jaba.2003.36-309

Rapp, J. T., & Vollmer, T. R. (2005). Stereotypy I: A review of behavioral assessment and treatment. *Research in Developmental Disabilities, 26,* 527–547. doi:10.1016/j.ridd.2004.11.005

Reed, D. D., & Kaplan, B. A. (2011). The matching law: A tutorial for practitioners. *Behavior Analysis in Practice, 4,* 15–24. doi:10.1007/BF033

Rispoli, M., Camargo, S., Machalicek, W., Lang, R. and Sigafoos, J. (2014), Functional communication training in the treatment of problem behavior maintained by access to rituals. *Journal of Applied Behavior Analysis, 47,* 580–593. doi:10.1002/jaba.130

Rodriguez, N. M., Thompson, R. H., Schlichenmeyer, K., & Stocco, C. S. (2012). Functional analysis and treatment of arranging and ordering by individuals with an autism spectrum disorder. *Journal of Applied Behavior Analysis, 45,* 1–22. doi:10.1901/jaba.2012.45-1

Saini, V., Miller, S. A., & Fisher, W. W. (2016). Multiple schedules in practical application: Research trends and implications for future investigation. *Journal of Applied Behavior Analysis, 49,* 421–444. doi:10.1002/jaba.300

Smith, R. G., & Iwata, B. A. (1997). Antecedent influences on behavior disorders. *Journal of Applied Behavior Analysis, 30,* 343–376. doi:10.1901/jaba.1997.30-343

Tiger, J. H., Hanley, G. P., & Bruzek, J. (2008). Functional communication training: A review and practical guide. *Behavior Analysis in Practice, 1,* 16–23. doi:10.1007/BF033

Tyner, S., Brewer , A., Helman, M., Leon, Y., Pritchard, J., & Schlund, M. (2016). Nice doggie! Contact desensitization plus reinforcement decreases dog phobias for children with autism. *Behavior Analysis in Practice, 9,* 54–57. doi:10.1007/s4061

Vaz, P., Volkert, V. M., & Piazza, C. C. (2011). Using negative reinforcement to increase self-feeding in a child with food selectivity. *Journal of Applied Behavior Analysis, 44,* 915–920. doi:10.1901/jaba.2011.44-915

Woods, K. E., Luiselli, J. K., & Tomassone, S. (2013). Functional analysis and intervention for chronic rumination. *Journal of Applied Behavior Analysis, 46,* 328–332. doi:10.1002/jaba.24

COMPETENCY 7. PROGRAM AND PROBE FOR GENERALIZATION AND MAINTENANCE

Generalization is the degree to which a behavior change (e.g., something you taught the client or a behavior problem you decreased) transfers to the relevant context(s) for the behavior without explicit training. Maintenance refers to the longevity of the behavior change. As a competent behavior analyst, you should begin your assessment and treatment planning with generalization and maintenance in mind. You would program for both generalization of skills and their maintenance in your intervention planning. Otherwise, your time and efforts, as well as the client's, would be wasted, because trained skills are meaningful only if they can be applied to everyday situations. Therefore, for this competency, we identify two component skills: (a) program and probe for stimulus and response generalization and (b) program and probe for maintenance. Diagram 9.7.1 provides some benchmarks to help you gauge your skill development in this competency.

DIAGRAM 9.7.1   Competency benchmarks for programming and probing for generalization and maintenance.

<u>**Elementary Skills**</u>

- ■ Can define generalization and maintenance
- ■ Can discriminate between stimulus and response generalization and give examples of each
- ■ Can discriminate between contrived and naturally occurring contingencies
- ■ Can list schedules of reinforcement that would support generalization and maintenance of established behaviors
- ■ Can explain the relationship between fluent responding and maintenance
- ■ Can list procedures that would support generalization of the targeted skills and alternative/incompatible behaviors (e.g., multiple exemplar training, program common stimuli)

<u>**Intermediate Skills**</u>

- ■ Can describe how to conduct generalization and maintenance probes
- ■ Can implement procedures that would support generalization of the targeted skills and alternative/incompatible behaviors (e.g., multiple exemplar training, program common stimuli)
- ■ Can conduct generalization and maintenance probes as programmed and directed
- ■ Can develop a measurable criterion for generalization and maintenance of targeted skills and alternative/incompatible behaviors

<u>**Advanced Skills**</u>

- ■ Can select and incorporate an appropriate procedure into treatment plans to program and probe for generalization of behavior change based on client's repertoire and the best available scientific evidence
- ■ Can incorporate naturally existing contingencies into treatment plans to program and probe for maintenance of behaviors based on client's repertoire and the best available scientific evidence
- ■ Can involve caregivers/teachers to support generalization and maintenance of behavior change
- ■ Can explain the difference between generalization and maintenance and the purpose of different procedures to support generalization of behavior change to a caregiver or teacher using non-technical language
- ■ Can teach others how to implement a variety of procedure that would support generalization and maintenance of the skills using BST (e.g., multiple exemplar training, program common stimuli, building fluency)
- ■ Can teach others how to probe for generalization and maintenance of the skills using BST (e.g., multiple exemplar training, program common stimuli)
- ■ Can make changes to treatment plans by graphing and analyzing generalization and maintenance data

Continuing Education & Professional Development

Competency 7. Example Case Scenario for Teaching Component Skill

(1) *Scenario*: You are asked by your supervisor to develop a treatment plan to teach receptive identification of objects from the natural environment (e.g., couch, chair) to your client, a 3-year-old girl. You had conducted the initial assessment with your supervisor and know that you will be using Discrete Trial Instruction and pictures of the objects. Your supervisor informs you that, as best practice, you need to program for generalization of the targeted stimuli from the onset of the teaching sessions.

(2) *Baseline assessment of your skills*

    a. Given that there are many different methods of programing for generalization of taught behaviors, your supervisor may ask you to:

        i. List some of the methods that would be relevant to teaching receptive identification of objects.

        ii. Provide a rationale for using each method.

        iii. Describe how you would incorporate the selected method into Discrete Trial Instruction.

        iv. Describe when and how the generalization probes would be conducted.

        v. Develop a criterion to indicate the point at which you would say the client is exhibiting generalization of receptive identification of objects.

    b. Your supervisor would evaluate your skills at baseline using a performance monitoring checklist and provide feedback as needed.

        i. If you did not meet the criteria set by your supervisor for competency, your supervisor may ask you to do the following:

            1. Review chapters in textbooks that address generalization.

            2. Search and review articles that address generalization for the specific skill that you are targeting in your protocol.

        ii. When you meet the criteria set by your supervisor for the competency, your supervisor may begin training you on how to develop the treatment plan that incorporates the generalization method(s) you suggested and work with you to select stimuli for teaching the skill.

(3) *Training*

    a. Model

        i. Your supervisor would:

            1. Provide you with a sample treatment plan that incorporates a generalization method to ensure programming for generalization at the onset of the intervention.

2. Provide a PMC that lists all of the required components of a plan.

3. Go over the PMC with you.

b. Competency check

    i. You would develop the technological treatment plan for teaching receptive identification of objects, include a list of targets, and present the treatment plan to your supervisor for review.

    ii. Your supervisor would provide you with feedback using the PMC.

- When your written plan meets the criteria on the PMC (e.g., 80% or more of the noted steps completed correctly), you would move to sharing the plan with the caregiver and train the behavior technician on implementation of the written plan.

c. Rehearsal and feedback

    i. Your supervisor would play the role of the client's caregiver or the staff person you are training. You will complete all the training steps.

    ii. You would present the treatment plan including how you are going to support generalization of the skill you were assigned.

    iii. Your supervisor would provide feedback on two areas:

        1. Performance on PMC items for sharing the information with a parent.

        2. Other areas in which the supervisor feels you did well or could improve upon (e.g., tone, pacing between segments, documentation of progress, responses to questions, clarity of the statements you made).

- If you complete the training PMC at 80% or greater fidelity, you would move to the generalization component.

- If you complete it at less than 80% fidelity, you would complete the role-play again.

- This will continue until you meet the competency criteria.

(4) *Generalization*

    1. Completion of training of a related procedure (going over the treatment plan with the caregiver) would be determined by your supervisor based on your performance with the caregiver and the behavior technician.

    2. Your supervisor would use the same PMC as the one used for your training to evaluate your performance and give you feedback.

Competency 7. Possible Group Supervision Activities

Group supervision can be devoted to reviewing and giving feedback on how each individual in the group programmed for generalization and maintenance. The questions that would come up during peer review may be the same ones you were encouraged to ask yourself in the earlier case scenario. That is, what are some of the generalization methods that would be relevant to the target behavior? What is the person's rationale for using the method he or she selected? When and how does the person recommend that the generality probes are conducted? And, finally, does the person have a criterion to indicate the point at which the client is considered to be exhibiting generalization of the target skills?

Competency 7. Specific Task Lists for the Component Skills and Additional Resources

In addition to the case scenario and suggestions for group supervision activities, we outline the tasks you need to accomplish to meet each component skill in Competency 7. Competency Task Lists 9.7.1 and 9.7.2 are intended to help you initiate tasks and select activities to complete with your supervisor. Again, we encourage you to hold conversations with your supervisor(s) to determine which of these tasks, or any additional tasks, are appropriate for you at each stage of your supervision experience.

COMPETENCY TASK LIST 9.7.1   CONSIDER INITIATING AND COMPLETING THE FOLLOWING TASKS FOR THE COMPONENT SKILL OF PROGRAMMING AND PROBING FOR STIMULUS AND RESPONSE GENERALIZATION, WITH YOUR SUPERVISOR

	(Mark done or record benchmark)
I. Review BACB ethical guidelines	
A. Before beginning to work with your first client (as an implementer) and before developing your first treatment plan, review the following ethical guidelines and discuss with supervisor i. 1.0 Responsible Conduct of a Behavior Analyst ii. 2.0 The Behavior Analyst's Responsibility to Clients iii. 4.0 The Behavior Analyst and the Individual Behavior Change Program iv. 6.0 The Behavior Analyst and the Workplace v. 8.0 The Behavior Analyst's Responsibility to Colleagues vi. 9.0 The Behavior Analyst's Ethical Responsibility to Society vii. 10.0 The Behavior Analyst and Research	
II. Plan for generalized behavior change	

A. For each skill acquisition or behavior reduction plan, choose a strategy to program for generalized behavior change based on assessment results and the best available scientific evidence
• Consult with supervisor and offer a rationale and supporting articles for your choice
• Discuss the limits of each procedure with supervisor and address the limits in the plan
• Discuss with supervisor and take into account:
  i. Client's preferences and current repertoires
  ii. Environmental and resource constraints
B. Incorporate technological and conceptually systematic procedures for achieving generalization in your skills acquisition and behavior reduction plans
• Develop observable and measurable goals that will address generalization
• Incorporate naturally existing contingencies in the plans
  i. Involve significant others and caregivers in your plan for generalization
  ii. Use one or a combination of the strategies listed here to support stimulus and response generalization across people and settings:
  a. Teach sufficient examples (stimulus and response; e.g., tact or mand training)
  b. General case analysis (e.g., doing laundry)
  c. Programming common stimuli (e.g., job training)
  d. Programming indiscernible contingencies
  e. Using "Don't do it" teaching examples	

(continued)

COMPETENCY TASK LIST 9.7.1   *(continued)*

	(Mark done or record benchmark)

f. Programming behavior traps
     g. Incorporating self-management skills
 C. Have the supervisor use a written program performance checklist to evaluate whether the generalizations are behavior-analytic in nature and give feedback
   • Make needed changes and place the final product and the feedback in this tab	

D. Use behavior skills training to train the staff on how to implement the plans i. Develop and use performance monitoring checklists to monitor procedural integrity during implementation of treatment plans	
E. Evaluate the effectiveness of interventions through ongoing data collection and analysis and make data-based decisions	

COMPETENCY TASK LIST 9.7.2   CONSIDER INITIATING AND COMPLETING THE FOLLOWING TASKS FOR THE COMPONENT SKILL OF PROGRAMMING AND PROBING FOR MAINTENANCE, WITH YOUR SUPERVISOR

	(Mark done or record benchmark)
I. Review BACB ethical guidelines	

A. Before beginning to work with your first client (as an implementer) and before developing your first treatment plan, review the following ethical guidelines and discuss with supervisor:
   i. 1.0 Responsible Conduct of a Behavior Analyst
   ii. 2.0 The Behavior Analyst's Responsibility to Clients
   iii. 4.0 The Behavior Analyst and the Individual Behavior Change Program
   iv. 6.0 The Behavior Analyst and the Workplace
   v. 8.0 The Behavior Analyst's Responsibility to Colleagues
   vi. 9.0 The Behavior Analyst's Ethical Responsibility to Society
   vii. 10.0 The Behavior Analyst and Research	

(continued)

COMPETENCY TASK LIST 9.7.2 *(continued)*

	(Mark done or record benchmark)
II. Plan for and probe for maintenance	

A. For each skill acquisition or behavior reduction plan, choose a strategy to maintain the behavior change in the natural environment using the best available scientific evidence
 • Consult with supervisor and offer a rationale and supporting articles for your choice
 • Discuss with supervisor and take into account:
    i. Client's preferences and current repertoires
    ii. Environmental and resource constraints
    iii. Social validity of the intervention	

B. Incorporate technological and conceptually systematic procedures for achieving maintenance of socially appropriate behaviors • Develop observable and measurable goals that will address maintenance • Incorporate naturally existing contingencies in the plans • Involve significant others and caregivers in your plans **C.** Have the supervisor use a written program performance checklist to evaluate whether the strategies are appropriate and behavior-analytic in nature, and give feedback i. Make needed changes and place the final product and the feedback in this tab	

D. Develop performance monitoring checklists that include measurable components of the maintenance plan
    i. Have the supervisor use performance monitoring checklists to evaluate the objectivity of performance checklist and give feedback
    ii. Make needed changes and place the final product and the feedback in this tab	

Additional Resources to Consider

Chandler, L. K., Lubeck, R. C., & Fowler, S. A. (1992). Generalization and maintenance of preschool children's social skills: A critical review and analysis. i, 415–428. doi:10.1901/jaba.1992.25-415

Fragale, C. L., O'Reilly, M. F., Aguilar, J., Pierce, N., Lang, R., Sigafoos, J., & Lancioni, G. (2012). The influence of motivating operations on generalization probes of specific mands by children with autism. *Journal of Applied Behavior Analysis, 45,* 565–577. doi:10.1901/jaba.2012.45-565

Freeland, J. T., & Noell, G. H. (2002). Programming for maintenance: An investigation of delayed intermittent reinforcement and common stimuli to create indiscriminable contingencies. *Journal of Behavioral Education, 11,* 5–18. doi:10.1023/A:101432910

Greer, R. D., Stolfi, L., Chavez-Brown, M., & Rivera-Valdes, C. (2005). The emergence of the listener to speaker component of naming in children as a function of multiple exemplar instruction. *The Analysis of Verbal Behavior, 21,* 123–134. doi:10.1007/BF033

Horner, R. H., Dunlap, G., & Koegel, R. L. (Eds.). (1988). *Generalization and maintenance: Lifestyle changes in applied settings.* Baltimore, MD: Paul H. Brookes Publishing.

Johnston, J. M. (1979). On the relation between generalization and generality. *The Behavior Analyst, 2,* 1–6. doi:10.1007/BF03391833

Marzullo-Kerth, D., Reeve, S. A., Reeve, K. F., & Townsend, D. B. (2011). Using multiple-exemplar training to teach a generalized repertoire of sharing to children with autism. *Journal of Applied Behavior Analysis, 44,* 279–294. doi:10.1901/jaba.2011.44-279

Mesmer, E. M., Duhon, G. J., & Dodson, K. G. (2007). The effects of programming common stimuli for enhancing stimulus generalization of academic behavior. *Journal of Applied Behavior Analysis, 40,* 553–557. doi:10.1901/jaba.2007.40-553

Sprague, J. R., & Horner, R. H. (1984). The effects of single instance, multiple instance, and general case training on generalized vending machine use by moderately and severely handicapped students. *Journal of Applied Behavior Analysis, 17,* 273–278. doi:10.1901/jaba.1984.17-273

Stokes, T. F., & Baer, D. M. (1977). An implicit technology of generalization. *Journal of Applied Behavior Analysis, 10,* 349–367. doi:10.1901/jaba.1977.10-349

COMPETENCY 8. CONDUCT EXPERIMENTAL EVALUATIONS AND ONGOING ASSESSMENTS OF INTERVENTIONS

It is the ethical duty of every behavior analyst to advocate for evidence-based, most-effective treatment procedures for his or her clients. However, it is difficult to find research results that have shown effectiveness of a treatment procedure for participants who exactly match your client (e.g., in age, gender, family situation, history of reinforcement). Therefore, it is imperative that you also use clinical judgment to select treatment procedures that match the client's preferences and needs. Additionally, it is important that you take the client's natural environment and the resources available into consideration when you plan your intervention. Therefore, you must conduct ongoing reviews, monitor the client's progress, and evaluate the effects of your treatment to be confident that your intervention is working. This process requires the integration of many of the previous competencies. To conduct evaluations of your current intervention plan effectively, you must be competent in measuring the target behavior, representing the data visually, analyzing the data presented, accessing evidence-based treatment plans, and then adjusting those plans based on the data that are presented. Oftentimes the first iteration of a behavior intervention is not perfect. In such a case, implementing the skills listed next can be the catalyst for the program to be successful. For this competency, we identify four component skills: (a) evaluate the effectiveness of the behavioral programs, (b) conduct treatment fidelity checks, (c) evaluate effectiveness of components of an intervention package, and (d) compare effectiveness of different treatments. Diagram 9.8.1 provides some benchmarks to help you gauge your skill development in this competency.

DIAGRAM 9.8.1 Competency benchmarks for evaluating and conducting ongoing assessments of interventions.

<u>**Elementary Skills**</u>

- Can define and give examples of independent and dependent variables
- Can define and give examples of internal and external validity
- Can list different type of experimental designs (e.g., reversal/withdrawal, alternating treatments)
- Can discriminate between different types of experimental designs (e.g., correctly identifies reversal/withdrawal design)
- Can list the defining features of single-subject experimental designs (e.g., individuals serve as their own controls, repeated measures, etc).

<u>**Intermediate Skills**</u>

- Can list the strengths and weakness of different type of experimental designs in relation to experimental control and target behaviors
- Can use seven dimensions of Applied Behavior Analysis to evaluate whether researched articles are behavior analytic in nature
- Can identify experimental designs used in research article by examining the graphs and the information provided in the methods section
- Can explain the difference between component and parametric analyses
- Can identify the correct experimental design in relation to the purpose and type of intervention/assessment (e.g., will identify alternating treatment design to determine if topography or selection-based mands are the best communication mode for a client)

<u>**Advanced Skills**</u>

- Can select and use correct single subject experimental design to show experimental control between independent and dependent variables
- Can design and supervise implementation of component and parametric analysis with various clients
- Can design and supervise implementation of various type of single subject designs to address client needs (e.g., multiple baseline, alternating treatments, etc.) while maintaining experimental control

Continuing Education & Professional Development

Competency 8. Example Case Scenario for Teaching Component Skill: Evaluating Intervention Effectiveness

(1) *Prerequisites*

    a. Accurately define level, trend, and variability.

    b. Identify the following items in a graphed data set:

        i. Upward, downward, and stable trend

        ii. Stable and variable data paths

        iii. Level changes

    c. Describe and utilize methods to determine level, trend, and variability of graphed data sets.

    d. Create graphs for specific experimental designs:

        i. Reversal

        ii. Multiple baseline

        iii. Alternating treatments

        iv. Changing criterion

(2) *Baseline assessment of your skills*

    a. Your supervisor would provide you with a data set, intervention fidelity data (from staff), and the written procedures for a behavior reduction or skill acquisition procedure.

    b. You would be responsible for the following tasks:

        i. Enter the data into a program for graphing.

        ii. Create a graph to best represent the data set.

        iii. Identify the current trend, level, and variability of the data set presented in the chart.

        iv. Identify the current trend, level, and variability of the fidelity data presented in the chart.

        v. Propose the next steps to take for the intervention/skill acquisition procedure based on the current features of the data set (trend/level/variability/time).

    c. Your supervisor would evaluate you in the following ways:

        i. Data entry = duration of time to complete data entry and accuracy (tracked by total number of errors).

            1. Criteria to be established by your supervisor based on the data set.

        ii. Graph creation = 90% or higher on graphing performance monitoring checklist (PMC).

        iii. Accuracy of statements regarding trend, level, and variability for intervention data set.

            1. Criteria and correct responses to be determined by your supervisor.

      iv. Accuracy of statements regarding trend, level, and variability for fidelity of implementation data.

         1. Criteria and correct responses to be determined by your supervisor.

      v. Evaluation of proposed steps given the information presented.

         1. Criteria and correct responses to be determined by your supervisor.

    d. If you meet the set criteria at baseline, you will move to the generalization phase.

      i. If you do not meet set criteria, you will move to the training phase.

(3) *Training*

    a. **Instruction and model**

      i. Your supervisor would provide you with a data set, intervention fidelity data (from staff), and the written procedures for a behavior reduction or skill acquisition procedure.

         1. Your supervisor would additionally provide the graphed data.

         2. Your supervisor would describe his or her interpretation of the data with regard to trend, level, and variability.

         3. Your supervisor would describe to you at least two potential courses of actions to take based on the provided information.

    b. **Rehearsal and feedback**

      i. Your supervisor would provide you with a data set (different from that provided in the baseline and instruction/model phases), written intervention, and staff fidelity data.

         1. The baseline process would be repeated until competency (set per supervisor criteria) is met.

(4) *Generalization*

    a. Your supervisor would assess this by using current client data.

      i. You would do the following:

         1. Identify a client program/intervention to evaluate.

         2. Collect staff fidelity data if such data are not readily available. Enter the data into a program for graphing.

         3. Create a graph to best represent the data set.

         4. Identify the current trend, level, and variability of the data set presented in the chart.

         5. Identify the current trend, level, and variability of the fidelity data presented in the chart.

         6. Propose the next steps to take for the intervention/skill acquisition procedure based on the current features of the data set (trend/level/variability/time).

         7. Implement the proposed steps.

         8. Evaluate the efficacy of the changes made to the program.

PERFORMANCE MONITORING CHECKLIST 9.8.1   PMC FOR EVALUATING GRAPHICAL REPRESENTATION OF DATA

Creating Behavior Graphs	Yes	No
1. The graph has a title that describes the data it depicts		
2. The graph represents the data correctly (e.g., bar graph for categorical or nominal data, line graph for continuous data such as sessions or days)		
3. The *y*-axis is the same range across participants		
4. The *y*-axis is labeled correctly (e.g., percentage of correct responses)		
5. The *x*-axis is labeled correctly (e.g., sessions)		
6. The *x*-axis ticks appear aligned with the data points		
7. There are condition labels (e.g., baseline, DRA, withdrawal) that represent the condition (or independent variables)		
8. There are condition phase lines between conditions (for each independent variable): solid lines between conditions with clear IV change and dashed lines between conditions that share components		
9. The data path is not connected across the conditions		
10. The grid lines on the graphs have been removed		
11. The graph for each subject aligns with the ones below it (sessions line up)		
12. *x*-Axis ticks appear aligned with the data points		
13. The graph contains a legend if there are multiple dependent variables or data paths		

Competency 8. Possible Group Supervision Activities

Researchers have a peer-review process for publishing the results of their studies in journals and at conferences. Such outlets enable researchers to show their work to peers with expertise in that particular area and to solicit feedback. The peer-review process is very helpful for catching errors and helping researchers evaluate each other's work objectively. Group supervision provides a similar forum for peer review. Your supervisor may ask that you de-identify your case reports and present a summary of the data to your peers to solicit feedback about the efficacy of your intervention. Your peers can help you troubleshoot if your client is not learning at the rate he or she should be or if the problem behavior appears resistant to change. Engaging in the peer review of case reports and graphs of the data is very helpful for you in learning about various cases and how you could troubleshoot if you are ever in a similar situation as a peer.

Competency 8. Specific Task Lists for the Component Skills and Additional Resources

In addition to the case scenario and suggestions for group supervision activities, we outline the tasks you need to accomplish to meet each component skill in Competency 8. Competency Task Lists 9.8.1 to 9.8.4 are intended to help you initiate tasks and select activities to complete with your supervisor. Again, we encourage you to hold conversations with your supervisor(s) to determine which of these tasks, or any additional tasks, are appropriate for you at each stage of your supervision experience.

COMPETENCY TASK LIST 9.8.1   CONSIDER INITIATING AND COMPLETING THE FOLLOWING TASKS FOR THE COMPONENT SKILL OF EVALUATING THE EFFECTIVENESS OF BEHAVIORAL PROGRAMS, WITH YOUR SUPERVISOR

	(Mark done or record benchmark)
I. Review BACB ethical guidelines	

A. Review the following ethical guidelines and discuss with supervisor
      i. 1.0 Responsible Conduct of a Behavior Analyst
      ii. 2.0 The Behavior Analyst's Responsibility to Clients
      iii. 4.0 The Behavior Analyst and the Individual Behavior Change Program
      iv. 6.0 The Behavior Analyst and the Workplace
      v. 8.0 The Behavior Analyst's Responsibility to Colleagues
      vi. 9.0 The Behavior Analyst's Ethical Responsibility to Society
      vii. 10.0 The Behavior Analyst and Research	

II. Effectiveness of treatment plan, data collection, display, and data-based decision making	

A. For each written treatment plan, propose an appropriate design that will allow evaluation of the effectiveness of the behavioral programs
      • Example: Suppose you are using an intervention to address a problem behavior that occurs in two different settings. You would propose a multiple probe or baseline across settings design to evaluate if there is a functional relationship between your intervention and the problem behaviors.
        o Discuss the proposed design with supervisor and obtain feedback
        o Make necessary changes to the designs and include the final products in this tab
      • Use the title of treatment plans to label each design	

(continued)

234

COMPETENCY TASK LIST 9.8.1   *(continued)*

	(Mark done or record benchmark)

B. Use the proposed design to systematically arrange interventions (IV) and to demonstrate their effects on target behaviors (DV)
 C. Provide for ongoing documentation of behavioral services
     o During implementation of interventions, collect appropriate data and generate graphs
     o Obtain feedback on construction of graphs
     o Make necessary changes and include the revised graphs in this tab	

D. Base decision making on data displayed in various formats o Discuss the visually displayed ongoing treatment data with supervisor **E.** Using baseline logic, evaluate the effectiveness of the treatments and make changes to the treatment plans	

III. Experimental designs

Indicate "Yes" or "No" for each design

Used withdrawal designs	
Used reversal designs	
Used alternating treatments (i.e., multielement) designs	
Used changing criterion designs	
Used multiple baseline designs	
Used multiple probe designs	
Used combinations of design elements	
Used Standard Celeration Charts (SCCs)	
Used cumulative record	

235

COMPETENCY TASK LIST 9.8.2   CONSIDER INITIATING AND COMPLETING THE FOLLOWING TASKS FOR THE COMPONENT SKILL OF MEASURING PERFORMANCE FIDELITY, WITH YOUR SUPERVISOR

	(Mark done or record benchmark)
I. Review BACB ethical guidelines	

A. Review the following ethical guidelines and discuss with supervisor
  i.   1.0 Responsible Conduct of a Behavior Analyst
  ii. 2.0 The Behavior Analyst's Responsibility to Clients
  iii. 4.0 The Behavior Analyst and the Individual Behavior Change Program
  iv. 6.0 The Behavior Analyst and the Workplace
  v.   8.0 The Behavior Analyst's Responsibility to Colleagues
  vi. 9.0 The Behavior Analyst's Ethical Responsibility to Society
  vii. 10.0 The Behavior Analyst and Research	

II. Design and use effective performance monitoring systems	

A. For each written treatment plan, design a performance monitoring checklist for monitoring procedural integrity
  o Obtain feedback from supervisor and make needed changes
  o Include the final product in this tab	

B. Use performance monitoring checklists to evaluate implementation of the skills acquisition and behavior reduction programs in the field
  o Provide corrective feedback
  o Obtain supervision during use of checklists and feedback
  o Use performance monitoring checklists during scheduled supervision visits with implementers
  o Include the completed checklists in this tab (make sure to de-identify personal information)	

C. Use performance monitoring checklists to evaluate fidelity of *data collection* in the field o Include the completed checklists in this tab (make sure to de-identify personal information)	
D. Use performance monitoring checklists to evaluate fidelity of *preference assessment* in the field o Include the completed checklists in this tab (make sure to de-identify personal information)	

PERFORMANCE MONITORING CHECKLIST 9.8.2 EXAMPLE PERFORMANCE CHECKLIST YOU AND YOUR SUPERVISOR CAN USE TO GAUGE YOUR PERFORMANCE IN THIS COMPONENT SKILL

Program Implementation Fidelity PMC	Yes	No
(1) Data sheet is prepared prior to beginning program		
(2) All stimuli for program are within reach of the BI		
(3) SR is within arm's reach of BI but unavailable to the participant		
(4) Waited for participant to make eye contact/gained participant attention		
(5) Delivered SD according to specific program instructions		
(6) Waited a maximum of 5 seconds for participant to respond		
(7) Child response (score only one item, depending on prompt level used)		
(a) **IF CORRECT:** Delivered SR within 3 seconds		
(b) **IF NR/INCORRECT:** Redelivered SD and prompted at least intrusive level for program		
(c) **IF NR/INCORRECT to SD + Prompt 1:** Redelivered SD and prompted at second prompt level for program		
(d) **IF NR/INCORRECT to SD + Prompt 2:** Redelivered SD and prompted at third prompt level for program		
(8) SR delivered at correct magnitude per prompt level required (+ or prompt level = full magnitude, − = none delivered)		
(9) Consequence delivered within 5 seconds of correct/prompted response		
(10) Data collected within 5 seconds of SR delivery		
(11) Data collected correctly based on prompt level required		
(12) Next SD delivered within 30 seconds (unless moving to a break)		

COMPETENCY TASK LIST 9.8.3   CONSIDER INITIATING AND COMPLETING THE FOLLOWING TASKS FOR THE COMPONENT SKILL OF EVALUATING EFFECTIVENESS OF COMPONENTS OF AN INTERVENTION PACKAGE, WITH YOUR SUPERVISOR

	(Mark done or record benchmark)
I. Review BACB ethical guidelines	
A. Review the following ethical guidelines and discuss with supervisor 　i.　1.0 Responsible Conduct of a Behavior Analyst 　ii.　2.0 The Behavior Analyst's Responsibility to Clients 　iii.　4.0 The Behavior Analyst and the Individual Behavior Change Program 　iv.　6.0 The Behavior Analyst and the Workplace 　v.　8.0 The Behavior Analyst's Responsibility to Colleagues 　vi.　9.0 The Behavior Analyst's Ethical Responsibility to Society 　vii.　10.0 The Behavior Analyst and Research	
II. Conduct a component analysis to determine the effective components of an intervention package	
A. For treatment plans that consist of multiple procedures, design a component analysis to determine the effectiveness of different components of the intervention package **B.** Discuss the proposed design with supervisor and obtain feedback 　o　Make necessary changes to the designs and include the final products in this tab 　　•　Use the title of treatment plans to label each design	
C. Use the proposed design to systematically arrange different components to demonstrate their effects on target behaviors 　o　Collect appropriate data and generate graphs 　o　Obtain feedback on construction of graphs 　o　Make necessary changes and include the revised graphs in this tab **D.** Base decision making on data displayed in various formats 　o　Discuss the visually displayed ongoing treatment data with supervisor **E.** Using baseline logic, evaluate the effectiveness of the different components and make changes to the treatment plans	

(continued)

COMPETENCY TASK LIST 9.8.3 (*continued*)

III. Experimental designs

	Indicate "Yes" or "No" for each design
Used withdrawal designs	
Used reversal designs	
Used alternating treatments (i.e., multielement) designs	
Used changing criterion designs	
Used multiple baseline designs	
Used multiple probe designs	
Used combinations of design elements	
Used Standard Celeration Charts (SCCs)	
Used cumulative record	

COMPETENCY TASK LIST 9.8.4   CONSIDER INITIATING AND COMPLETING THE FOLLOWING TASKS FOR THE COMPONENT SKILL OF COMPARING THE EFFECTIVENESS OF DIFFERENT INTERVENTIONS, WITH YOUR SUPERVISOR

	(Mark done or record benchmark)
I. Review BACB ethical guidelines	

A. Review the following ethical guidelines and discuss with supervisor
   i.   1.0 Responsible Conduct of a Behavior Analyst
   ii.   2.0 The Behavior Analyst's Responsibility to Clients
   iii.   4.0 The Behavior Analyst and the Individual Behavior Change Program
   iv.   6.0 The Behavior Analyst and the Workplace
   v.   8.0 The Behavior Analyst's Responsibility to Colleagues
   vi.   9.0 The Behavior Analyst's Ethical Responsibility to Society
   vii. 10.0 The Behavior Analyst and Research	

(*continued*)

COMPETENCY TASK LIST 9.8.4 *(continued)*

	(Mark done or record benchmark)
II. Conduct a component analysis to determine the effective components of an intervention package	

A. Design an intervention that uses an alternating treatment design to establish the effectiveness of two or more treatments on the DV
    B. Discuss the proposed design with supervisor and obtain feedback
    o Make necessary changes to the designs and include the final products in this tab
      • Use the title of the treatment plan to label each design	

C. Use the proposed design to alternate different treatments to demonstrate their effects on target behaviors
    o Collect appropriate data and generate graphs
    o Obtain feedback on construction of graphs
    o Make necessary changes and include the revised graphs in this tab
    D. Base decision making on data displayed in various formats
    o Discuss the visually displayed ongoing treatment data with supervisor
    E. Using baseline logic, evaluate the effectiveness of the different components and make changes to the treatment plans	

III. Experimental designs

Indicate "Yes" or "No" for each design

Multielement design	
Simultaneous design	

Additional Resources to Consider

Bailey, D. B. (1984). Effects of lines of progress and semi logarithmic charts on ratings of charted data. *Journal of Applied Behavior Analysis, 17,* 359–365. doi:10.1901/jaba.1984.17-359

Barlow, D. H., & Hayes, S. C. (1979). Alternating treatments design: One strategy for comparing the effects of two treatments in a single subject. *Journal of Applied Behavior Analysis, 12,* 199–210. doi:10.1901/jaba.1979.12-199

Cooper, L. J., Wacker, D. P., McComas, J. J., Brown, K., Peck, S. M., Richman, D., . . . Millard, T. (1995). Use of component analyses to identify active variables in treatment packages for children with feeding disorders. *Journal of Applied Behavior Analysis, 28,* 139–153. doi:10.1901/jaba.1995.28-139

Fisher, W. W., Kelley, M. E., & Lomas, J. E. (2003). Visual aids and structured criteria for improving visual inspection and interpretation of single-case designs. *Journal of Applied Behavior Analysis, 36,* 387–406. doi:10.1901/jaba.2003.36-387

Hagopian, L. P., Fisher, W. W., Thompson, R. H., Owen-DeSchryver, J., Iwata, B. A., & Wacker, D. P. (1997). Toward the development of structured criteria for interpretation of functional analysis data. *Journal of Applied Behavior Analysis, 30,* 313–326. doi:10.1901/jaba.1997.30-313

Hains, A. H., & Baer, D. M. (1989). Interaction effects in multielement designs: Inevitable, desirable, and ignorable. *Journal of Applied Behavior Analysis, 22,* 57–69. doi:10.1901/jaba.1989.22-57

Johnston, J. M., & Pennypacker, H. S. (1993). *Strategies and tactics of behavioral research* (2nd ed.). Hillsdale, NJ: Erlbaum.

Kazdin, A. E. (1982). *Single-case research designs: Methods for clinical and applied settings.* New York, NY: Oxford University Press.

Klein, L. A., Houlihan, D., Vincent, J. L., & Panahon, C. J. (2017). Best practices in utilizing the changing criterion design. *Behavior Analysis in Practice, 10,* 52–61. doi:10.1007/s4061

Park, H., Marascuilo, L., & Gaylord-Ross, R. (1990). Visual inspection and statistical analysis in single case designs. *Journal of Experimental Education, 58,* 311–320. doi:10.1080/00220973.1990.10806545

Roane, H. S., Fisher, W. W., Kelley, M. E., Mevers, J. L., & Bouxsein, K. J. (2013). Using modified visual inspection criteria to interpret functional analysis outcomes. *Journal of Applied Behavior Analysis, 46,* 130–146. doi:10.1002/jaba.13

Ward-Horner, J., & Sturmey, P. (2010). Component analyses using single-subject experimental designs: A review. *Journal of Applied Behavior Analysis, 43,* 685–704. doi:10.1901/jaba.2010.43-685

Wine B., Freeman T. R., & King A. (2014). Withdrawal versus reversal: A necessary distinction? *Behavior Intervention, 30,* 87–93. doi:10.1002/bin.1399

COMPETENCY 9. TRAIN ANOTHER INDIVIDUAL TO CONDUCT A PROCEDURE

As a behavior analyst, chances are you will be in a position to supervise and train other individuals. Therefore, it is imperative that part of your supervised experience is devoted to helping you become a competent supervisor and trainer so that you feel well prepared for your role. The distinction between supervisor and trainer boils down to this: As a trainer, you are responsible for the initial acquisition of the skill. As a supervisor, you are concerned with the generalization and maintenance of the skill. As a behavior analyst, it is likely you will wear both of these hats, often-times as you work with the same individuals. Researchers have found that effective staff training generally consists of instructions, modeling, practice, and feedback until a predetermined mastery criterion is achieved, which are all components of a competency-based behavioral skills training (BST; Parsons et al., 2012). This approach to training requires that you develop performance monitoring checklists (PMCs) for the tasks you aim to train, find opportunities for directly observing your staff perform the skills, model the correct behaviors, and provide feedback effectively.

Effective delivery of performance feedback is not easy. In fact, researchers have found that more than 80% of supervisors, or managers, shy away from providing corrective feedback. However, if your supervisor observes you providing feedback to a supervisee and provides you with feedback for how you delivered feedback, you are much more likely to feel confident about the feedback you give your staff. In my own research, I have found that individuals have a hard time delivering feedback when they do not have the knowledge (the skill for which they are giving feedback), the right tool (PMCs), or experience providing feedback that has improved behavior effectively. Therefore, for this competency, you are to design and use competency-based training for persons who are responsible for carrying out behavior change procedures. Diagram 9.9.1 provides some benchmarks to help you gauge your skill development in this competency.

DIAGRAM 9.9.1 Competency benchmarks for evaluating the training of another individual to conduct a procedure.

Elementary Skills

■ Can state the reasons for using behavior-analytic supervision and the potential risks of ineffective supervision

■ Can define behavior skills training

■ Can state the advantages of using behavior skills training

■ Can list the components of behavior skills training and state advantages and disadvantages of each component

■ Can explain the purpose of using Performance Monitoring Checklists and list different types of Performance Monitoring Checklists (e.g., weighted vs. unweighted)

Intermediate Skills

■ Can develop Performance Monitoring Checklists to be used for monitoring implementation of skill acquisition and behavior reduction treatment plans

■ Can evaluate the effectiveness of training by quantifying and graphing data obtained from Performance Monitoring Checklists

■ Can assist supervisor during Behavior Skills Trainings

Advanced Skills

■ Can conduct assessment of supervisee's skills

■ Can develop supervision goals and set clear performance expectation based on assessment of the supervisee's skills

■ Can use all components of BST and Performance Monitoring Checklists to train personnel, caregivers/teachers to competently perform assessment and intervention procedures

■ Can evaluate the effectiveness of supervision of personnel by quantifying and graphing data obtained from client outcomes and supervisee repertoires, and use functional assessment approach (e.g., performance diagnostics) and function-based strategies to improve personnel performance

---

Continuing Education & Professional Development

Competency 9. Example Case Scenario for Teaching Component Skill: Training Another Person on a Procedure

(1) *Scenario*

    a. You are training a new team member, Charlie, on implementing a differential reinforcement of alternative behavior (DRA) for physical aggression. The alternative behavior being reinforced is manding for a break from the activity. You are responsible for preparing Charlie to implement this procedure with a client in the field.

   i. You will be completing the following items:

      1. Determine Charlie's current level of competence with the procedure.

      2. Create a training plan to be implemented with Charlie and evaluate Charlie's performance.

      3. Create a plan to evaluate the generalization and maintenance of Charlie's skills.

(2) *Baseline assessment of your skills*

  a. Your supervisor would provide you with a copy of the DRA procedure to be used for this exercise.

  b. Complete the following:

     i. List all the steps to be completed in training.

     ii. Role-play the training procedure with your supervisor in the role of Charlie.

     iii. Your supervisor would evaluate your performance using the performance monitoring checklist (PMC) for behavior skills training (BST).

  c. If you reach the criteria for competency (at least 80% of required steps from PMC completed correctly) in the writing out of steps, you would move directly to step 2 of training.

     i. If you reach the criteria for competency (at least 80% of required steps from PMC completed correctly) during the role-play, you would move to implementation with a staff person.

     ii. If you do not meet the criteria for either area, you would begin with training step 1.

(3) *Training*

  a. **Step 1: Creating the training process**

     i. Instruction

      1. Your supervisor would give you a copy of the PMC for BST.

       a. You would follow along on the PMC as your supervisor models the process of training to you.

       b. You and your supervisor would review each step of the PMC.

        i. Example = Steps 1 and 2: Trainer presented written instructions to trainee. Instruction steps were presented in a sequential manner.

         1. Explanation: By presenting written steps in a sequential manner, your trainee will have a reference material to review if he or she forgets a specific step.

     ii. Model

      1. You would act in the role of the trainee using the provided script.

2. You would gather data on your supervisor's performance using the PMC provided.

iii. Competency check

1. You would write out all of the steps you would follow to train another individual.

a. Your supervisor would provide you with feedback on your process.

2. If your written process matches that on the PMC in 80% or more of the noted steps, you would move to step 2.

b. **Step 2: Rehearsal**

i. *Role-play*

1. Your supervisor would play the role of Charlie, the staff person you are training. You would complete all the training steps.

a. Your supervisor would play the role of the staff person based on his or her experience.

2. You would be responsible for completing the training from start to finish.

a. Once you have completed the training, you would discuss with your trainee your plan for tracking generalization and maintenance of the skill.

3. Your supervisor would provide feedback on two areas:

a. Performance on PMC items

b. Other areas in which the supervisor feels you did well or could improve upon (e.g., tone, pacing between segments, documentation of progress, responses to questions, clarity of the statements you made)

4. If you complete the training PMC at 80% or greater fidelity, you would move to the generalization component.

a. If you complete it at less than 80% fidelity, you would complete the role-play again.

b. This would continue until you meet the competency criteria

(4) *Generalization*

a. Completion of training of a related procedure (behavior reduction procedure) with a trainee.

i. Your supervisor would use the same PMC as the one used for your training.

ii. The trainee may also be given a feedback form to evaluate your performance based on his or her perspective.

PERFORMANCE MONITORING CHECKLIST 9.9.1   PMC FOR TRAINING USING BST

Training Procedure with BST PMC			
Date			
Baseline			
(1) Informed the trainee of the training topic			
(2) Asked the trainee if he or she has any experience with the specific procedure			
(a) If trainee says no, proceeded to step 3			
(b) If trainee says yes, completed performance monitoring checklist (PMC) for procedure			
(3) Informed trainee of his or her performance			
(a) If trainee meets criteria, move to generalization phase			
(b) If trainee does not meet criteria, move to instructions phase			
Instructions			
(1) Delivered written instructions to the trainee			
(2) Written instructions presented steps in a sequential manner			
(3) Written instructions contained no instances of mentalistic language			
(4) Written instructions contained all required steps for the procedure			
(5) Language used was appropriate for the individual being trained on the procedure			
(6) Delivered the rationale for the procedure to the trainee			
(7) Delivered a comprehension check for trainee's understanding of instructions			
(8) Solicited questions about the procedure from the trainee			
Modeling			
(1) At least two individuals participated in the model of the procedure			
(2) Used a script to organize the model for the trainee			
(3) Model included all steps from the written instructions			
(4) Model included steps to take for all likely responses from participant			
(5) If mistake was made during model, the trainee was corrected immediately and the step was repeated			

(continued)

PERFORMANCE MONITORING CHECKLIST 9.9.1   *(continued)*

(6) Completed a comprehension check regarding at least two portions of the model			
(7) Solicited questions about the model from the trainee			
Rehearsal			
(1) Set criteria for movement to generalization phase (e.g., 5 opportunities at 100% fidelity)			
(2) Informed trainee of criteria and showed trainee PMC being used to evaluate performance			
(3) Took data on trainee's rehearsal using a PMC			
(4) Rehearsal contained opportunities for trainee to respond to all likely responses from participant			
(5) Delivered feedback on each error made in rehearsal (80% or more errors based on supervisor's observations)			
(6) Feedback covered items found on PMC			
(7) Rehearsal continued until criteria for moving to generalization were met			
Feedback			
(1) Delivered empathic statement at start of feedback			
(2) Reviewed trainee's response to previously delivered feedback (e.g., was previous feedback implemented correctly)			
(3) Delivered a minimum of one statement regarding each aspect of the rehearsal done well			
(4) Feedback delivered with specific language and praise (e.g., "Great work with arranging the field again after an incorrect response")			
(5) No occurrences of a "but" or "however" statement (e.g., "You did really well with thing X BUT you did thing Y poorly")			
(6) Delivered a minimum of one statement regarding each aspect of the rehearsal that can be improved			
(7) Accurately identified an area for improvement to trainee			
(8) Following identification of area, gave instructions and/or a model for how to improve			
(9) Solicited questions from trainee regarding feedback delivered			
(10) Completed a comprehension check of trainee understanding of feedback			
(11) Solicited questions from trainee regarding feedback			

(continued)

PERFORMANCE MONITORING CHECKLIST 9.9.1 (*continued*)			
(12) Trainee repeated rehearsal opportunity to implement feedback			
(13) Noted if feedback was implemented accurately by the trainee			
(14) Produced a permanent product of all feedback to be delivered to trainee			
Total Yes/41			

Competency 9. Possible Group Supervision Activities

Your supervisor may use group supervision time to have you use BST to train your peers and to provide you with feedback on your BST or feedback-giving skills.

Competency 9. Specific Task Lists for the Component Skills and Additional Resources

In addition to the case scenario and suggestions for group supervision activities, we outline the tasks you need to accomplish to meet each component skill in Competency 8. Competency Task List 9.9.1 is intended to help you initiate tasks and select activities to complete with your supervisor. Again, we encourage you to hold conversations with your supervisor(s) to determine which of these tasks, or any additional tasks, are appropriate for you at each stage of your supervision experience.

COMPETENCY TASK LIST 9.9.1   CONSIDER INITIATING AND COMPLETING THE FOLLOWING TASKS FOR THE COMPONENT SKILL OF DESIGNING AND USING COMPETENCY-BASED TRAINING FOR PERSONS WHO ARE RESPONSIBLE FOR CARRYING OUT BEHAVIOR CHANGE PROCEDURES, WITH YOUR SUPERVISOR

	(Mark done or record benchmark)
I. Review BACB ethical guidelines	
A. Review the following ethical guidelines and discuss with supervisor i. 1.0 Responsible Conduct of a Behavior Analyst ii. 2.0 The Behavior Analyst's Responsibility to Clients iii. 4.0 The Behavior Analyst and the Individual Behavior Change Program iv. 6.0 The Behavior Analyst and the Workplace v. 8.0 The Behavior Analyst's Responsibility to Colleagues vi. 9.0 The Behavior Analyst's Ethical Responsibility to Society vii. 10.0 The Behavior Analyst and Research	
II. Develop an evidence-based staff training	
A. Design competency-based trainings for direct staff that includes the following components: o Description of the target skill and purpose o Technological written plan describing how to perform the target skill o Demonstration of the target skill o Opportunity for trainees to practice the target skills o How performance feedback will be given during practice o Set clear criteria for mastery of the skill in the training setting o Set clear criteria for mastery of the skill on the job **B.** Obtain feedback from supervisor and make needed changes o Include the final product in this tab	
C. Conduct small-group training using the competency-based training o Include participant ratings of the group training	
III. Provide on-the-job training and supervision for behavior-change agents	
A. Conduct on-the-job BST after small-group instruction o Use the performance monitoring checklists to evaluate implementation of skills in the field o Give feedback to implementers using the checklists o Obtain supervision during on-the-job BST **B.** Provide weekly supervision to direct staff that includes: o Data collection o Monitoring procedural integrity and corrective feedback o Data analysis and data-based decision making	

(continued)

COMPETENCY TASK LIST 9.9.1 *(continued)*

	(Mark done or record benchmark)
o Modification of existing programs o Development and implementation of new programs o Orderly termination of services when they are no longer required	

IV. Develop professional presentations (optional)

A. Submit an abstract for consideration to a professional conference or organization (sample performance monitoring checklist)

B. Present empirical research findings, a conceptual paper, or a professional topic at professional conference or organization (see sample performance monitoring checklist)

Condition	S#	S#	S#	Notes
1. **Begun with a positive statement** about general affect, timing, preparation, and so on	Y N	Y N	Y N	
2. **Transitioned quickly between things** (observation to giving feedback, session to session, attendees)	Y N	Y N	Y N	
3. **Provided FB on each TB for condition** (total # of Y/ Y + N)				
If correct, noted and praised (for S#2 & 3, only note as correct if performed incorrectly in the previous session)	/	/	/	
If incorrect, stated specifically what the trainee did (modeled correct behavior if requested)	/	/	/	
4. **Provided FB on data collection (only session 1. unless attendee needs more feedback)**				
If correct, confirmed and praised	Y N	Y N	Y N	
If incorrect, reviewed data collection with attendee	Y N	Y N	Y N	
5. **Provided FB on the use of a timer (only session 1. unless attendee needs more feedback)**				
If correct, confirmed and praised	Y N	Y N	Y N	
If incorrect, reviewed use of a timer with attendee	Y N	Y N	Y N	
6. **Ended FB session with a positive statement**	Y N	Y N	Y N	
7. **Asked if the therapist had any other questions**	Y N	Y N	Y N	
8. **Answered questions correctly** (explained function of each step if asked—note the number of questions)	Y N	Y N	Y N	
9. **Was generally flexible** (diverted from a script when providing feedback and/or answering questions when needed)	Y N	Y N	Y N	

(continued)

COMPETENCY TASK LIST 9.9.1   (continued)

Condition	S#	S#	S#	Notes
10. **Balanced and spent equal time** (as much as possible) on positive statements versus incorrect responses	Y N	Y N	Y N	
Total (# of correct / 10) **Mastery criteria (100%)**				

Additional Resources to Consider

Carr, J. E., Wilder, D. A., Majdalany, L., Mathisen, D., & Strain, L. A. (2013). An assessment-based solution to a human-service employee performance problem: An initial evaluation of the Performance Diagnostic Checklist—Human Services. *Behavior Analysis in Practice, 6*, 16–32. doi:10.1007/BF033

Chok, J. T., Shlesinger, A., Studer, L., & Bird, F. L. (2012). Description of a practitioner training program on functional analysis and treatment development. *Behavior Analysis in Practice, 5*, 25–36. doi:10.1007/BF033

Codding, R. S., Feinberg, A. B., Dunn, E. K., & Pace, G. M. (2005). Effects of immediate performance feedback on implementation of behavior support plans. *Journal of Applied Behavioral Analysis, 38*, 205–219. doi:10.1901/jaba.2005.98-04

Fiske, K. E. (2008). Treatment integrity of school-based behavior analytic interventions: A review of the research. *Behavior Analysis in Practice, 1*, 19–25. doi:10.1007/BF033

Gresham, F. M. (1989). Assessment of treatment integrity in school consultation and prereferral intervention. *School Psychology Review, 18*, 37–50.

Gresham, F. M. (2004). Current status and future directions of school-based behavioral interventions. *School Psychology Review, 33*, 326–343.

Kuhn, S. A. C., Lerman, D. C., & Vorndran, C. M. (2003). Pyramidal training for families of children with problem behavior. *Journal of Applied Behavior Analysis, 36*, 77–88. doi:10.1901/jaba.2003.36-77

Miles, N. I., & Wilder, D. A. (2009). The effects of behavioral skills training on caregiver implementation of guided compliance. *Journal of Applied Behavior Analysis, 42*, 405–410. doi:10.1901/jaba.2009.42-405

Parsons, M. B., & Reid, D. H. (1995). Training residential supervisors to provide feedback for maintaining staff teaching skills with people who have severe disabilities. *Journal of Applied Behavior Analysis, 28*, 317–322. doi:10.1901/jaba.1995.28-317

Parsons, M. B., Rollyson, J. H., & Reid, D. H. (2012). Evidence-based staff training: A guide for practitioners. *Behavior Analysis in Practice, 5*, 2–11. doi:10.1007/BF033

Reed, F. D. D., Hirst, J. M., & Howard, V. J. (2013). Empirically supported staff selection, training, and management strategies. In *Handbook of crisis intervention and developmental disabilities* (pp. 71–85). New York, NY: Springer.

Reid, D. H., Parsons, M. B., & Green, C. W. (2012). *The supervisor's guidebook: Evidence-based strategies for promoting work quality and enjoyment among human service staff.* Morganton, NC: Habilitative Management Consultants.

Sanetti, L. M. H., Luiselli, J. K., & Handler, M. W. (2007). Effects of verbal and graphic performance feedback on behavior support plan implementation in a public elementary school. *Behavior Modification, 31*, 454–465. doi:10.1177/0145445506297583

Sarokoff, R. A., & Sturmey, P. (2004). The effects of behavioral skills training on staff implementation of discrete trial teaching. *Journal of Applied Behavior Analysis, 37*, 535–538. doi:10.1901/jaba.2004.37-535

Shapiro, M., & Kazemi, E. (2017). A review of training strategies to teach individuals Implementation of behavioral interventions. *Journal of Organizational Behavior Management, 31*(1), 32–62. doi:10.1080/01608061.2016.1267066

Ward-Horner, J., & Sturmey, P. (2012). Component analysis of behavior skills training in functional analysis. *Behavioral Interventions, 27*(2), 75–92. doi:10.1002/bin.1339

Weinkauf, S. M., Zeug, N. M., Anderson, C. T., & Ala'i-Rosales, S. (2011). Evaluating the effectiveness of a comprehensive staff training package for behavioral interventions for children with autism. *Research in Autism spectrum disorders, 5*(2), 864–871. doi:10.1016/j.rasd.2010.10.001

Weldy, C. R., Rapp, J. T., & Capocasa, K. (2014), Training staff to implement brief stimulus preference assessments. *Journal of Applied Behavior Analysis, 47*, 214–218. doi:10.1002/jaba.98

COMPETENCY 10. REPRESENT AND DISSEMINATE THE FIELD OF BEHAVIOR ANALYSIS

This competency is about how you relay what we do as behavior analysts when you interact with clients, their families, and other individuals who are not behavior analysts (e.g., school personnel, occupational and speech therapists, your friends, the community at large). It is not a secret that despite the growth of behavior analysis, our field continues to face many challenges when it comes to our image. Because we are a young profession, you are an ambassador for our field and need to educate others about the qualifications of individuals who are behavior analysts. You need to be able to inform individuals who want to know more about our profession about our code of ethics, the certification requirements of our field, the extensive training and supervised experience you had to undergo to practice, and our commitment to increasing our clients' freedom and quality of life. The vitality and continued growth of the profession of behavior analysis rely on your ability to interact with others in a manner that is genuine, welcoming, collaborative, and professional. In addition, you need to try to bust the myths and misconceptions about our profession (e.g., behavior analysts don't care about people's feelings, are arrogant, or only deal with simple behaviors) by setting a great example of compassion, humane care, humility, and openness to ideas that are different than yours.

As a behavior analyst, you also need to work on your "bedside manner." This is an older phrase, typically used in the medical profession, to refer to how a health care professional builds rapport with patients and their family members, relays information about diagnosis and medical procedures, and communicates patients' progress. How a health care professional interacts with patients, their loved ones, and other stakeholders influences continuity of care, treatment acceptability, and how family members cope with difficult news. The same is true for our profession. As a behavior analyst, you are likely to work with at-risk populations and family members, teachers, and other stakeholders who may be under much duress. Parents want to understand their children and to work with professionals who care for them. They do not want to work with professionals who want to control their child or to debate those professionals on how to operationally define choice (see Bailey, 1991). You will need to communicate with parents and caregivers using lay language and put them at ease when they feel confused about the treatment protocol. You also need to have a cultural competence such that you are respectful of cultures other than yours and open to learning how culture affects each of your clients' treatment needs and the decisions their caregivers make. Lastly, you may need to train other individuals (e.g., teachers, teaching aids, caregivers) to help you carry out the behavior plan for a client. This training often goes beyond the nuts and bolts of the procedure into the realm of treatment acceptability and fidelity. Taking into consideration your audience and his or her needs when you are training can result in more effective outcomes. Therefore, for this competency, we have identified two component skills: (a) develop and present a training module to individuals unfamiliar with behavior analysis and (b) explain behavioral concepts and philosophy using nontechnical language. Diagram 9.10.1 provides some benchmarks to help you gauge your skill development in this competency.

DIAGRAM 9.10.1 Competency benchmarks for representing and disseminating behavior analysis.

Elementary Skills

- Accurately answers questions about what behaviors analysts do and their qualifications
- Accurately answers questions about terms and concepts in applied behavior analysis
- Accurately answers questions about behavior assessments and behavior interventions
- Accurately answers questions about the history and philosophy of behavior analysis
- Can define active listening and explain its main components
- Can define treatment acceptability and social validity and how they affect client services
- Can explain what is meant by bedside manners
- Can explain what is meant by cultural competence

Intermediate Skills

- Can identify the function of a question posted by a speaker
- Can ask for clarification without offending the speaker
- Can identify limitations and areas that need improvement in our own profession
- Can answer questions about what behavior analysts do, their qualifications, their overarching mission, and the profession with minimal behavioral terminology
- Can answer questions about terms and concepts in applied behavior analysis with minimal behavioral terminology
- Can explain the procedures in behavior assessments and behavior interventions with minimal behavioral terminology
- Can role-play active listening accurately
- Can explain how treatment acceptability and social validity affect treatment

---

Advanced Skills

- Can answer questions about the profession, concepts, and procedures using lay terms
- Can provide multiple examples that are relevant to a listener
- Can shed behavior analysis in a positive light by relaying its humane perspectives
- Demonstrates cultural competence
- Demonstrates skills in active listening
- Interacts with clients, caregivers, and other professionals on the multidisciplinary team in a manner that appears genuine and collaborative

---

Continuing Education & Professional Development

Competency 10. Example Case Scenario for Teaching Component Skill: Disseminating ABA to Non-Behavior Analyst Audiences

(1) *Scenario*

    a. You have been asked to make a presentation on group contingencies to a group of teachers at a local elementary school. The purpose of this presentation is to introduce group contingencies and evaluate if they would be interested in a more formalized training on implementation.

        i. You would be responsible for:

          1. Researching relevant information for the training

          2. Create the training presentation

          3. Create any supplemental materials

          4. Presenting the training to this audience

          5. Evaluating the quality of your training

    b. This activity will specifically address your training skills (numbers 4 and 5)

(2) *Baseline*

    a. Prior to engaging in all steps to create and present the training, your supervisor would conduct a baseline (and possibly training) on how to present such a training.

    b. Your supervisor would assign you a training to present to a group of peers.

        i. This training would have been created by your supervisor to isolate your skills with in-person training.

        ii. All supplemental materials would be made available to you.

    c. During the training, your supervisor would evaluate your training ability using the group training performance monitoring checklist (PMC).

    d. If you score at or higher than 80% on the PMC, you would move to the generalization phase.

        e. If you score lower than 80% on the PMC, you will move into the training phase.

(3) *Training*

    a. Your supervisor would provide you with the PMC for training.

        i. Your supervisor would solicit questions from you regarding the PMC and its specific use for evaluating a trainer.

    b. Your supervisor would bring you to a training conducted either by your supervisor or by an individual arranged by your supervisor.

        i. Your supervisor would have you evaluate the training using the PMC.

          1. If observing another individual, your supervisor would conduct interobserver agreement on the training using the PMC.

   c. After completion of the observation, your supervisor would assign you to read the following article for a discussion of how to apply to your training ability:

      i. Friman, P. C. (2014). Behavior analysts to the front! A 15-step tutorial on public speaking. *The Behavior Analyst, 37*(2), 109–118. doi:10.1007/s40614-014-0009-y

   d. Your supervisor would provide you with an option to choose from five precompleted trainings (chosen at the discretion of your supervisor)

      i. You would choose one training option.

      ii. You would present this training to your supervisor.

         1. Your supervisor would evaluate you using the PMC.

         2. If you perform at the required criteria, you would move to the next phase (letter e. below).

           3. If you do not meet the required criteria, your supervisor would provide you with feedback and you would attempt a second training from the previous options (letter d).

   e. Your supervisor would provide you with the choice of the previous trainings (letter d) and have you present to a group of at least three peers.

      i. You would choose one training option.

      ii. Your peers would evaluate your performance through data collection of specific trainer behaviors.

         1. Your supervisor would evaluate you using the PMC.

         2. Your peers would evaluate you using the data collected as well as their subjective opinions of the training.

         3. If you perform at the required criteria (based on supervisor PMC), you would move to the next phase (e).

           4. If you do not meet the required criteria, your supervisor would provide you with feedback and you would attempt a second training from the previous options (d).

(4) *Generalization*

   a. After completion of all individual activities for this competency area (see items 1–5 under Scenario):

      i. Your supervisor would assign you a specific training topic.

      ii. You would create the training from start to finish.

      iii. If you meet all requirements for the steps, move to step b.

         iv. If you do not meet all the requirements, you will attempt again with the same training topic.

   b. Your supervisor would have you create the training for the scenario listed earlier.

PERFORMANCE MONITORING CHECKLIST 9.10.1 PMC FOR TRAINING USING BST

Group Training PMC			
Date			
Preparation			
(1) Date, time, location, and attendees for training were confirmed at least 24 hours in advance			
(2) If using PowerPoint or another presentation program, ensured all animations, transitions, and hyperlinks were working			
(3) All participant materials were prepared and ready for use in the training (either printed or online)			
(4) Trainer arrived at least 30 minutes prior to scheduled time			
(5) Trainer had space set up for training prior to arrival of first participant			
Training materials			
(1) Training materials were relevant to the presentation			
(2) Training materials contained fewer than five total spelling and/or grammar mistakes			
(3) At least 80% of the materials presented to participants were introduced to the participants			
Training structure			
(1) Trainer introduced self and described qualifications to give talk			
(2) Trainer introduced topic to be covered			
(3) Trainer described objectives of training and any results/ competencies that would be obtained			
(4) Trainer transitioned appropriately between topics (e.g., connected topics together, told story about next topic) for 75% or more of the counted transitions			
(5) Topics were presented in a logical order given the goals of the training			
(6) Trainer concluded the training with a reiteration of the main points			
(7) Trainer completed the training in the stated time frame			
Trainer and participant behaviors			
(1) Trainer maintained vocal volume to be heard by all participants in 80% or more of measured intervals (MTS: 5 minutes)			
(2) Trainer solicited participation from group at least once every interval in 80% or more of measured intervals (PITS: 5 minutes)			

(continued)

257

PERFORMANCE MONITORING CHECKLIST 9.10.1 *(continued)*			
(3) Trainer answered questions from group appropriately (not necessarily knowing the answers) in 80% of presented questions			
(4) At least 50% of audience had eyes oriented at speaker or presentation in 80% of measured intervals (MTS: 5 minutes)			
(5) Trainer emitted five or fewer umms, uhhs, or similar words per 1 hour of presentation time			
(6) Trainer used language inappropriate given the audience (to be defined based on audience) less than once per hour of presentation time			
End of training			
(1) Trainer presented evaluation forms to audience at conclusion of training			
(2) Trainer remained to answer questions until all participants have left the training			
(3) Trainer reviewed all evaluation forms and determined at least two areas of improvement based on forms			
Total Yes/24			

BST, behavior skills training.

Competency 10. Possible Group Supervision Activities

Your supervisor may decide to use group supervision meetings to give you time to mock your training and solicit feedback from your peers. Furthermore, your supervisor may have you role-play common scenarios (e.g., a caregiver who is confused about why you must conduct a functional analysis prior to making treatment recommendations) with peers, or with your supervisor, as other members of the supervision group watch, make notes, and provide feedback.

Competency 10. Specific Task Lists for the Component Skills and Additional Resources

In addition to the case scenario and suggestions for group supervision activities, we have outlined the tasks you need to accomplish to meet each component skill in Competency 10. Competency Task Lists 9.10.1 and 9.10.2 are intended to help you initiate tasks and select activities to complete with your supervisor. Again, we encourage you to hold conversations with your supervisor(s) to determine which of these tasks, or any additional tasks, are appropriate for you at each stage of your supervision experience.

COMPETENCY TASK LIST 9.10.1 CONSIDER INITIATING AND COMPLETING THE FOLLOWING TASKS FOR THE COMPONENT SKILL OF DEVELOPING AND PRESENTING A TRAINING MODULE TO INDIVIDUALS UNFAMILIAR WITH BEHAVIOR ANALYSIS, WITH YOUR SUPERVISOR

	(Mark done or record benchmark)
I. Review BACB ethical guidelines	
A. Review the following ethical guidelines and discuss with supervisor 　i. 1.0 Responsible Conduct of a Behavior Analyst 　ii. 2.0 The Behavior Analyst's Responsibility to Clients 　iii. 4.0 The Behavior Analyst and the Individual Behavior Change Program 　iv. 6.0 The Behavior Analyst and the Workplace 　v. 8.0 The Behavior Analyst's Responsibility to Colleagues 　vi. 9.0 The Behavior Analyst's Ethical Responsibility to Society 　vii. 10.0 The Behavior Analyst and Research	
II. Develop an evidence-based staff training	
A. Design and conduct competency-based trainings for parents and/or teachers using a combination of presentations, demonstrations, and opportunities for trainees to practice the target skills 　o Set clear criteria for mastery of the skill in the training setting 　o Set clear criteria for mastery of the skill in the natural environment 　o Provide feedback in all settings B. Assess learning outcomes through tests and demonstrations 　o Include assessment results in this tab C. Obtain feedback from supervisor and make needed changes	

COMPETENCY TASK LIST 9.10.2   CONSIDER INITIATING AND COMPLETING THE FOLLOWING TASKS, FOR THE COMPONENT SKILL OF EXPLAINING BEHAVIORAL CONCEPTS USING NONTECHNICAL LANGUAGE, WITH YOUR SUPERVISOR

	(Mark done or record benchmark)
I. Review BACB ethical guidelines	

A. Review the following ethical guidelines and discuss with supervisor
  i.   1.0 Responsible Conduct of a Behavior Analyst
  ii. 2.0 The Behavior Analyst's Responsibility to Clients
  iii. 4.0 The Behavior Analyst and the Individual Behavior Change Program
  iv. 6.0 The Behavior Analyst and the Workplace
  v.   8.0 The Behavior Analyst's Responsibility to Colleagues
  vi. 9.0 The Behavior Analyst's Ethical Responsibility to Society
  vii. 10.0 The Behavior Analyst and Research	

II. Provide behavior-analytic services in collaboration with others who provide services to your clients.	

A. Collaborate with other professionals who provide services to your client
  o   Reduce problem behaviors to allow other professionals to work on skill acquisition
  o   Provide treatment data to parents to share with physicians for clients who are taking psychotropic medications
B. Explain behavioral concepts using nontechnical language
  o   During meetings with other professionals and parents, use nontechnical language to explain:
    • Assessment results
    • Treatment plans
    • Data analysis and progress	

Additional Resources to Consider

Bailey, J. S. (1991). Marketing behavior analysis requires different talk. *Journal of Applied Behavior Analysis, 24*(3), 445–448. doi:10.1901/jaba.1991.24-445

Becirevic, A. (2014). Ask the experts: How can new students defend behavior analysis from misunderstandings? *Behavior Analysis in Practice, 7*(2), 138–140. doi:10.1007/s40617-014-0019-y

Critchfield, T. S. (2014). Ten rules for discussing behavior analysis. *Behavior Analysis in Practice, 7*(2), 141–142. doi:10.1007/s40617-014-0026-z

Foxx, R. M. (1996). Translating the covenant: The behavior analyst as ambassador and translator. *The Behavior Analyst, 19*(2), 147–161. doi:10.1007/BF03393162

Jarmolowicz, A., Kahng, S. W., Ingvarsson, E. T., Goysovich, R., Heggemeyer, R., & Gregory, M. K. (2008). Effects of conversational versus technical language on treatment preference and integrity. *Intellectual and Developmental Disabilities, 46,* 190–199. doi:10.1352/2008.46:190-199

Morris, E. K. (2014). Stop preaching to the choir, publish outside the box: A discussion. *The Behavior Analyst, 37*(2), 87–94. doi:10.1007/s40614-014-0011-4

Rolider, A., & Axelrod, S. (2005). The effects of "behavior-speak" on public attitudes toward behavioral interventions. A cross-cultural argument for using conversational language to describe behavioral interventions. In W. L. Heward, T. E. Heron, N. A. Neef, S. M. Peterson, D. M. Sainato, G. Y. Cartledge, . . . J. C. Dardig (Eds.), *Focus on behavior analysis in education* (pp. 283–293). Upper Saddle River, NJ: Pearson/Merrill Prentice Hall.

Rolider, A., Axelrod, S., & Van Houten, R. (1998). Don't speak behaviorism to me: How to clearly and effectively communicate behavioral interventions to the general public. *Child & Family Behavior Therapy, 20,* 39–56. doi:10.1300/J019v20n02_03

Schlinger, H. D. Jr. (2015). Training graduate students to effectively disseminate behavior analysis and to counter misrepresentations. *Behavior Analysis in Practice, 8*(1), 110–112. doi:10.1007/s40617-014-0028-x

Todd, J. T. (2014). Some useful resources for students who are tempted to bring enlightenment to errant non-behaviorists. *Behavior Analysis in Practice, 7*(2), 143. doi:10.1007/s40617-014-0027-y

Pulling It All Together

As you go through the competencies with your supervisor, we recommend that you have a method to track your progress so that you can review your own work and see your gains over time. During supervision, it is very likely that you will develop several iterations of each of the documents you are learning to develop as a behavior analyst, including but not limited to operational definitions of target behaviors, data sheets for skill acquisition and behavior reduction programs, graphs summarizing data you obtained, and intervention protocols. We recommend that at the end of your supervision experience, you put together a portfolio of your work to demonstrate your mastery of the 10 competencies. You can create either a hard-copy or an electronic copy of your portfolio. The main purpose of asking you to develop a portfolio is to enhance your learning experience and to provide you with the opportunity to gather what you have learned during your supervision experience, reflect on your experiences, and demonstrate your gains across the competencies. With a portfolio, you get to keep track of what you have learned and reflect on your educational journey as an emerging behavior analyst. Therefore, the portfolio provides you with opportunities to make connections between your coursework, your supervision experiences, and your goals, both short and long term. In short, developing a portfolio of your work enables you to culminate your supervision experience.

In this chapter, we briefly outline some information regarding ePortfolios. However, you can follow these general tips with regard to the core content and organization of a portfolio no matter how you decide to collect and archive your materials.

WHAT ARE ePORTFOLIOS?

An ePortfolio is an electronic collection of your accomplishments and reflections. Creating an ePortfolio is like building your own website. You can insert images, sound, video, text, and mixed-media formats (Siegle, 2002). The function is to teach you how to present yourself, as a professional, online. One advantage of using an electronic portfolio versus hard-copy portfolio is that it is easier to store and share electronic work. Rather than having to carry copies of documents to demonstrate your competency in specific areas, you can share a link with potential employers or other individuals. In addition, you gain basic technology skills in developing a webpage by building your ePortfolio (MacDonald, Liu, Lowell, Tsai, & Lohr, 2004). Giving access to your portfolio is also easy. You can choose to keep your portfolio private and provide a link to individuals whom you select to view your site. Alternatively, you can make your portfolio public. Also, because your work is electronically digitized, you can use images and color without additional costs. Essentially, your ePortfolio serves as collated digital evidence of your learning of the competencies (Blair & Godsall, 2006; Mason, Pegler, & Weller, 2004).

WHY USE AN ePORTFOLIO?

The ePortfolio sets the occasion for you (the supervisee) to organize your thoughts, reflect on your learning process, and document the outcomes you have achieved. The ePortfolio can be either archived for your personal use or shared with future employers or doctoral committees. The benefits to you, depending on the time and effort you spend, may be any of the following:

- Personalizing your learning experience
- Drawing connections between your various learning experiences over the graduate program and beyond
- Seeing your own progress over time, which is encouraging
- Enhancing your critical thinking about your training and your journey to come

The benefits to faculty, the graduate program, or your supervisor may be any of the following:

- Evaluating the outcomes of supervision becomes easy.
- Seeing the supervisee's growth rate and final gains is very encouraging.
- Gaining insight into how the supervisee experienced and interpreted activities related to supervision is helpful.

HOW DO I GET STARTED?

There are several different sites you can use to make an ePortfolio (e.g., Google sites, Evernote, WordPress, and Weebly). You can also use your personal webpage if you already have one, either through a personal paid account or through your university account. If you use your university account, be sure to find out how long you have access to the site after you graduate. Also, some universities have recently adopted an online portfolio software platform such as Portfolium (portfolium.com), which makes developing and sharing portfolios easier.

For the past 5 years, we have used Google sites for ePortfolios because Google accounts are free and our graduates have unlimited access to their portfolios. If you and your supervisor decide you would like to use a free online application, such as Google, to develop your webpage, you can get started by going to www.sites. google.com and following the tutorials offered by the developers (see, for example, sites.google.com/site/eportfolioapps/online-tutorials-sites/sites-how-to). For Google ePortfolios, several universities have developed easy-to-use self-instructional written guides for their undergraduate and graduate students (see, for example, www. montclair.edu/media/montclairedu/oit/documentation/eportfolios/Google-Sites-ePortfolio-3-13-PF-Final.pdf). In addition, you can find step-by-step video tutorials (e.g., Latisha Alford, "How to Create a Free Professional ePortfolio Using Google Sites," youtu.be/1j-x3-VbGVg).

KEY ELEMENTS OF AN ePORTFOLIO

All ePortfolios should contain authentic drafts of documents that provide evidence of your learning. One key element of any portfolio is an introduction, home, or cover page that introduces readers to the portfolio and provides a clear summary of the materials displayed and the connections between them. Your summary page should include the following elements:

- Reflection on your experiences using the evidence you have provided
- Interpretations or self-assessment of changes over time
- Self-evaluation of strengths and limitations across competencies
- Articulation of short- and long-term professional goals (sometimes called mission statements)
- Synthesis of the work demonstrated and its connection(s) to professional goals

PULLING IT ALL TOGETHER IN YOUR ePORTFOLIO FOR CULMINATING YOUR SUPERVISION EXPERIENCE

You and your supervisor can discuss which documents you should archive and the content you should place in your final portfolio. To help you decide, we have provided several examples of ePortfolios in the Additional Resources section. We typically recommend that you have an introductory page that introduces audiences to your portfolio. You can also place an abstract, or a summary, of what the audience will see when they review the subpages (or tabs) of your portfolio. In addition, we recommend that you place your most recent curriculum vitae and evidence of your progression across the 10 competencies. Therefore, at a minimum, your portfolio would include the following elements:

1. A professional picture of you and/or a personalized webpage
2. A home page with an abstract or cover letter (with a link to your curriculum vitae)
3. Ethics and professional conduct
4. Behavior measurement
5. Behavior assessment
6. Evidence-based treatment planning
7. Skill acquisition intervention planning
8. Behavior reduction intervention planning
9. Generalization and maintenance
10. Evaluating effectiveness and procedural integrity
11. Training others to implement procedures
12. Dissemination

ADDITIONAL RESOURCES

- Google sites make creating and sharing group websites easy. See www.google.com/sites/help/intl/en/overview.html

Some example ePortfolios from previous students:

- sites.google.com/site/jenniferfriederportfolio/home
- sites.google.com/site/chelseacarterefolio/home
- sites.google.com/site/mahsamesbahhesari/home

REFERENCES

Blair, R., & Godsall, L. (2006). One school's experience in implementing e-portfolios: Lessons learned. *Quarterly Review of Distance Education, 7*(2), 145.

MacDonald, L., Liu , P., Lowell, K., Tsai, H., & Lohr, L. (2004). Graduate student perspectives on the development of electronic portfolios. *Tech Trends, 48*(3), 52–55.

Mason, R., Pegler, C., & Weller, M. (2004). E-portfolios: An assessment tool for online courses. *British Journal of Educational Technology, 35*(6), 712–727.

Siegle, D. (2002). Technology: Creating a living portfolio: Documenting student growth with electronic portfolios. *Gifted Child Today, 25*(3), 60–64.

Index

CPSIA information can be obtained
at www.ICGtesting.com
Printed in the USA
BVHW011831130722
642077BV00023B/307

9 780826 139122